THE MIND IN CONFLICT

Charles Brenner, M.D.

THE MIND IN CONFLICT

by
Charles Brenner, M.D.

INTERNATIONAL UNIVERSITIES PRESS, INC.
NEW YORK

Second Printing 1983

Library of Congress Cataloging in Publication Data

Brenner, Charles, 1913–
The mind in conflict.

Bibliography, p.
Includes index.
1. Conflict (Psychology) 2. Psychoanalysis.
3. Psychology, Pathological. I. Title.
BF503.B73 1982 150.19'5 82-21391
ISBN 08236-3365-9

Manufactured in the United States of America

CONTENTS

CHAPTER 1

INTRODUCTION

The exposition of psychic conflict in this book is based on what psychoanalysts, beginning with Freud, have observed of human psychic functioning and development. It is appropriate, therefore, to begin with an account of the nature of psychoanalysis as a method of psychological investigation and of its place in the field of science.

The beginning of psychology as an area for systematic inquiry is attributed by consensus to Aristotle. If we add the speculations of poets, mystics, and religious thinkers on man's nature or soul to Aristotle's account of the subject and to the accounts of scholars and philosophers who, like him, were animated by a spirit of scientific inquiry, it is clear that for thousands of years, both before and after Aristotle, psychology has been a matter of major concern to mankind. It is, therefore, an astonishing fact that psychoanalysis has, in less than a century, contributed more to the understanding of human psychology than did all the studies and speculations put together that preceded Freud's great discoveries. His *Interpretation Of Dreams* (1900) inaugurated an epoch in psychology as surely as Newton's *Principia* did in physics and Darwin's *Origin Of Species* did in biology. What made such an extraordinary advance possible?

The answer is twofold. It was the combination of the psychoanalytic method and the psychoanalytic situation. Freud, though trained as a neurologist, had the good fortune to undertake to treat mentally ill patients whose illnesses, as he discovered, were psychogenic. The therapeutic situation of analyst and patient proved to be a source of psychological data whose value was and still is unsurpassed. It is a source, however, which yields its data only when a special method of study and investigation is used, and it was one measure of Freud's genius that it was he, and he alone of the many who undertook to treat patients suffering from psychogenic illnesses, who devised and developed the psychoanalytic method from its origins in hypnosis (Freud, 1925b).

It is not my intention to present a detailed account of the psychoanalytic method. For reasons given elsewhere (Brenner, 1976) I believe that such an account can never be a truly satisfactory one. Personal experience in using the method is a *sine qua non* to an adequate understanding of it, as is the case with every specialized method of scientific investigation. For my present purpose the most summary account of the psychoanalytic method will suffice. The method is simply this. The subject, a patient, says as freely as possible whatever comes to his or her mind, having agreed at the start to renounce any conscious attempt to edit it, while the analyst directs his or her attention as exclusively as possible to the task of understanding the nature and origins of the patient's psychological difficulties and of communicating that understanding to the patient.

The application of the psychoanalytic method is not a simple matter. It requires much in the way of education, experience, and skill on the part of an analyst if it is to be done well enough for its results to be therapeutically useful and scientifically reliable. As a method, however, it is an extremely simple one in comparison with many scientific methods and techniques. It requires no artificial aids, no special tools or apparatus whatever. Only time and privacy are necessary. It is simply a method of observing the sequence of a person's conscious mental life, as reported by that person under conditions that reduce to a minimum the influence of extraneous stimuli.

Despite its relative simplicity, the psychoanalytic method has proved to be fruitful in a measure far beyond what could have been anticipated. It is only reflection, based on experience with the method, that offers an explanation for its fruitfulness.

Experience has shown that the method of psychoanalysis is the only method which is as yet available for the study of human psychology which does two things. First, it provides access on a large scale to the truly important aspects of man's mental life, i.e., to his uniquely personal motives, memories, and current experiences. Second, it makes possible an independent, objective appraisal of those aspects of mental life. It is the combination of these two properties that makes the psychoanalytic method so superior to its two competitors, introspection and the methods of academic psychology.

This assertion demands explanation. Introspection, after all, has been used since time immemorial as a method of psychological investigation. Those who espouse its use even argue its superiority over the method of psychoanalysis for the reason that a description of a mental event can never convey precisely the quality and vividness of the event as an experience. Yet the data of introspection, often referred to as subjective data, have long been discredited on purely empirical grounds as unreliable. Subjective and unreliable have come to be synonymous.

Why this should be so was never clear before psychoanalytic data were available, however. As soon as they became available, the answer was obvious. Everyone, without exception, is at considerable pains to deceive himself or herself about his or her own motives, past experiences, and current plans or wishes for the future. It is for this reason that the data of introspection are so unreliable. They are, invariably, systematically falsified, supressed, or both. It is no wonder, therefore, that a psychoanalyst can gain more accurate, more useful, and more informative data from a patients' verbal communications than anyone can from introspection.

As for academic psychology, its methods give extensive and reliable data only about aspects of mental life which are, in everybody's subjective assessment, of minor importance, as, for example, studies of the psychology of sensory perception. Academic psychologists who have attempted to use the psychoanalytic method in situations which are not therapeutic ones have been disappointed in their hopes, for obvious reasons. No one will speak to a stranger without consciously editing his or her thoughts hour after hour and day after day unless he or she has an urgent need to do so. A psychoanalysis, beyond its mere beginning, is possible only if the subject is a patient. It is not possible to divorce a psychoanalyst's therapeutic activities from his or her scientific, investigative activities (Freud, 1927).

What, then, is the nature of the data the psychoanalytic method makes available? On what sort of facts are the theories of psychoanalysis based?

The data themselves are no different qualitatively from those of introspection and of everyday observation of the people about us. They are describable as wishes, fears, fantasies, dreams, physical sensations, and so on, expressed in words and gestures. It is the range and content of psychoanalytic data that are unique. Their nature is not unique at all. They are commonplace psychological data. As such they are, to be sure, different in certain respects from data of other branches of science, e.g., physics and neurophysiology. This fact has misled some psychoanalysts to the conclusion that psychoanalysis is not a branch of natural science at all, but a science *sui generis*, since it has to do with language and meaning. In addition, there are philosophers of science who are critical of psychoanalytic theories, and who mistakenly characterize psychoanalysis as speculation rather than as a branch of science. This they do despite the fact that they are themselves without experience in using the method that provides the basis for the theories they criticize. I have dealt at length with these and similar objections elsewhere (Brenner, 1968, 1973a, 1980). Here I shall merely repeat my conclusions. They are that psychoanalysis is a branch of psychology and, as such, a part of science as a whole. It is the study of one aspect of cerebral functioning by the method best suited to the purpose. Its data are unique in some respects, but so are the data of every branch of science. Were they not, there would be no reason to keep separate one branch from another. Thus, for example, as long as the data of physics and those of chemistry were substantially different from one another, they constituted separate branches of science. When their data substantially coincided, there was no longer reason to separate them. They merged. Similarly for biology, which has, in the course of recent decades, merged with physics-chemistry. With respect to psychoanalysis, by contrast, its data are still different enough from those available by other methods of investigation to warrant treating it as a separate branch of science. That it is a branch of science, however, there can be no doubt. Moreover, what a psychoanalyst does with the data which derive from applying the psychoanalytic method is no different from what any scientist does with his or her data. An analyst postulates the same cause-and-effect relationships with respect to psychoanalytic data as a physicist, for example, postulates with respect to the data available to him or her. Like every other scientist, a psychoanalyst is an empiricist, who imaginatively infers functional and causal relations among his data, avoiding, if possible, generalizations that are inherently inconsistent with one another as well as those that are incompatible with well supported conclusions from other branches of science. The generalizations or hypotheses thus formed constitute psychoanalytic theory. Some are well substantiated by abundant data, some are less well substantiated, but all are empirically based hypotheses which are wholly comparable with those in every other branch of science. It was to these facts that Freud (1933) referred when he wrote that psychoanalysis has no philosophical outlook, no *Weltanschauung* other than that of science as a whole.

It follows from these considerations, among other things, that psychoanalytic hypotheses, like all scientific hypotheses, are subject to revision as relevant new data become available. Hypotheses, that is to say, theories that are either contradicted by new facts or are made implausible by them, must be amended or discarded and new ones framed. The better the fit between data and theory, the better able one is to look for new facts to test that theory and to use as a basis for its improvement. As Freud (1915b) wrote, in a paper on the theory of drives, one can construct many different theories to explain the available facts, but it is the fit between theory and facts that determines which theory is to be preferred. There should be, as he put it, a substantial, meaningful relation between data and hypothesis if one is to take the latter seriously and use it as the basis for further investigation.

It is in this spirit that I present the theory of psychic conflict contained in this volume. The concept of psychic conflict was one of Freud's earliest discoveries. By his own account, as soon as Freud gave up the technique of hypnosis as his method of investigating the origin of psychogenic symptoms, he encountered the phenomenon he called resistance, which he explained by the assumptions of conflict and repression (Freud, 1925b). His first paper on the subject, "The Neuropsychoses of Defence" appeared in 1894, a year before the publication of *Studies On Hysteria*.

Although the concept of psychic conflict occupied an important position in psychoanalytic theory from the very start, it was not truly central to Freud's theory of neurosogenesis prior to 1926. Before that time Freud attributed primal or infantile repression to factors other than anxiety and conflict. By this I mean that he believed anxiety to be a consequence of a failure of repression, not the motive for repression.[1] It was only in 1926, in "Inhibitions, Symptoms and Anxiety," that Freud gave to anxiety and conflict the centrally important or key roles in the psychoanalytic theory of neurosogenesis which they have occupied ever since that time. He related anxiety to a series of dangers associated with childhood instinctual life and identified its function in initiating defense and conflict, both then and subsequently throughout the life of every individual.

His revision of this important aspect of psychoanalytic theory proved to be most fruitful for the subsequent development of psychoanalysis. It enabled psychoanalysis to change from a psychology of dreams and of neurotic symptoms to a psychology with indispensable contributions to make to the entire range of human psychology. It enabled psychoanalysis to change, in other words, from what had been essentially a psychopathology to a general psychology. At the same time it had valuable consequences for psychoanalytic practice. It initiated the change from what was primarily id analysis to analysis of the relevant aspects of ego and superego functioning as well. As a result, the range of applicability of analysis was widened (Stone, 1954) and the safety and reliability of its technique were much improved.

Over half a century has passed since 1926. During that time many analysts have made additional contributions to the

[1]For a fuller discussion of these and other changes in Freud's theory, see Arlow and Brenner, 1964, and Brenner, 1957a.

psychoanalytic theory of psychic conflict. Notable among them are Anna Freud (1936), Fenichel (1941), and Hartmann and Kris (1945), later joined by Loewenstein (1946, 1949). Singly and together they contributed greatly to a better understanding of defense, to the technique of ego and superego analysis, to the theory of aggression, and to the role of aggression in psychic conflict. Nevertheless, the chief elements of Freud's conceptual framework have remained unchanged since 1926.

In 1975 I proposed a substantial change in the psychoanalytic theory of conflict. I asserted, on the basis of psychoanalytic data, that it is *unpleasure* that is responsible for defense and conflict in connection with infantile instinctual wishes and, further, that this unpleasure is of two kinds, anxiety and what I call depressive affect (Brenner, 1975a).

Like the change in the theory of conflict Freud introduced in 1926, I believe that the one I first proposed in 1975 and which is more fully developed in this book will be fruitful for the future development of psychoanalytic theory and technique. Among other things, it throws important new light on the psychopathology of depressive illness, on psychosexual development in the phallic-oedipal phase, and on hitherto unexplored areas of superego functioning.

In the following pages I have set down as fully and as precisely as possible what I believe can be said about psychic conflict on the basis of the evidence available at the present time. My chief reason for doing so is this. A thorough understanding of psychic conflict is equally indispensable to one who hopes to become proficient as a psychoanalyst and to one who wishes to understand the contribution of psychoanalysis to human psychology. One can neither practice psychoanalysis skilfully nor master its theories without such an understanding.

The plan of the book conforms to my understanding of what conflict is: its components, their interaction, and its consequences in mental life. Its components are several. They include drive derivatives, anxiety and depressive affect, defense, and various manifestations of superego functioning. These components interact in ways governed by the pleasure-unpleasure principle. The consequences of conflict are compromise formations. On all of these subjects I have altered or revised psychoanalytic theory—as it was in 1975—to conform as satisfactorily as possible to currently available data. I have tried in each instance to show the necessity for changing previously existing theories, to document the basis for the changes I propose, and to illustrate the advantages of the new over the old. Some of the alterations are substantial ones. In order to orient the reader, I shall list the major changes I have made and describe them briefly.

First as to the drives. Here the major changes have to do with the nature and source of the drives and with the relation between the aims of the drives and ego development. All psychic phenomena are aspects of cerebral functioning. The drives are as much so as any other, but no more so than the rest. Drives have no unique, extracerebral source or sources. They are not phenomena on a supposed frontier between mind and body, for the reason that no such frontier exists. The concept of the drives is a psychological one. It is, quite properly, based on psychological data, which is to say, on psychoanalytic data. The aims of the drives, moreover, are related to ego maturation and development in a more substantial and intimate way than is usually recognized.

The changes in the theory of anxiety have already been mentioned. As I have said, they furnished the original impetus for writing this book. I believe that consequences of major importance for both the theory and the practice of psychoanalysis follow from the recognition that unpleasure aroused by drive derivatives is of two kinds, anxiety and depressive affect, and that each plays a role in the initiation of conflict.

Like the changes in drive theory, the changes I have made in the theory of defense have, in part, been set forth in earlier publications (Brenner, 1975b, 1976). The chief one is that defense is definable by its consequence, not by the method used to achieve it. Every aspect of ego functioning can be used and is used to reduce unpleasure associated with drive derivatives and/or superego demands. Every so-called defense mechanism can be used and is used to further gratification of a drive derivative. To speak of defense mechanisms is, therefore, ambiguous and misleading. In addition, defense is not concerned solely with warding off drive derivatives and superego prohibitions or demands. Defense may also be directed against the unpleasure of anxiety and depressive affect, against their ideational content, or against both.

Object loss, loss of love, and castration are the calamities of early childhood. As Freud (1926) pointed out, they are the ideational content of anxiety aroused by drive derivatives. What I add is that they are also the ideational content of depressive affect aroused by drive derivatives. In addition, I offer two generalizations which are both important enough and unfamiliar enough to be included in this preliminary summary. The first is that depressive affect associated with psychic conflict is neither invariably nor exclusively a consequence of real or fantasied object loss. It can result from any of the calamities of childhood: object loss, loss of love, or castration. Second, though the calamities make their appearance in sequence during the course of psychic development, the earlier ones do not disappear as the subsequent ones come on the scene. Each persists throughout childhood and, indeed, throughout life. In particular, all are important during the oedipal period and, what is more, all are closely interrelated (Brenner, 1959).

As for the chapter on superego formation and functioning, I call attention in advance to three points. One is that much more is subsumed under the heading of guilt than the type of anxiety to which Freud (1926) referred, namely fear of punishment. Guilt is related as closely to depressive affect as it is to anxiety. The second concerns the role of libidinal drive derivatives in superego formation and functioning. They are far more important than has been recognized in the literature on the subject since the introduction of the concept of the superego by Freud in 1923. The third is that both the origins and the functioning of the superego must be understood in terms of the theory of psychic conflict that is the subject of this book. The superego takes its origin from conflict. It is itself a consequence of conflict—a compromise formation. It is for this reason that, in its later functioning, it contributes to conflict in complex and diverse ways. To cite but one example, it functions at times to reduce unpleasure, at times to produce unpleasure. The fact is, the theory of superego formation and functioning has remained largely unchanged since Freud set it forth (Freud,

1920, 1923, 1924b). It was never revised in the light of his subsequent understanding of conflict (Freud, 1926). It must be revised as I have done here for it to conform to what is known at present of its role in psychic functioning.

So much by way of an orienting summary. I begin my exposition of the components of psychic conflict and its consequences in psychic life with a discussion of the concept of drives.

CHAPTER 2

THE DRIVES

In *The New Introductory Lectures On Psycho-Analysis*, Freud wrote, "The theory of the drives is what might be called our mythology. The drives are like mythical creatures, magnificent in their indefiniteness. In our work we cannot disregard them for a moment, yet we are never sure that we have a clear view of them." (Freud, 1933, p. 95. The translation given differs slightly from that of Strachey.) I believe it is possible to offer a view of some aspects of drive theory that is, if not wholly clear, at least significantly more definite and less mythic than has been the case in the past. I shall try to do so in what follows.

FREUD'S IDEAS ON THE NATURE AND SOURCE OF THE DRIVES

Freud conceived of the mind as an apparatus that can be activated by stimuli of two kinds, sensory stimuli from the environment and bodily stimuli of a special sort. These latter Freud called drives for the reason that they impel or drive the mental apparatus to activity in accordance with the pleasure principle. This is the role that Freud assigned to the drives in psychoanalytic theory. The drives provide impetus. They drive the mind to activity.

In accordance with this idea, Freud believed that psychoanalytic data by themselves can never be an adequate basis for a satisfactory theory of the drives. It was his conviction, to which he held fast till the end of his life, that a drive is something somatopsychic, something whose source is somatic and whose effect is psychic. It is, he wrote, something ". . . on the frontier between the mental and the somatic . . . a measure of the demand made upon the mind for work in consequence of its connection with the body" (Freud, 1915b, p. 122).

In the theory Freud evolved over a period of fifteen years, he identified two separate drives: libido and aggression. To each he attributed a somatic source. In the case of libido, the sources are what Freud called the erogenous zones. In the case of aggression, the source is a death drive which is common to all living matter. In addition, Freud ascribed distinctive aims to the two drives. The aim of libido, he said, is to achieve an experience of pleasure. The aim of aggression is death and destruction of self, of object, or of both (Freud, 1905b, 1915b, 1920, 1924a).

The principal erogenous zones Freud identified as sources of libido are genitals, anus, and mouth. The secondary, or subsidiary ones are skin and organs of special sense such as eyes, ears, and olfactory organs. Part of the evidence for assuming that these body parts are sources of libido is nonanalytic. One need not be an analyst to relate libido to the genitals, for example, or to know that certain sensations, such as touch, sight, smell, and sound, can be sexually stimulating. Nor need one rely on analytic data to include mouth and anus among the principal erogenous zones. It is enough to observe the sexual perversions to be convinced that these parts of the body can serve a principal sexual function. Observation of the sexual behavior of children likewise supports Freud's formulation about the sources of libido, i.e., the relation of libido to the erogenous zones.

In fact, in his pioneer work on the subject, the "Three Essays on Sexuality," Freud (1905b) used all the evidence just referred to in support of his assertion that mouth, anus, genitals, and, less importantly, skin, taste, smell, sight, and hearing are erogenous zones and, as such, the somatic sources of libido. That is to say, he adduced evidence from generally available knowledge, from observations on sexual perversions, and from the sexual behavior of children to support his libido theory. To them he added psychoanalytic evidence. He had discovered that the unconscious fantasies of neurotic patients correspond to the sexual wishes and activities of children and of perverts. Subsequently analytic evidence has become available which indicates that the same is true of the unconscious fantasies of persons who are not neurotic. The oral, anal, phallic, and other libidinal wishes of early childhood persist as driving forces in the mental life of every adult. It was, in fact, precisely the psychoanalytic data, which he was the first to discover, that originally led Freud to formulate his libido theory. Only psychoanalytic data indicate the full scope of the role of libido as a driving, motive force in mental life from infancy to old age. Not that sexual appetite was ignored as a motive before Freud—obviously not—but it was Freud who demonstrated its universality, its early beginnings, its manifold disguises, and the importance in everyone of its relation to parts of the body other than the genitals themselves. To demonstrate *these* characteristics, psychoanalytic data are essential. Freud, and only Freud, could demonstrate them in 1905–1915 because he and he alone had the psychoanalytic data essential to the task.

What I wish to emphasize in reviewing matters that are so familiar is this. Freud did not wish to rely on psychoanalytic data for the part of his libido theory that has to do with its source or origin, since he believed that source to be a somatic one. Wholly reliable data on that score, he believed, could come only from other than analytic observations. They might come, for example, from the observation of sexual behavior, from a better knowledge of the nature and function of sexual hormones, from comparative physiological and anatomical studies, and the like. For this reason he welcomed as evidence in support of the intensity of phallic wishes in the oedipal period the report, later discredited, that the gonads of four-to-five-year-old children are larger relative to total body weight than are those of children in either the preoedipal or the latency periods. Even Ferenczi's (1923) fanciful explanation of the relation between latency and the recent ice age seemed to Freud to be worthy of serious attention. It was not at all to his liking that it is *psychoanalytic* data which are the principal support for so much of psychoanalytic libido theory. He wished it were otherwise and he tried to base as much of it as seemed to him possible on other than psychoanalytic data.

With all of this in mind it is not hard to understand why Freud postulated hormonal and other somatic processes in the erogenous zones as the source of libido. As psychoanalysts we are so used to this formulation that we rarely question it. It seems self-evident or, at the least, so plausible as to be readily acceptable.

The *connections* between libido as a driving force in mental life and those parts of the body Freud designated as erogenous zones are indisputable and intimate. Psychoanalytic data leave no room for doubt on these points. On the contrary, psychoanalysts know from repeated experience that the psychological importance of wishes related to these several parts of the body must be continually reaffirmed and emphasized for the reason that it is precisely such libidinal derivatives that give rise to unpleasure in early childhood and that have been vigorously warded off ever since. But this is not the same as saying that libido arises from mouth, anus, genitals, etc. Certain facts, as we have seen, are consistent with the theory that it does. Others, however, are less so.

Thus, for example, the increased urgency of libidinal wishes during puberty is perfectly consistent with Freud's theory. However, the same phenomenon at the time of menopause or climacterium is not. Nor, for that matter, can Freud's theory satisfactorily explain the efflorescence of sexual wishes during the oedipal period. As far as I know, there is not as yet reliable evidence of endocrine or other changes in the genital apparatus itself to support Freud's theory that the phallic-genital zone is the *source* of libido as a driving force in psychic life. There is no doubt that stimulation of any of the important zones can increase the urgency of libidinal wishes. But to recognize this is quite different from asserting that these zones are the sources of libido as a constant driving force in mental life. Everyday analytic experience demonstrates, for example, that events occurring in the context of the relationship between patient and analyst, such as an impending separation or the commencement of analysis, can powerfully increase, i.e., stimulate the urgency of libidinal wishes, but no one would conclude from such observations that the relationship between patient and analyst, i.e., the transference, is a source of libido, much less *the* source of it. In the same way, it is not truly convincing to conclude from the very intimate relation between erogenous zones and libidinal derivatives that the zones are the *source* of the libidinal drive. That they are intimately linked is certain. That one is the source of the other is less so.

I have not raised these doubts about Freud's libido theory with the intention of maintaining on their grounds alone that it is of dubious validity to assume, as Freud did, that the drives have the special characteristic of being somatopsychic or frontier phenomena in mental life. On the contrary, I believe that his assumption is plausible enough with respect to libido to justify one in holding fast to it for the time being despite whatever doubts of its validity may be raised by objections of the sort I have mentioned. It is not until one turns from libido theory to the theory of aggression that the evidence against the frontier concept of drives becomes irrefutable. As long as libido was the only drive, i.e., before 1920, it could be argued that the frontier concept was tenable. That it is tenable no longer, i.e., within the framework of the dual drive theory, is a conclusion I believe is inescapable.

Consider first of all the nature of the evidence on which Freud based his theory that aggression is no less a driving force in mental life than is libido. It must be confessed at the start that this is a matter on which one cannot be quite certain. Freud himself never said explicitly what evidence persuaded him that aggression is properly viewed as a drive. One can say, however, that it is very likely that it was psychoanalytic evidence. I do not think it was the brutal massacre of millions of soldiers in the war of 1914–1918, shocking as that massacre was to every cultured European, especially to one who, like Freud, had sons at the front. Nor do I think that the experiments of microbiologists on generations of paramecia was what suggested the theory of aggression to Freud, despite the importance he gave to those experiments in his argument in *Beyond the Pleasure Principle*. If one reads what Freud wrote in the years just before and just after 1920, I believe one cannot escape the impression that the theory of aggression was suggested by the accumulation of psychoanalytic evidence concerning the importance of self-directed aggression in mental life, evidence derived from Freud's studies of melancholia, of sexual perversions, especially masochism, and, above all, from his studies of the nature and function of the superego (Arlow and Brenner, 1964, pp. 45-46). In other words, Freud's theory of aggression was suggested to him by the same clinical data as those that inspired "Mourning and Melancholia," "A Child Is Being Beaten," "The Ego and the Id," and "The Economic Problem of Masochism," works which span the period 1915–1924.

If this inference is correct, it means that the basis for the theory of aggression was psychoanalytic, a basis which, be it noted, Freud deemed inadequate for the purpose. If aggression is a drive, it must be a frontier phenomenon and it may not be based primarily on psychoanalytic evidence. So Freud reasoned, and it was because of this reasoning that he constructed the argument in favor of aggression as a drive, as he did in *Beyond the Pleasure Principle*.

What Freud did was to adduce evidence in favor of the existence in all living matter of a drive to return to the inorganic state. By this I mean he argued in favor of a death drive that is inherent in all living matter. The manifestation in mental life of this omnipresent death drive, he maintained, is the instinctual drive of aggression. Though not related to any specific or localized body parts or processes, as libido is to the erogenous zones, aggression, according to Freud, is related to the death drive inherent in every cell of the body. In this way he attempted to base the concept of aggression as a drive in mental life on a foundation other than psychoanalytic evidence.

In summary, then, one may say the following. Fundamental to Freud's concept of a drive is that it is something somatopsychic. It is something on the frontier between mind and body. The source of a drive, Freud believed, is a somatic process, e.g., excitation of nerve endings in an erogenous zone, in the case of libido. In the case of aggression, still according to Freud, the somatic process is the universal tendency of living matter to die. Freud understood very well that the classification of drives into libido and aggression derived from his clinical experience as a psychoanalyst, i.e., from psychoanalytic data. In the case of libido he specified the nature of the psychoanalytic evidence involved. It came from data about childhood sexuality, about sexual perversions, and about unconscious, especially pathogenic, sexual fantasies in adults. In the case of aggression he was not specific, but one can reasonably assume the psychoanalytic evidence came from analysis of instances of self-directed aggression and of sadomasochistic phenomena. What is essential to bear in mind, however, is that Freud believed that no satisfactory theory of drives could be based on psychoanalytic evidence alone, since he started with the premise that a drive must have its source in one or more bodily processes.

For reasons given in more detail below, I believe the weight of available evidence is strongly in favor of Freud's dual instinct theory. The same cannot be said, however, either of his concept of drives as something on the frontier between mind and body or of the generalization he used to support and validate the concept of aggression as an instinctual drive in mental life, namely, that in all living matter there is a drive to death, an inborn tendency to return to a lifeless, inorganic state. I shall discuss the concept of drives as frontier phenomena shortly. First, however, I shall consider the validity of the concept of a death drive.

Implicit in the concept of a drive to die is the idea of a clear distinction between life and death. The concept of a death drive rests on the assumption that life and death are as separate and opposed to one another biologically as are a wish for sensual pleasure, i.e., libido, and a wish to destroy, i.e., aggression, in the psychological sphere. In fact, however, there is no such clear distinction between life and death, speaking biologically. There is a very sharp one, speaking psychologically. In men's minds, life and death are indeed polar opposites; not so in biology.

Life and death, living and dead, organic and inorganic are not chemically distinct or sharply separable from one another. On the contrary, the evidence that has accumulated over many decades, from the time of the synthesis of urea by Wöhler in 1828 to the most recent discoveries of molecular biologists, has steadily added support to the view, by now inescapable, that there is no discontinuity between what is living and what is not.

It is clear that there is a continuum between physical-chemical systems we call simple and inorganic and those we call living plants or animals. There is no point at which life enters a physical-chemical system. There is, simply, a gradual change in physical-chemical properties from one system to the next in the series that begins with what is called inorganic and ends with what is called living matter. Life and death have no such importance or meaning in biology as a whole as each of us, for very personal reasons, attributes to them and as Freud assumed in his generalization about a death drive and, incidentally, about a life drive as well. To be sure, one can point to the obvious fact that there frequently are changes in physical-chemical systems from those we call living because of certain of their properties, to those we call lifeless because of their properties. Living things do become lifeless. However, this offers no useful support of Freud's generalization. The idea of life and death as meaningful, contrasting, distinct properties of physical-chemical systems is essential to his argument. His theory took its origin from the distinction in mental life between sensual wishes, i.e., wishes for pleasure through physical closeness, physical stimulation, and love, on the one hand, and wishes to hurt, to kill, and to destroy, on the other. It is these psychoanalytic or, more broadly, these psychological data that suggested the distinction Freud made between libido and aggression as drives in mental life. It is these data that support that distinction. Freud sought to support the contrast between the two in mental life by making a parallel contrast between life and death as biological phenomena. Life and death are thus key concepts in Freud's drive theory. They cannot be dispensed with if the theory is to stand. It is questionable enough to assume, as Freud did, that a presumed tendency of cells to die can be the basis for such complex psychic phenomena as aggressive and destructive wishes. When one realizes in addition that death and life are not precisely definable concepts and are not to be separated physicochemically as aggression and libido are separated and contrasted with one another psychologically, one must conclude that Freud's death drive theory is wholly unsatisfactory as a basis for postulating an aggressive drive in mental life.

AN ALTERNATIVE THEORY

I believe, as Freud did, that data do exist that support the concept of aggression as an instinctual drive in man, just as there are data that support the concept of a libidinal drive. They are not, however, data from fields of biology other than the field of psychology. Quite to the contrary; they are psychological data. More exactly, they are psychoanalytic data, i.e., data that derive from the application of the psychoanalytic method. Without that method, without the data it can furnish, the dual theory of instinctual drives which Freud proposed would have little to support it. It is psychoanalytic data that speak so strongly for Freud's theory, not data from other fields of biology.

Freud himself understood very well that psychoanalytic data support his dual instinct theory. What troubled him was his conviction that psychoanalytic data alone cannot serve as a satisfactory basis for a theory of instinctual drives, a conviction derived from the concept of a drive as a phenomenon on the frontier between mind and body. Thus the first question to be decided is whether a drive is a frontier phenomenon, i.e., a measure of the demand made on the mind for work in consequence of its connection with the body, in contrast with other features of psychic life which are purely psychological phenomena. Must one have recourse to other than psychoanalytic data in formulating a theory of drives, as Freud maintained is the case, or are drives psychological phenomena that can be validated or invalidated by psychoanalytic data?

There is no question that Freud was right in emphasizing the inseparable connection between mind and body. In his own day everyone who was trained as he was in neuropathology and neurophysiology was irresistibly led to the same position as Freud in this respect; further accumulation of knowledge in the intervening years has consistently confirmed its correctness. What I suggest is not that Freud was wrong in linking mind to body, but rather that he did not go far enough in doing so.

All of psychology is an aspect of the functioning of the central nervous system. There is no frontier between mind and body. The idea that there is one is but a relic of the time when the separateness of mind and body was arguable, of the time when one might maintain that they are separate with some show of reason. That time is long past. The idea of mind as something separate from body is no more than a disguised version of the age-old belief in an incorporeal soul. As soon as one discards the remnants of this belief, it is clear that all available evidence supports the view that mind is an aspect of cerebral functioning. One can say that the brain is the organ of the mind as truly as that the lungs are the organs of respiration, and the heart the organ of circulation. Mind is impossible without brain. The evidence accumulated during the past 150 years by neurophysiologists, by neuropathologists, by comparative neurologists, and by developmental psychologists leaves no doubt of the correctness of this statement. The mind, i.e., psychology, is as much a somatic phenomenon as are respiration and circulation, even though we know so much more about how the heart and lungs cause circulation and respiration than we do about how cerebral activity causes psychological phenomena.

Since all mental functioning is somatic, it is unnecessary and, in some respects, even misleading to separate one group of psychological phenomena from others by labeling them as somatic in nature. True as it is that the aspect of mental functioning which Freud correctly distinguished from the rest as the drives are somatically dependent psychological phenomena, this characteristic does not distinguish them from other psychological phenomena. All psychological phenomena are somatically dependent. All are an aspect of brain functioning. Some are related to specific body parts in special ways. Some are intimately associated with hormonal and other, similar aspects of extracerebral chemistry. Nevertheless, however important their special characteristics may be in these and other respects, all are an aspect of body functioning. The term somatopsychic is tautologous. Everything psychic is somatic as well. One need not hesitate, therefore, to base a theory of drives on psychoanalytic data, despite Freud's reluctance to do so himself.

This view gains further support from the fact that the aspects of drive theory which are currently used in psychoanalytic practice are those that derive from psychoanalytic data, not those that are related to such other evidence as a presumed protoplasmic death drive. For example, it would seem to most analysts today to be both inadequate and unsatisfactory to explain a patient's self-destructive behavior as due to an increase in the intensity of his death drive. Such an explanation follows naturally from the idea that aggression is the reflection in psychic life of the human organism's death drive; at one time it was an explanation that was commonly used by psychoanalysts. This is no longer the case. At present, when analysts attempt to explain or to understand a patient's self-destructive behavior, they use the parts of the psychoanalytic theory of aggression which are derived from psychoanalytic data. They explain such behavior in terms of murderous childhood wishes, of fears of retribution, of fears of loss, and of penitential, self-punitive trends. None of these depend on the assumption that a death drive is common to all living matter. They depend essentially on data furnished by application of the psychoanalytic method. More than this, in attempting to understand self-destructive wishes and behavior, analysts also take into account the libidinal derivatives that are invariably involved. It has long been recognized (e.g., Jones, 1911, 1912) that such wishes and behavior have libidinal determinants as well as aggressive ones. Analysts proceed in their clinical work in accordance with that recognition. The one thing analysts do not make use of in their day-to-day clinical work is the theory of a protoplasmic death drive.

Granting all of this, the question that immediately arises is obvious. If one dispenses with the protoplasmic death drive as evidence for aggression as a driving force in mental life, on what evidence will one base it? What psychoanalytic evidence is one to use and how is one to use it?

Everyone knows from simple observation of himself and others that wishes play an important part in psychic life. When one has a patient in analysis, i.e., when one can apply the psychoanalytic method, one can observe much more fully the role of wishes in mental life, what those wishes really are, their relation to early childhood wishes, and the history of their development and transformation in later childhood and adolescence. That is to say, the evidential basis for psychoanalytic drive theory is the conscious and unconscious wishes of patients as disclosed by the psychoanalytic method of observation.

It should be noted that each observation is personal and unique. It is the wish of a particular patient for a particular kind of gratification from or at the hands of a particular person under particular circumstances. A patient's wish is never "an oral wish," for example. It is a wish for gratification of a special kind, e.g., nursing or swallowing a penis. It is a wish that has a uniquely personal history, a uniquely personal form, and a uniquely personal content. Nor is a wish ever just "an aggressive wish." It is always a wish to do something to somebody, again with a special history, a special content, and a special form.

When the aggregate of such data from many analyses is surveyed certain generalizations are possible. One generalization is that such wishes fall readily into two broad groups, libidinal and aggressive. Another is that there are both libidinal and aggressive elements in every wish. Another, that the history of such wishes goes back to the early years of childhood, i.e., they are persistent or modified infantile wishes. Still another, that libidinal wishes have often to do with pleasurable stimulation of the erogenous zones.

Taken together, these generalizations make up the psychoanalytic theory of drives. By this I mean that psychoanalytic data support Freud's formulation that there are two driving forces or motivations which are fundamentally important in mental life, libidinal and aggressive; that both are active from the beginning of mental life; and that the libidinal drive has a special relation to the erogenous zones. As already noted, this differs from what Freud thought and wrote about drives in only one way. He postulated noncerebral, somatic processes as the sources of the drives. In other words, he declined to rely on psychoanalytic data alone as a basis for drive theory, although it is clear, when one reviews it, that Freud's drive theory was, in fact, based on psychoanalytic data in respect to every part except that having to do with the sources of the two drives.

In 1905, when he first formulated libido theory, only Freud himself had had extensive experience with the psychoanalytic method. Even in 1915 there was only a handful of analysts with much experience. Moreover, the method itself was less developed than it has become since, so that it is fair to presume that its results were less reliable and less precise than they are at present. By now, in contrast with the situation at the beginning of this century, there are hundreds of psychoanalysts, each of whom has had more than two decades of experience with the psychoanalytic method on a total of thousands of patients. It was prudent in 1915 to be modest, even skeptical about the importance and reliability of purely psychoanalytic evidence, especially when used as a basis for drawing conclusions about the nature of the very wellsprings of human motivation. The same skepticism is not necessary today. Psychoanalysts should, of course, welcome evidence from other branches of biology which confirms psychoanalytic drive theory, whether it be from human physiology, from comparative psychology (Panel, 1956), or from any other discipline. They should likewise take care not to propose or maintain theories about drives—or anything else—which are at odds with established facts and theories from other branches of science (see Brenner, 1968). There is, however, no need to defer the development of theories based on psychoanalytic data, either wholly or principally, until evidence concerning them is available from other, related disciplines, as Freud maintained is the case for the theory of drives.

The fact is that the psychoanalytic method is the method *par excellence* of studying the aspect of brain functioning that is called mind or psyche. Neurophysiology studies certain aspects of brain functioning, psychoanalysis studies others. If one is interested in the psyche, if one is interested in human psychology, the best way of studying it is psychoanalysis. It is possible that things may change. The time may come when other methods of study are more fruitful for psychology than the method of psychoanalysis, but that time is not yet here. At present psychoanalysis is the best method we have of studying the aspects of brain functioning called the psyche.

In light of all these considerations, what can be said, on the basis of the available data, concerning the nature and the source of the libidinal and aggressive drives, respectively?

As to their nature, the answer is simple and straightforward. The drives, as properly conceptualized in psychoanalytic theory, are psychological phenomena. To call them somatopsychic is to indulge in mere tautology.

As to their sources, neither has any special source as far

as is known at present. Both are ways of conceptualizing certain aspects of human psychology, based primarily on psychoanalytic data.

It is important to emphasize the following with respect to libido, however. Libido is closely tied to and influenced by what Freud called the erogenous zones as well as by various sexual metabolites. These are facts of great significance in both normal and pathological mental functioning. Moreover, it is a relationship that must be emphasized in any presentation of the subject of the drives for a very special reason. Everyone, including patients in analysis, is more than eager, though often unconsciously so, to deny and to disprove the sexual significance of mouth, anus, and genitals, especially during the years before puberty. In other words, the relation of these parts of the body to psychosexual life and to psychosexual development should be specially emphasized precisely because it is so apt to be repressed, pushed aside, or otherwise defended against. Emphasis is necessary to counteract defensive de-emphasis. Nonetheless, it is worth repeating that there is no convincing evidence that the erogenous zones are, in fact, the sources of the libidinal drive. To be sure, wishes for satisfaction of one sort or another are profoundly influenced by many factors, among which stimulation of the erogenous zones figures largely. Wishes are made more urgent by such stimulation, as well as by certain hormones or, for that matter, by words and memories. However, such stimulation, hormones, etc., are not sources of libido. They influence libidinal wishes. They do not give rise to libido. Libido, like all other psychic phenomena, including aggression, derives from the functioning of the brain. It is one of the features of the aspect of brain functioning we call the mind.

DRIVE ECONOMY AND PSYCHIC ENERGY

As already noted, the essence of psychoanalytic drive theory is that aggression and libido are driving forces that motivate mental activity. It was because he considered their motivational, impelling attribute their most important, indeed, their essential characteristic that Freud called them drives. It was in this context that he introduced the term psychic energy, a term he borrowed from the language of physics to denote the capacity of the drives to impel the mind to work.

Psychic energy bears its name only by virtue of the analogy just described (see Brenner, 1973b, pp. 18-19). There is no other relation between psychic energy and energy as defined by physicists than one of analogy. Psychic energy is not a form of physical energy as are, for example, kinetic energy, potential energy, or electrical energy. It is not measurable in gram-centimeters. Its flux cannot be described by the differential equation that defines entropy for physicists. Psychic energy is a term that refers only to the concept that there are driving forces in the mind which are identified as libido and aggression for the reasons set forth above. The capacity of these forces to set the mind to work in the direction of achieving gratification is what is called psychic energy.

Unless one is ready to assume that the drives never fluctuate in intensity, one must attribute a dimension of magnitude to psychic energy, i.e., there must be some quantitative or economic (from the German: *ökonomisch*) aspect to that part of drive theory expressed by the concept of psychic energy. There is no way at present of measuring the intensity of a drive, however. It is not currently possible to give to psychic energy a numerical value. Even to estimate its magnitude in the grossest way, i.e., to say whether it is now greater and now less, is rarely possible, at least with any satisfactory degree of assurance. The quantitative aspect of drive theory—the quantification or measurement of psychic energy—is still an area for future exploration. What is important in the meantime in order to avoid misunderstandings that can lead one far astray, is to realize that psychic energy is unrelated to physical energy except by the analogy specified above.

AIMS OF THE DRIVES—DRIVE DERIVATIVES

Drive derivative, drive representation, and drive representative are synonyms. I use the first for the sake of convenience only. The other two terms are equally appropriate.

The distinction between drive and drive derivative is essential to any discussion of the aims and objects of the drives.

The distinction is this. A drive derivative is a wish for gratification. It is what one observes in a patient or, to be more precise, it is what one infers about a patient via the psychoanalytic method. A drive derivative is unique, individual, and specific. The concept of drive, on the contrary, is a generalization about drive derivatives based on many individual observations and inferences. It applies to all persons, in the sense that it indicates what characteristics or qualities are common to the wishes of people in general, irrespective of their individual experiences or personal histories.

A drive, therefore, is a psychological generalization, a theoretical construct that serves the purpose of explaining the nature of peoples' basic motivations, of their prime impetus to mental activity; a drive derivative refers to a particular example or instance of drive activity. To say of a patient that he has libidinal conflicts, or aggressive ones, is to say but little. Everyone has both. Even to specify that a patient's wishes are oral, anal, or phallic is to add but little more. What is important with respect to each patient is to learn as much as possible about the libidinal and aggressive drive derivatives which are dynamically important at the moment, including their relation to childhood derivatives and to subsequent experiences and development. What is important, in other words, is to learn as much as possible about what a patient wishes, about who is involved in his wishes, and about how and why he has just those particular wishes about those particular persons.

Critics of the psychoanalytic theory of the drives have often charged that it is impersonal and mechanistic. The facts do not justify the charge. Such critics either ignore or misunderstand the distinction between drive and drive derivative. The former is impersonal and general. The latter is personal and specific. Drive theory includes both.

With this distinction in mind, one can proceed to a discussion of drive aims. I begin with aggression.

Freud (1920, 1923, 1930, and elsewhere) identified the aim of aggression as destruction of whatever is the object of the drive. This is in keeping with his concept that aggression is the psychological counterpart of a universally present death drive. It is worth noting in this connection that the equivalence, death

= destruction, is a psychological one. It is an equivalence that arises from man's imagination. It is not a physical fact. On the contrary, in the part of the physical world which constitutes man's immediate environment, there is no such thing as destruction of any material object, whether alive or inanimate.

Hartmann et al. (1949, p. 18) were more cautious than Freud about the aim of aggression. They suggested that there may be different aims, each corresponding to a different degree of drive discharge. They seem to have inclined toward the view that "full" discharge corresponds to death or destruction of the object, but they did not explicitly commit themselves to that position.

Stone (1971, 1979) is still less in agreement with the idea that the aim of aggression is to destroy. While he recognizes the strength and importance of aggressive and destructive wishes in mental life, he feels their aims are so diverse as to raise serious doubts concerning the very concept of aggression as a drive.

There are few if any other exceptions to the rule, however, that psychoanalytic writers accept the view that the aim of the aggressive drive is "destruction of the object." This is true even of those authors who do not subscribe to Freud's original reason for this conclusion, namely, that aggression corresponds to a death drive in all living matter.

What can be said about the aim of the aggressive drive on the basis of psychoanalytic data? In attempting to answer this question the following considerations should be kept in mind.

The psychoanalytic method depends on communication and, primarily, on verbal communication, i.e., on language. Its application yields reliable results concerning the mental processes of individuals who are sufficiently developed to acquire and, in most instances, to use language (Arlow and Brenner, 1966; A. Freud, 1969, pp. 38ff.). As psychoanalysts, we have information concerning the psychic processes of such people which is both extensive and reliable. Our information about young children is much less certain and extensive, since we cannot apply the psychoanalytic method directly in such cases. Our ideas about their psychology depend on observation of behavior alone, as it does with animals other than man. It is tempting to attribute to infants psychological processes that resemble those with which we are familiar in older individuals who are accessible to the psychoanalytic method (e.g., Klein et al., 1952). A number of authors (Waelder, 1937; Glover, 1947; Brenner, 1968) have indicated the pitfalls and impropriety of such an approach, so appealing at first glance. The fact is that we have as yet far less reliable information concerning the psychology of the early period of postnatal life than we should like to have, despite the several programs of study that have been conducted in recent years by psychoanalytically trained observers.

These considerations are pertinent to the problem under discussion in the following way. It is assumed that the sexual and aggressive drives are active and operative from the first days of life. This follows from the belief that the drives are constitutionally determined. Thus oral tensions and gratifications are attributed to babies from the onset of postnatal life, although, to be sure, Freud (1905b, p. 222; 1914, p. 87; 1915b, p. 126) pointed very early to the likelihood that infantile sexuality has a root in early experience as well as in constitutional endowment, a relation he indicated by the term anaclitic. Despite these hints in an opposite direction, analysts have nearly all continued in the assumption that the drives are active from the very first days of postnatal life and that they are, therefore, fundamentally independent of experience, even though much modified by experience in the course of psychic development (Freud, 1915b).

How correct is the assumption that a drive is more nearly independent of experience than the aspects of mental functioning subsumed under the heading ego?

It appears that these matters are not as simple as has been widely supposed. Certainly with respect to aggression it is not possible as yet to draw any certain conclusions concerning its characteristics during the period of life prior to an age at which psychoanalysis can be used as a method of observation. What is known about the drive of aggression is what has been learned from the psychoanalysis of children and of adults. It does not derive either from physiology or from observations on the behavior of infants. However much one may wish to go beyond the limits of present knowledge, one must recognize the uncertainty of one's conclusions if the attempt is made.

On the basis of psychoanalytic data one is forced to conclude that the aims of aggression vary from one stage of life to another. The most familiar variations are those that parallel the variation of libidinal aims in the progression of the libidinal phases. One speaks with assurance of oral, anal, and phallic aggressive aims, all of which, like the corresponding libidinal aims, are observed to be active in mental life well into the oedipal period and beyond, i.e., well into that time of life which can be studied directly by the psychoanalytic method.

In addition, intellectual development brings with it the possibility for alterations in the aim of aggression. A child's wish to make another feel the same pain as it feels, or to kill someone, are aggressive aims which, after a certain age, are so common as to merit the term universal, yet the probability is that they do not occur at all in the mind of a very young child. Before a certain age, as Freud (1900, pp. 19, 254-255) pointed out long ago, death is a meaningless word. The recognition that others feel as oneself feels is likewise absent in the very young. It is only in the course of development, in consequence, that a child becomes capable of such aggressive aims as the universal ones just mentioned. It may be also pertinent to recall in passing the clinically important observation that when one encounters fantasies of death and killing in one's work with a patient, one must bear in mind the fact, documented long ago, that death may symbolize castration. A child's wish to kill, like a fear of being killed, often expresses a fantasy of genital mutilation and penetration in addition to a primarily aggressive wish.

On the basis of the available psychoanalytic evidence, then, one is justified in saying that aggressive aims vary with mental development and experience and, as has been noted repeatedly, it is psychoanalytic evidence that justifies the assumption of an aggressive drive.

Such a complex state of affairs with respect to the aims of aggression seems to offer a regrettable contrast to what is known about the libidinal drive, whose aims are thought of as the same from one individual to the next and as understandable and expressible in physiological-anatomical terms rather than in psychological ones. Yet are there not similarities as well as differences?

The differences are clear. Libidinal excitement and pleasure are bound to the erogenous zones, to use Freud's term, by genically determined, constitutional endowment. The pattern of orgasm is likewise largely determined by genically inherited factors. At the same time it must be remembered that even orgastic patterns are often greatly modified by psychological factors as well. They may be grossly altered by psychic conflicts which are significantly related to ego functions and to experience. The same is true for the relative importance of one or another of the erogenous zones, as well as for the details of just what stimulation is necessary for gratification. Much attention has been paid by psychoanalysts to the importance of experience in determining libidinal objects. Much less attention has been paid to its importance with respect to libidinal aims, though these are also dependent on experience in no small measure, as psychoanalytic data attest.

Freud (1905b, 1915b) early called attention to the variety of the libidinal aims of childhood, to progressive alterations in their relative importance, and to the fact that their final organization does not take place until puberty. When one considers the part played in this complicated development by experiential and related psychological factors, it is reasonable to conclude that there are substantial similarities between the aggressive and the libidinal drives with respect to the variety and developmental alterations of their aims. To take account of the similarities should not, to be sure, lead one to discount the differences. Both similarities and differences are important to keep in mind.

Loewald (1972) has also called attention to the importance of early experiential influences in drive development. In his view, the drives develop from the inevitable interactions between mother and infant. This way of conceptualizing the nature and origin of the drives appears to ignore the distinction between drive and drive derivative—between drive and wish. It is not clear what the advantages are to altering drive theory in this way. As was noted earlier, there are no psychoanalytic data about this very early time of life. Any hypothesis about the dawn of psychic life is necessarily speculative.

In summary, the following conclusion is in order at the present stage of knowledge of the subject of the aims of the drives. The aims of both the libidinal and the aggressive drive are influenced by experiential factors reflected in ego development. The details of this influence and its differences with respect to the two drives remain to be explored more fully. It may prove to be the case, for example, that the close relation between the aim of aggression and the aims of the libidinal component drives is in part due to the fact that wishes connected with these libidinal aims so often cause fear or other intense unpleasure to children. After a certain age, a child hurts, or wants to hurt, someone else by doing to him or her what hurts or frightens the child.

AGGRESSION AND THE PLEASURE PRINCIPLE—REPETITION COMPULSION

Freud's (1920) original view was that aggression is beyond the pleasure principle, whence the name of the monograph. According to this formulation, the discharge of aggression, unlike the discharge of libido, is unaccompanied by pleasure in and of itself. Only when it is fused with libido, i.e., erotized and directed toward representations of external objects, was aggression considered by Freud to give rise to pleasure when discharged (Freud, 1920, p. 63; 1923, pp. 40ff.; 1930, p. 119).

More recent authors have expressed a different opinion concerning aggression and the pleasure principle, an opinion first stated clearly by Hartmann et al. (1949). They suggested that aggression bears the same relation to pleasure and to unpleasure as does libido. They advanced the view that, generally speaking, the discharge of aggression gives rise to pleasure and that the accumulation and lack of discharge of aggression give rise to unpleasure. This is a change that has both theoretical and practical consequences.

The most important of the former has to do with the idea that a compulsion to repeat (repetition compulsion) is a characteristic of the drives. This idea is associated with Freud's concept of aggression as beyond the pleasure principle—as a derivative of a universal death drive. If pleasure is associated with gratification of derivatives of aggression, it is unnecessary to ascribe the repetitive nature of either aggressive or libidinal wishes to a repetition compulsion, as Freud proposed to do in 1920.[1] Instead, the repetitive nature of drive derivatives, both libidinal and aggressive, is explained by the pleasure principle. According to the pleasure principle, unsatisfied drive derivatives, i.e., unsatisfied wishes of drive origin, persistently seek gratification. In particular, and of special importance practically, childhood wishes which remain ungratified because they arouse unpleasure and conflict remain active and continually drive the person in the direction of gratification, a direction that may lead to any of the familiar consequences that such psychic conflicts have, for example, symptom formation or self-punishment. All of this is adequately explained by the pleasure principle without assuming, in addition, a special compulsion to repeat. If aggression is *not* beyond the pleasure principle, it is unnecessary to assume a repetition compulsion.

DRIVES IN PSYCHIC CONFLICT—DRIVES AND EGO FUNCTIONS

In Freud's opinion (1930, p. 139) libido and aggression play different roles in neurotic symptom formation: libido gives rise to the symptoms themselves and aggression gives rise to the related self-punitive and self-destructive trends.

Freud's formulation served the useful purpose of emphasizing the great role of aggression in superego functioning. A large part of what can be identified as self-directed aggression in mental life is related to superego functioning, i.e., to prohibitions of the satisfaction of drive derivatives, to a sense of guilt, to a need for punishment, and to related phenomena. However, most analysts are agreed that derivatives of aggression in general, i.e., not merely self-directed aggression, play a large role not only in symptom formation, but in all psychic conflicts related to drive derivatives. To put the matter succinctly, observable clinical data justify placing aggression and libido on an approximately equal footing with respect to un-

[1]For similar conclusions, though more elaborately based, see Kubie (1939) and Schur (1966).

pleasure and conflict, just as they justify the view that satisfaction of derivatives of aggression, like the satisfaction of libidinal derivatives, gives rise to pleasure.

It is to be noted in this connection that Melanie Klein maintained that aggression is the prime, if not the only source of anxiety and conflict (Klein, 1948). This view is, by now, widespread. It does not, I believe, accord with available psychoanalytic data. Either libidinal or aggressive wishes in early childhood can give rise to intense unpleasure leading to conflict. Daily analytic experience demonstrates that this is so. The fact that libidinal and aggressive wishes are so closely intertwined in the mental lives of adult patients, as indeed they are in the mental lives of all adults, does not justify ignoring either as a source of unpleasure. Both are invariably involved, though sometimes the one or the other appears to be more important.

In addition, Klein's formulation has undesirable, practical consequences. It readily gives rise to a belief that love is good and wholesome in psychic life, while hate is unwholesome. It is hard to escape the conclusion that those most influenced by Klein's ideas believe this to be the case. Whether they do or not, however, nothing is further from the truth. Both libidinal and aggressive derivatives play their part in psychic conflict. In consequence, both participate in the formation of neurotic symptoms and neurotic character traits, i.e., of pathological compromise formations, as well as of the compromise formations regarded as normal, i.e., normal character traits, normal thought and behavior, and normal mental life as a whole. All of this will be discussed at greater length in subsequent chapters.

There are two other features of the role of drives in psychic conflict that must be mentioned. One concerns the idea of conflict between drive derivatives, the other, the idea of conflict due to an inherent or basic antagonism between ego and drives.

Drive derivatives are never in conflict because their aims are disparate or even logically incompatible. This is something that Fenichel (1945a, p. 129) clearly stated long ago. Despite this, it is still overlooked at times, often with regrettable practical consequences. However disparate their aims, wishes that originate in the drives can be gratified in succession or even simultaneously without conflict. Opposite aims are readily tolerated.

Drive derivatives conflict only when one is used to ward off another. If, for example, murderous wishes give rise to anxiety, to guilt, or to depressive affect, loving wishes may be used defensively to ward them off. In every reaction formation there is a dynamic relation of this sort between drive derivatives that are in conflict with one another. What is important to realize is that they are in conflict because one is used defensively to ward the other off in order to eliminate or to alleviate unpleasure. Drive as defense against drive plays a large role in many clinical situations. Drive in conflict with drive, except for purpose of defense, does not occur. A clear appreciation of this fact is of great practical importance in clinical work. For instance, no severe ambivalence conflict can be properly understood without it. The same is true, I believe, for cases of sexual perversion and for many neurotic character disorders. In all of these the gratification of one or more drive derivatives serves an important defensive function. In ambivalence conflicts, for example, loving wishes are not merely gratifying as such. They also serve to defend against cruel, vengeful drive derivatives and vice versa. In the same way, the gratification of feminine wishes in a case of sexual perversion in a male is not only gratifying as such. It also serves the purpose of defense against other sexual wishes which arouse intense anxiety or depressive affect. The same is true, with suitable changes, for many neurotic character disorders. Whenever one drive derivative is in conflict with another, it is because the one serves a defensive purpose as well as achieving gratification as such.

To turn to the second feature mentioned above, to the idea of an inherent antagonism between ego and drives, the hypothesis that there is a fundamental opposition between the two, i.e. between the two agencies, ego and id, was emphasized by Anna Freud (1936). She later modified her views in this regard, giving credit to Hartmann for having called her attention to the one-sidedness of what she had written earlier. As she put it, "The ego's role as an ally of the id precedes that of an agent designed to slow up and obstruct satisfaction" (A. Freud, 1952, p. 236).

I believe that even the opinion just quoted does not do full justice to the facts of the case. What psychoanalytic theory subsumes under the heading of ego functions is separable or distinguishable from drives and drive derivatives only in situations of conflict. Ego functions are the executants of the drives and their derivatives (Brenner, 1973b, p. 41). They are inseparable and indistinguishable from them except when a drive derivative arouses unpleasure and, for that reason, defense.

It is my impression that the clinical data giving rise to the mistaken idea that ego and drives are antagonistic to one another are data of the following sort. Children, as well as some adults who resemble children in this respect, may be thrown into a turmoil which is marked by considerable disorganization of their relation to their environment by the appearance of intense anxiety or other unpleasure associated with an exciting drive derivative. Their subjective experience is that excitement leads to their being upset and unable to think sensibly or to act rationally, and it is perfectly appropriate to interpret to them, in such a case, the relation between wish (drive derivative) and functional incapacity. It is quite a different matter to infer from such clinical data that the patients in question are disabled by the mere intensity of their drive derivatives, rather than by anxiety or depressive affect deriving from their wishes and the consequent defensive reaction, which in such cases includes defensive regression of ego functioning (see Arlow and Brenner, 1964, Chapter 6). Whether in children or in adults, *disorganization of ego functioning resulting from wishes that give rise to intense unpleasure is not simply the consequence of the patient's ego being overwhelmed by drive derivatives. The experience such patients describe and the behavior they manifest, usually referred to as fragmentation of the ego, as disintegration of the ego, as loss of ego boundaries, etc., are symptoms of conflict, like any others. They are* not *endopsychic perceptions or their empathically perceived equivalents. They are compromise formations of the usual sort as far as their dynamic structure is concerned, however unusual they may be in intensity and with respect to the severity of their consequences.*

DRIVE FUSION

The final topic to be considered in this chapter is the theory of the fusion and defusion of the drives. The German word

Freud usually employed in this connection (*Mischung*) is slightly more ambiguous than the English word fusion. It means either mixture or alloy, whereas fusion means only the latter.

If one assumes, as Freud did, that aggression is the reflection in psychic life of a universal death drive, the concept of fusion is an attractive possibility. In the physical sphere, one can assume that the fusion of the two drives accounts for the immortality of germ plasm and makes possible the reproduction of the species. In addition, it seemed to Freud that clinically observable facts in connection with identification and with regression in general support the fusion-defusion theory from the psychological side.

Freud had already demonstrated that identification plays a large role in both melancholia and in superego formation (Freud, 1917a, 1923). Identification, Freud said, is a primitive form of object relation. The appearance of identification in melancholia and in superego formation is therefore to be attributed to regression. One can explain the increase of self-directed aggression in cases of melancholia, then, if one assumes that regression leads to a defusion of the drives, the unmixed aggression being once more self-directed, as Freud assumed it to be originally, before it became mixed with libido and turned outward in the normal course of development after birth.

If one does not follow Freud in relating aggression as a drive in mental life to a universal death drive, it is difficult or impossible to decide whether aggression and libido are separate at birth and become mixed in the course of development, as Freud asserted is the case, or whether they are indistinguishable at birth and become separate and distinguishable factors in mental life in the course of development, an alternative suggestion made by Fenichel (1935, pp. 367ff.), Jacobson (1964, p. 13), and others. The psychoanalytic data are not such as permit a decision. One cannot, as I have observed more than once, gather reliable, pertinent evidence by the use of the psychoanalytic method before a considerable degree of psychic development has taken place, nor are reconstructions of very early psychic events thoroughly convincing.

Moreover, identification has been found to be of much more general importance in mental life and development than was apparent when Freud (1917a) wrote *Mourning and Melancholia*. It is not a primitive mechanism that recurs regressively only in connection with object loss. On the contrary, even in superego formation, identification with a feared and envied rival is principally dependent on factors other than object loss (see Chapter 8). Identification plays a large role normally as well as pathologically in many of the object relations of later life as well as in the early ones, and it is not always accompanied by an increase in self-directed aggression. In some instances, as, for example, in group formation, it leads to diminution of self-directed aggression and turning of aggression outward. In other instances no major shift is discernible in the aims and object of aggression. It appears, therefore, that the clinical facts connected with the phenomenon of identification are not compellingly in support of Freud's theory of drive fusion.

Another set of phenomena that have been adduced in support of the theory of drive fusion has to do with ambivalence. It has been asserted that psychoanalytic observations demonstrate that ambivalence is maximal in the earliest, oral phase of life and minimal in the postoedipal, genital phase, at least when psychosexual development is normal. In the psychoanalytic literature of a few decades ago one frequently comes across the opinion that one of the chief goals of psychoanalytic therapy is to assist patients to achieve a stage of postambivalent object relations, a stage that was either relinquished as a result of regression at the onset of the patients' neuroses or one they never achieved in any substantial measure.

No one can doubt the clinical significance of ambivalence, nor overlook the important role it plays in many aspects of pathological psychic conflicts. However, it is as yet unproven that there is a normal progression from ambivalence to nonambivalence in the first years of life, a progression which, if it were to be demonstrated, would offer considerable support to Freud's theory of drive fusion, since it would fit so well with it and be so readily explained by it. The available psychoanalytic evidence speaks more strongly in a different direction, however. It favors the conclusion that psychic conflicts which are related to intense feelings of love and hate toward the same individual arise in most persons during or after the third year of life, i.e., in the course of the oedipal phase of development. One cannot disprove the possibility that ambivalence as a potent force in mental life regularly antedates the oedipal period. One can say only that what psychoanalytic evidence is available speaks in favor of the view that ambivalence is usually at its peak during the oedipal period rather than in favor of the view that it is by then in decline from a previously higher level of intensity.

In fine, what evidence is available at present is not sufficient to support a decision in favor of either of the two possibilities that have been offered. One cannot say whether aggression and libido are separate at the start of psychic development and gradually mix or fuse in the course of it, or whether the two differentiate gradually from a common matrix.

SUMMARY

The neurophysiology of the drives is as obscure today as it was in 1933, when Freud compared them to mythic creatures, but the drives are no different in this respect from all other psychic phenomena. Neurophysiological and neurochemical methods of investigation are not, as yet, very informative methods of studying any of the psychological phenomena in which psychoanalysts are interested. Psychoanalysis is by far the most useful method of studying those phenomena, which is to say that psychoanalytic data are the most satisfactory basis for theories about any of them, including the drives. The concept of drives in mental life is properly based on psychoanalytic data plus other readily available subjective and behavioral data.

On the basis of psychoanalytic data one can say the following about the drives:

They are generalizations drawn from the psychoanalytic study of wishes.

They drive the mind to activity. They are the wellsprings of human motivation.

They comprise two categories, libidinal and aggressive.

They are active from the earliest time in psychic life of which we have reliable knowledge.

Drive derivatives always contain both libidinal and aggressive components, as far as is known.

It is uncertain whether libido and aggression are separate or commingled in the dawn of psychic life.

The drives have no special, extracerebral source. Like all other psychic phenomena, they are an aspect of cerebral functioning. However, libido has a close and special relation to genitals, mouth, anus and, to a lesser extent, touch, sight, smell, and sound.

Psychic energy is not a form of physical energy. It is an analogue of it. Psychic energy cannot be quantified or measured with any precision.

Drive derivatives are substantially influenced by experience, especially with respect to aims and objects. There is, in other words, a more important relation between the drives and ego development than is usually realized.

Both aggression and libido are within the pleasure principle, not beyond it.

Derivatives of both give rise to unpleasure and conflict on occasion.

There is no inherent antagonism between ego and drives. When it occurs, disruption of ego functioning is a symptom, to be analyzed like any other symptom.

Drive derivatives are in conflict only when one is used to relieve anxiety or depressive affect aroused by another.

CHAPTER 3

AFFECTS

The phenomena subsumed under the headings of drives and drive derivatives are concerned with seeking and achieving pleasure. The pleasure principle is fundamental to the whole of the psychoanalytic theory of psychic functioning. According to that principle the mind functions in such a way as to attain pleasure and to avoid unpleasure. Since drive gratification is pleasurable and frustration, or lack of gratification, is unpleasurable, it follows that, according to psychoanalytic theory, the mind functions to achieve gratification of drive derivatives as fully and as promptly as possible. Yet in situations of psychic conflict precisely the reverse appears to be the case. The mind functions in such a way as to postpone, to prevent, and to limit the gratification of one or several drive derivatives. To be more precise, in situations of psychic conflict one part of psychic functioning is intent on achieving gratification of a drive derivative while another aims at preventing it.

How does this come about? How does it happen that the ego, which develops as the executant of the drives, as the agency for the gratification of drive derivatives, can on occasion oppose them and prevent their being gratified?

The answer to this question involves a detour into the theory of affects, since it is a question that can be answered only if one has a correct understanding of the nature of affects in general and of unpleasurable affects in particular. In this chapter, therefore, I shall present as much of the theory of affects as is necessary for an understanding of their role in psychic conflict. My presentation is based on an earlier exposition of the subject (Brenner, 1974c). Before that time much was known about anxiety and its role in conflict and much had been written about it, but very little had been written about affects other than anxiety. There was no theory of affects in the psychoanalytic literature prior to 1974 adequate to the task of explaining their role in psychic conflict. The one I offered was the first to do so.

It is a theory based on psychoanalytic data. It asserts that affects are complex mental phenomena which can best be understood in developmental terms. Their antecedents are sensations of pleasure and unpleasure, the most important of which are the sensations associated with the lack of gratification of a drive derivative, so-called drive tension, and with the gratification of a drive derivative, i.e. with drive discharge. Such sensations of pleasure and unpleasure are the undifferentiated matrix from which the entire gamut of the affects of later life develop.

At an early stage of psychic development memories and other ideas become associated with the sensations of pleasure and unpleasure connected with drive derivatives. The resulting complex of sensation and ideas is an affect. The continuing development of affects and their differentiation from one another depend on ego and, later, on superego development. In fact, the development and differentiation of affects is an important chapter in ego development.

Thus any affect includes (a) sensations of pleasure, of unpleasure, or of a mixture of the two plus (b) thoughts, memories, wishes, fears—in a word, ideas. *Ideas and sensation together constitute an affect* as a psychological phenomenon.

To avoid misunderstanding, the following should be noted. First, anxiety is not to be differentiated from other affects in any of the above respects. Second, whatever the affect, either the pleasure-unpleasure, the ideas, or both may be wholly or partly unconscious or otherwise warded off.

This bare outline may be amplified as follows.

1. DEVELOPMENTAL PROPOSITIONS

A. SENSATIONS OF PLEASURE AND UNPLEASURE

It seems reasonable to conclude from the available evidence, both subjective and objective, that sensations of pleasure and of unpleasure associated with drive derivatives in adult life are not significantly different from sensations of pleasure and of unpleasure associated with drive derivatives in the early stages of psychic development. However, attention must be paid to a possible exception, one which has to do with sexual gratification. Most persons do not experience orgasm before puberty. Does the pleasure of orgasm differ in kind from the pleasure of sexual gratification before orgasm is possible?

This question is an important one. Should it turn out that the correct answer is affirmative, significant consequences would be entailed for the psychoanalytic theory of affects. At present, unfortunately, we have no reliable evidence on which to base an answer. The available evidence is both scant and unreliable, consisting of occasional memories of experiences distant in time.

The best one can say on the subject is this. There is no doubt of the fact that the physical sensations which are part of the experience of orgasm are special to that experience. It is impossible to be sure at present, however, whether the *pleasure* in orgasm differs from other, earlier sensations of pleasure except in its extraordinary intensity. One cannot say with confidence that it differs in quality. It may be that there are developmental changes in sensations of pleasure and of unpleasure during the course of physical and psychic maturation, therefore, but at present there is no certain knowledge of any. The provisional formulation, made with due reservation, must be that the sensations of pleasure and of unpleasure which are associated with drive derivatives in adult life do not differ significantly from those of very early life. Pleasure and unpleasure have no developmental history, as far as is known at present. They are constitutionally determined. They are part of each person's endowment.

This is not to say that pleasure and unpleasure play no part in psychic development. Clearly they play a very large part which is of crucial importance. It is only to say that pleasure and unpleasure do not themselves change significantly in the course of development as far as is known. Pleasure and unpleasure sensations are present at the beginning of psychic life, whenever that dawn may come in the chronology of physical development. They are urgently important at that time and they remain so, as far as is known, without qualitative change throughout the rest of life.

B. IDEAS

The developmental history of the ideas which are part of every affect is obviously very different from the developmental history of pleasure and unpleasure sensations. By definition ideas are dependent on ego development and, later, on the development of the superego as well.

The ideational content of every affect involves memories, mental representations of objects, mental representations of one's own physical sensations, etc., whether the affect is joy or misery, yearning or dread. All such ideational elements are part of ego functioning. All have a progressive development from the early months of life, when psychic life has just begun and ego functioning is at its most primitive, through every stage of maturation to that which is called adult.

Thus, as far as present knowledge goes, the development of affects from infancy to adult life means the development of the ideas which are a part of affects. It is the ideational content that changes progressively and that accounts for the differences between primitive affects and those that are more mature—between those often called global and those called discrete or differentiated.

2. CLASSIFICATION OF AFFECTS

An important advantage of the new theory of affects has to do with classifying them and distinguishing one from the other. This can be done most usefully on the basis of the two components of every affect, i.e., pleasure-unpleasure sensations and ideas.

A first, broad classification of affects would separate them into those characterized by sensations of pleasure and those characterized by sensations of unpleasure (Glover, 1947). One must remember, however, that in any particular case such sensations may be repressed or otherwise defended against. Only psychoanalytic data offer the possibility of reliable and comprehensive information with respect to both pleasure-unpleasure sensations and ideas. An affect that is consciously perceived as pleasurable may prove to include hidden or disguised unpleasure as well, or vice versa. For this reason any classification should provide for a third category, namely, affects characterized by a mixture of sensations of pleasure and unpleasure.

Among affects, whether characterized by sensations of pleasure, by sensations of unpleasure, or by a mixture of the two, one can distinguish those whose ideational contents are similar in important respects. For example, one may agree to label as happiness (or joy) any affect that includes a sensation of pleasure and ideas of gratification of a drive derivative. Either the ideas or the sensation of pleasure may be unconscious or otherwise distorted or disguised. The sensation of pleasure may be mild or intense. The precise content of the ideas will necessarily vary from person to person and from instance to instance in the psychic life of a single person. Still, if the affect fulfills the conditions just described, i.e., if adequate data, usually psychoanalytic data, indicate a sensation of pleasure plus ideas of gratification of a drive derivative, the affect will be called happiness. Conversely, for an affect to be called happiness, it will have to conform to the definition, i.e., it must be made up of a sensation of pleasure and ideas of gratification of a drive derivative.

Within that definition, as already noted, there can be considerable variation from one instance to another. The feeling of pleasure may be slight or it may be intense. The gratification may be libidinal or aggressive; it may be oral, anal, or phallic. Either the pleasure or the ideas of gratification may be largely conscious or largely unconscious or otherwise defended against. In every instance, moreover, the ideas of gratification will be individual, i.e., specific for the person in question. Nevertheless, whatever the individual variations, an affect will be called happiness if, but only if it includes a sensation of pleasure and ideas of gratification of a drive derivative.

This way of classifying affects also allows one to distinguish varieties of a broad classification like happiness. If the sensation of pleasure is intense, the affect may be called ecstasy or bliss. If the ideas have to do with having defeated a rival or rivals, one may define the variety of happiness as triumph. Depending on the intensity of the pleasure and the nature of the associated ideas, one may define varieties of triumph as omnipotence, as self-satisfaction, as mild superiority, or as smugness.

Thus, speaking generally, the theory of affects presented here enables one to define pleasurable affects and to distinguish them from one another on the basis of (a) the intensity of the pleasurable sensation and (b) the content and origin of the associated ideas. The same holds true for unpleasurable affects. Among these, the affect that has been most often and most extensively discussed among psychoanalysts is anxiety. How is anxiety to be conceptualized or defined within the new theory of affects?

As it happens, the theory of affects I presented in 1974 grew out of a study of anxiety (Brenner, 1953). At that time I suggested the following definition of anxiety.

> Anxiety is an emotion (affect) which the anticipation of danger evokes in the ego. It is not present as such from birth or very early infancy. In such very early periods the infant is aware only of pleasure or unpleasure as far as emotions are concerned. As experience increases, and other ego functions develop (e.g., memory and sensory perception), the child becomes able to predict or anticipate that a state of unpleasure (a 'traumatic situation') will develop. This dawning ability of the child to react to danger in advance is the beginning of the specific emotion of anxiety, which in the course of further development we may suppose to become increasingly sharply differentiated from other unpleasant emotions [e.g., depression; p. 22].

According to the definition just quoted, then, anxiety is unpleasure plus a particular set of ideas: something unpleasurable is going to happen. In other words, it is unpleasure accompanied by ideas that in one way or another have to do with danger. Any affect, if it is to be called anxiety, must conform to this definition. As in the case of happiness, however, so in the case of anxiety different labels may be used to indicate variations both in the intensity of the unpleasure experienced and in the nature of the conscious and unconscious ideas associated with it. If the danger is perceived as acute or imminent, we may speak of fear; if the unpleasure is intense, of panic. If the unpleasure is mild and if the danger is perceived as slight, as uncertain, or as distant, we may well speak of worry or uneasiness. Thus, in the case of anxiety as in the case of any other affect, the theory of affects I have introduced enables one to define an affect and to distinguish one variety of it from another on the basis of psychoanalytic data which are accessible in a clinical situation. If the psychoanalytic method can be applied, an affect can be identified. In similar fashion, when one has data from many cases, one has a reliable basis for a satisfactory classification of affects.

Using anxiety as a paradigm has the great advantage of long familiarity with anxiety in a wide variety of clinical situations. The new theory can be validated by analytic experience with anxiety and the relation between theory and data can be easily appreciated. Every analyst is thoroughly familiar with the fact that, in the case of anxiety, the unpleasure may be unconscious even though the ideational content is conscious, at least in large part. Equally familiar are situations in which the unpleasure is conscious in large measure, but the ideational content of the affect is unconscious or otherwise warded off. Whenever a patient is conscious of no unpleasure in connection with thoughts of danger, we look for the reasons why that is the case. Whenever a patient is unaware what it is that he or she fears, we routinely direct our analytic efforts toward answering the questions, "What is this patient unconsciously afraid of?" and, "What are the origins of this patient's fears?"

The theory of affects I have presented goes a step further. It asserts that anxiety is but one example, that it is a paradigm rather than an exception. It asserts that in the respects just mentioned all affects are alike, and to analyze any affect means to explore its unconscious elements and origins, just as we customarily do with anxiety.

It should be noted that not all unpleasure associated with drive derivatives has an ideational content which is concerned with danger, i.e., with an impending calamity. Unpleasure may be associated with ideas of a calamity that has already happened, for example. I have called such an affect depressive affect in order to distinguish it from anxiety. Depending on the intensity of the unpleasure, one may speak of misery, of sadness, or of discontent. If the emphasis is on ideas of longing for a lost object, of wishing it were back, we may speak of loneliness. If, as Darwin (1872) said, "we have no hope of relief," we speak of despair. If the emphasis is on being scolded or being ridiculed, we speak of shame or humiliation, and so on.

As has been noted already, affects, at least in adult life, are often characterized by a mixture of sensations of pleasure and unpleasure, rather than by one or the other alone. In some experiences of anxiety, for example, both unpleasure and pleasurable excitement are conscious. These experiences have been explained as the result of a libidinization of anxiety, but this explanation does not do justice to the facts of the situation. The idea expressed by the term libidinization of anxiety is that, when anxiety appears in consciousness, it can, in certain cases, become itself a source of libidinal excitation. The facts are otherwise. Analysis shows that when an individual consciously feels both unpleasure and pleasure plus conscious ideas of an impending calamity, there are also unconscious ideas of gratification of a drive derivative. As an illustration, before going onstage, an actor was aware of pleasure, of unpleasure, and of an expectation of giving a performance which would be a dismal failure. That is to say, he had stage fright together with a conscious feeling of pleasurable excitement. What his associations revealed was not that his anxiety was the source of his conscious, pleasurable excitement. They revealed instead the expected memories of childhood experiences and fantasies of humiliation, of loss of love, and of castration plus unconscious fantasies of exhibitionistic gratification in the present—that he would be a great success, a cynosure, etc.—which were also related to childhood drive derivatives. It was not the patient's anxiety that was responsible for his conscious, pleasurable excitement. His anxiety had not become libidinized. What accounted for his conscious, pleasurable excitement were his unconscious fantasies of exhibitionistic, libidinal gratification.

When pleasure and unpleasure are mixed, they need not both be conscious. Either one or both may be unconscious or otherwise defended against. The same is true for any part of the ideational content of an affect. To use anxiety once more as a paradigm, in most experiences of anxiety which analysts encounter clinically there is at least unconscious pleasure and/or gratification as part of the total affective experience.

Clinical situations are usually quite complicated in this respect, as one might anticipate. Pleasure and unpleasure, gratification and calamity, are closely intertwined. For example, ideas of overcoming a rival often involve pity or compassion for the rival and an expectation of punishment for having defeated him. In such cases, the victor experiences a mixture of pleasure and unpleasure along with the associated ideas of wanting and fearing to win, of being the loser's rival and of being his ally, of dominating and of being dominated, or of castrating and being castrated.

In such complex situations, which make up so many of the affects in adults with which analysts are faced in their work, it matters little whether one speaks of mixed affects, as I have done, or of a mixture of affects. The difference is one of terminology more than of substance. Whichever terminology one prefers, one realizes, as one considers individual instances of affects encountered and analyzed in clinical situations, that affects are never precisely the same in any two individuals. They vary with respect to the intensity of pleasure and unpleasure, with respect to the mixture of the two, and with respect to the ideas which are part of each affect. No two persons can ever wish, fear, or remember precisely the same things. An affect is never the same for one person as for the next. Affects have common elements which can serve as a basis for classification. No more than this, however, can be meant when one classifies and names an affect.

It is equally important to bear in mind that only psychoanalytic data offer a satisfactory basis for classification. In other contexts than the study of affects it is a familiar clinical finding that conscious mental phenomena are only a part of the whole story. Similar conscious mental phenomena may have very different unconscious determinants in two different patients, while very similar unconscious determinants may be associated with very different conscious consequences in thought and behavior. The same is true for affects. When affects are classified or named on the basis of their conscious aspects alone, the result is ambiguity, confusion, or worse. The same name is often used for very different constellations of pleasure, unpleasure, and ideas. The reverse is also true. Different names turn out to refer to very similar affective states. As an example, we customarily call some affective states euphoria instead of simple joy, precisely in order to emphasize their close kinship with sadness or depression, just as we sometimes call courage a counterphobic reaction in order to emphasize its kinship with anxiety. These considerations will be discussed further in Chapter 4.

3. EXPRESSION OF AFFECT

The theory of affects presented here offers at least a partial answer to the question of variations from one person to another in the manifestations and expressions of affect. Why should it be that one person screams when frightened, another faints, and a third becomes nauseated? It is because of the long and close connection between affects and experience in the course of psychic development. Developmental influences in childhood can vary widely, with the result that ego development and later functioning vary widely as well. Processes of identification, of inhibition or exaggeration of function, of disguise and distortion, affect every aspect of ego development and functioning. They affect emotions (affects) both with respect to their ideational content, as has been seen, and with respect to their modes of expression. In this sense one must agree with Freud's (1916-1917) comparison between affective expression and an hysterical paroxysm. Both are determined by events of the past which unconsciously shape behavior in the present.

The same considerations help to explain the variations in the manifestations of affect from one culture to another. On the basis of what is known of the development of affects in individuals, one may assume that here too identification plays an important role. Children may be expected first to imitate, later to identify with and become like the significant adults in their environment with respect to manifestations of affect no less than with respect to various other aspects of behavior such as gait, speech, posture, and recreational and vocational interests (Brenner, 1973b, p. 216). The manifestations of affect must be unconsciously directed and influenced in their development in this and in other, similar ways, ways that differ in different societies or cultures and that lead to striking differences in the end results. There can be little doubt that many other factors enter into the process. However, an understanding of the connection between affective life and the whole complex sequence of psychic development offers at least a partial answer to the question of societal variations in the manifestation and expression of affect, just as it does to the question of individual variations.

4. DISCUSSION

The data on which a theory of affects can be based fall into three categories. The first is subjective. It includes experiences common to mankind. The second is behavioral. Under this heading are included both actions mediated by skeletal musculature under voluntary control and such phenomena as changes in pulse rate, blood pressure, respiration, bladder or bowel function, lachrymal secretion, and hormonal release or production. The third category includes observations of the behavior of animals other than man—behavior believed to be relevant to what we identify as affects or emotions in man. Briefly, then, the data are psychological, neurophysiological, and ethological.

It is clear that affects are psychological phenomena. They are part of conscious mental life. Historically, therefore, the first classifications of affects and the first attempts to study them systematically were based on introspection, since for a very long time introspection was the only method of study available.

I have already discussed the inadequacy of introspection as a method of psychological investigation as well as the explanation of its inadequacy, an explanation that was furnished only after psychoanalytic data became available (Chapter 1). To repeat only the conclusion, psychological data accessible to introspection are incomplete to begin with and have, in addition, been systematically and intentionally falsified.

The psychoanalytic method has not merely furnished an explanation of the unreliability of introspective data, however. It has also made it possible to gain access to psychological data which are complete enough and reliable enough to serve as a satisfactory basis for a theory of affects. Nevertheless, until I proposed one in 1974, no theory of affects had been based on psychoanalytic data alone, just as no psychoanalytic theory of drives was ever based primarily on psychoanalytic data prior to the one outlined in Chapter 2. Some attention had been paid to the developmental aspect of affects (Glover, 1947; Katan, 1972) and to the intimate association between affects and ideas (Novey, 1959; Lewin, 1961, 1965; Schur, 1969). Incidentally, though Novey, Lewin, and Schur emphasized that ideas and affects are closely linked, none of them concluded that ideas are a part of affects. On the whole, however, psychoanalysts who wrote about affect theory followed Freud (1915a, 1916-1917, 1919a), first, in emphasizing the relation between affects and the gratification and/or frustration of drive derivatives and, second, in the assumption that affects are preformed, constitutionally determined psychic phenomena. Freud himself, believing as he did in the inheritability of the effects of very intense environmental influences, attributed what he called the core of each affect to "the repetition of some particular significant experience . . . in the prehistory not of the individual but of the species" (1916-1917, p. 396).

As to the relation of affects to the flux of drive frustration and gratification, Freud's idea is correct, but incomplete. Affects are related not only to the gratification and the frustration of drive derivatives; they are also related to the maturation and development of ego and superego. It may be noted that Jacobson (1953) was the first to call attention to this aspect of affect theory.

As to the second of Freud's assumptions, the idea that affects are preformed, constitutionally determined psychic phenomena is not supported by the available evidence.

Consider first the available evidence from ethology. How far does it go in justifying the view that each affect is a different constitutional given in human psychic life? The answer is that ethological evidence offers very little to justify such a view. As Cannon (1929) and his associates demonstrated, there is no objective evidence that enables one to distinguish fear from rage or hunger, even in an animal whose central nervous system is as high in the evolutionary scale as a cat. The only basis for distinguishing the one from the other is subjective: "If I were a cat and were exposed to those stimuli, I would be frightened, angry, or hungry." It is possible to say with a reasonable degree of assurance whether an animal with a central nervous system large enough to have a convoluted cerebral cortex is experiencing pleasure or unpleasure. It is not possible to identify with assurance specific affects analogous to those assumed to be constitutional givens in human mental life.

Neurophysiological and behavioral evidence in humans themselves, whether infants or adults, is more informative than is the evidence of ethology, but it is still ambiguous. Lachrymal secretion may be associated with conscious pleasure, as in laughing till the tears come, or with unpleasure, as in sorrow. Screaming may be associated with rage, with physical pain, or with terror. Tachycardia appears with a variety of affects, both pleasurable and unpleasurable, as do hypertension, salivation, increased peristalsis. Even genital tumescence and lubrication are not invariably reliable signs of pleasurable sexual excitement.

As for introspection, I have already called attention to its unreliability and to the reason for it. To rely on introspection and intuition (often called empathy) to prove that each affect is a constitutional given, distinguishable from its near or distant relatives as such, is to trust a slender reed. Those who do so are really basing their classification of affects on verbal usage, as de Rivera (1977) and Dahl (1979) chose to do, or on lexical authority. Neither popular nor literary linguistic convention is a suitable basis for any psychological theory. It is certainly not an adequate basis for an acceptable theory of affects. To use it as a basis for one must lead in the end to confusion in theory and to errors in practice.

In short, at present the only adequate basis for a theory of the psychic phenomena called affects are psychoanalytic data, supplemented by what neurophysiology and ethology have to offer. The theory I propose is based on such data—primarily, of course, on psychoanalytic data. It is a theory that was suggested by and derives its chief support from what the psychoanalytic method has discovered and demonstrated about human psychic development and functioning. It is the best theory of affects currently available, simply because it derives from the application of the best method currently available for studying the mind and its functioning: the psychoanalytic method. A theory of affects that relies principally on psychoanalytic data must be superior to one that does not give those data first place.

In summary:

1. Affects are complex psychic phenomena that include (a) sensations of pleasure, unpleasure, or both, and (b) ideas. *Ideas and pleasure-unpleasure sensations together constitute an affect.*

2. The development of affects and their differentiation from one another depend on ego development. In fact, the differentiation of affects from immature and global to mature and specific is an important aspect of ego-maturational development.

3. This definition enables one to classify affects and to distinguish them from one another on the basis (a) of the intensity of the sensations of pleasure and/or unpleasure and (b) of the content and origin of the ideas that constitute each affect.

4. The concept of affects presented here offers at least a partial answer to the questions of variability of affective expression from one individual to another and from one culture to another.

The reader will recall that the account of affect theory just summarized is preliminary to a discussion of the role of affects in psychic conflict. In this chapter all affects, both pleasurable and unpleasurable, were considered. In the next chapter the focus will be on unpleasurable affects associated with drive derivatives.

Under certain circumstances, drive derivatives pressing for gratification arouse anxiety and depressive affect. Both of these are unpleasurable, sometimes intensely so. This is what accounts for the fact that the ego, which develops as the executant of the drives, as the agency for the gratification of drive derivatives, can on occasion oppose them. Such an opposition between ego and drive derivative is the essence of psychic conflict.

CHAPTER 4

AFFECTS AND PSYCHIC CONFLICT

The principal message of this chapter is that the unpleasurable affects that trigger psychic conflict are of two kinds, anxiety and depressive affect. As I noted at the end of Chapter 3, conflict occurs whenever gratification of a drive derivative is associated with a sufficiently intense, unpleasurable affect. I should add here that superego demands and prohibitions which arouse anxiety or depressive affect of sufficient intensity will also occasion conflict (Freud, 1923). This source of conflict will be discussed in detail later (principally in Chapter 8). I mention it here lest it seem to be unwittingly neglected in what follows.

Since either anxiety or depressive affect can figure in psychic conflict, it is essential, first of all, to distinguish between them. The distinction is based on ideational content. Both affects are unpleasurable. In this respect they are similar. It is only in their respective ideational contents that they differ.

Psychoanalytic data demonstrate that the ideational content of both affects has to do with events and with time. That is to say, it has to do with what is so unpleasurable and with whether it is happening, has happened, or will happen.

As for the unpleasurable events, they turn out to be the familiar calamities of childhood: object loss, loss of love, and castration—what Freud (1926) called the typical dangers of childhood psychic life. They are the same for depressive affect as for anxiety. Not so the temporal aspect. A sensation of unpleasure plus ideas that one, or more than one, calamity will happen is, by definition, anxiety. A sensation of unpleasure plus ideas that one, or more than one, calamity has happened is, again by definition, depressive affect (Brenner, 1974c).

When a sensation of unpleasure is accompanied by ideas that one, or more than one, calamity is happening, it is difficult to know whether the affect is better classified as anxiety or as depressive affect. Sometimes the one seems preferable, sometimes the other. For example, a child may feel, "Mother no longer loves me." This would be an affect characterized by unpleasure and the idea of a calamity in the present. For one child, however, the calamity in the present may have the ideational content, "She does not love me. She stopped long ago when [her] baby came," or, "She stopped yesterday when I wished she was dead." For another child the present calamity may have the ideational content, "She hates me. She does not love me any more. She will never love me again."

The first instance would be an example of depressive affect, in the opinion of most observers. The second would be classified by most as an example of anxiety. I think, however, that all would agree that it makes but little difference which label one applies to either—which is to say that anxiety and depressive affect can, at times, be indistinguishable varieties of unpleasure plus ideas about the occurrence of one or more of the calamities of childhood in the present.

When that is the case, when the distinction is merely an academic one, there is nothing to be gained by trying to decide whether the affect in question is better classified as anxiety or as depressive affect. In the great majority of cases, however, the distinction between the two is clear, and in those cases it is of great practical importance to reach a decision as to which affect is involved. It makes a significant difference to one's understanding of a patient's conflicts if the patient's unpleasure has to do with impending calamity, i.e., with danger, if it has to do with a calamity which has happened already, i.e., with present misery, or, as is often the case, if it has to do with both at the same time. When one classifies an unpleasurable affect as anxiety, one means that ideas of calamity are in the future, that the present situation is one of danger. When one classifies an unpleasurable affect as depressive affect, one means that the calamity has happened in the past, that the present situation is one of misery and suffering as a result.

As noted in Chapter 1, prior to the publication of my (1975a) article on the subject anxiety was considered to be the only affect that triggers psychic conflict (Freud, 1926). What kinds of data support my reformulation?

The following case material, which I offer as an illustration, is of a sort that is familiar to every analyst from clinical experience. Thus it not only illustrates the role of depressive affect in psychic conflict, it illustrates as well how abundant are the psychoanalytic data that demonstrate its role.

A patient in his mid-twenties, as he lay on the couch, would often pick at a sore on his hands or face, finger an old scar, rub a shoulder which had been injured some years earlier, or give some other indication of pain or injury. His attention was repeatedly directed to this behavior, and it gradually became apparent that all these gestures were unconsciously intended to gain my sympathy. In each case he had either told me or was about to tell me of actions or wishes that made him feel guilty and of which he believed that I, too, disapproved. His sores and injuries were unconscious evidences that he had already punished himself enough for his misdeeds and that he should be pitied and coddled rather than blamed and hated, as he expected to be.

As the unconscious motivation of his behavior on the couch emerged, it became apparent that it was a transference to the analysis of a pattern of behavior established well before his adolescence. Whenever he was engaged in aggressive or competitive behavior, he tended to injure himself, to make himself fail or lose, or both. When, on the contrary, he had suffered a severe reversal in his life, he could sometimes compete with much less inhibition. Eventually it was possible in the course of his analysis for him to be conscious of daydreams that had previously been unconscious altogether or had been briefly conscious but soon repressed. These daydreams accompanied every ambitious, competitive action he undertook. In them he imagined himself confronted by an older man who was invariably more powerful than he, whether physically or by virtue of his position in life. The main business of the daydream was a violent conflict between the patient and his opponent, which always ended with the patient being defeated. Sometimes the defeat was physical, sometimes not, but it was invariably complete. There was never any question who had won.

At the same time it became possible to understand the unconscious meaning of a repetitive element of his nocturnal dreams. He remembered only a small fraction of his dreams, but of the ones he did remember many had to do with fighting with other men. These dreams probably began in latency, or, at the latest, in early adolescence. In them the patient was always inhibited in attacking his opponents and was often unable to defend himself effectively. He could never strike an opponent forcefully, either with his fists or with a weapon. If he had a gun, it would not fire, and often he could not even run away.

There was evidence from many sources, therefore—from his behavior during his analytic sessions, from his past and present difficultues in every competitive situation, from his daydreams, and from his nocturnal dreams—that this patient both inhibited and punished himself for his competitive strivings, strivings directed unconsciously toward his powerful father and also, as it turned out, toward an older brother, who was the principal conscious enemy of his childhood.

What part was played by anxiety in all of this and what part by depressive affect?

In those real-life situations in which the patient inhibited his competitive strivings, as well as in the dreams in which he could not fight effectively, anxiety clearly played the role psychoanalytic theory customarily assigns to it. In each such instance a competitive wish was equated unconsciously with a murderous childhood wish to surpass and supplant his father or older brother. This aroused fear of retaliation, of loss of love, and of object loss—in his case, of being sent away forever—and he defended himself against his frightening wishes by a kind of reaction formation. He demonstrated that he was weak, stupid, ineffectual, and not to be taken seriously as a competitor. One can guess that he unconsciously castrated himself; indeed, fantasies of actual castration did occasionally erupt into conscious awareness at times of intense conflict over his competitive, murderous wishes.

However, anxiety and defenses against frightening, competitive wishes do not suffice to explain all of the patient's behavior. When he ached, when he, at first, unconsciously, begged to be coddled, when, after analysis had progressed further, he wept bitter tears of misery, he no longer *feared* he would be unloved; he was sure he *was* unloved. His yearning to be coddled, which meant, unconsciously, to be forgiven, did not stem from anxiety, but from a variety of depressive affect which fits best under the heading of remorse.

This aspect of his conflicts emerged even more clearly when, for example, he failed an important examination, when he was refused advancement in his career, or when I left him either to go on a vacation or for some other reason. On those occasions his behavior and associations during his analytic sessions revealed that he was making great efforts to remain unaware of his misery or to counteract it in some other way. What was intolerable was to be conscious of how miserable he was, to know how he really felt. When his career suffered a check, for example, he persuaded himself that he had been wrong to choose the career in the first place, that his true interests lay elsewhere, that the thing for him to do was to recognize his basic mistake and to rectify it by pursuing a different career or a different style of life altogether. Perhaps it was silly to pursue any career. Perhaps the only sensible way of life was the one many of his friends pursued, to despise the conventional ambitions of bourgeois morality and to wander about the world enjoying life as it came. The defensive function of the attitude expressed by this train of thought is obvious. On the several occasions when it occurred, it may be noted that it never succeeded in dispelling the patient's misery. It merely mitigated it. When its defensive function was interpreted to him, the patient's response was, "What should I do? Burst into tears?"

His characteristic response to my leaving him was more successful in avoiding any awareness of his misery. With great enthusiasm he would make vacation plans himself, plans that expressed the idea that, far from feeling lonely and unhappy at my absence, he was eager to get away and glad of an opportunity to do so, either to visit a friend or to take a trip with one. In other words, his reaction to my absence was his way of assuring himself he was happy, not unhappy, that he did not wish to accompany me, that he had his own place to go to, his own trip to take. As might be expected, it was also an unconscious way of taking revenge on me by being the active rather than the passive one of the two of us.

What is one to conclude from all of this? First of all, as has already been noted, some of the patient's reactions to his unconsciously murderous, consciously competitive wishes are readily understandable as defenses triggered by anxiety. In other instances, however, the psychological determinants and motives of his defenses are not understandable on that basis. In those cases the patient was not unconsciously afraid of what would happen as a result of his wish to supplant his father and brother. He was convinced he had indeed been punished for wishing to supplant them and for other bad wishes. His defenses were motivated not by a need to avoid or to minimize anxiety, but by a need to deny or put an end to his misery and unhappiness. Thus, while anxiety played the role customarily assigned to it in some of this patient's conflicts, in other conflicts, or in other aspects of the same conflicts, it was a variety of depressive affect—misery, unhappiness, or remorse—that gave rise to defense and conflict.

It would be easy to provide many more illustrations of the point I wish to make, namely, that either anxiety or depressive affect can play the role in psychic conflict which Freud assigned exclusively to anxiety. Such examples occur frequently in every analyst's practice, a fact that furnishes a solid observational basis for my assertion. Why, then, did Freud conclude otherwise? He did so because of the emphasis he continued to place, in 1926, on certain observations he had made much earlier, observations that have since been shown to be incorrect.

What misguided him was the connection he had made between anxiety and sexuality on the basis of observations which had led him in 1895 to the idea that, in susceptible individuals, sexual excitement without adequate gratification can, by itself, cause a neurosis which is characterized by constant or episodic anxiety. Freud (1895a; 1926, p. 110) called such a state an actual neurosis.[1] Because he was convinced there are such neuroses, he formulated his first theory about the origin and nature of neurotic anxiety, namely, that undischarged libido is, under certain circumstances, transformed into anxiety. In 1926 he explicitly rejected this idea, but he substituted for it the proposition that when the mental apparatus receives an influx of stimuli it cannot adequately bind and/or discharge, anxiety develops automatically, on a purely economic, i.e., on a purely quantitative, basis. Freud found this proposition necessary in order to explain the appearance of what he believed to be anxiety without ideational content, often referred to as contentless anxiety, in the actual neuroses. A psychological theory of anxiety, that is, a theory that defined anxiety as a response to danger, would have sufficed to explain the data of the psychoneuroses, as Freud himself pointed out. It could not, however, explain the genesis of anxiety without ideational content. It could not explain the genesis of anxiety that was simply the result of an excessive accumulation of libido, as Freud asserted is the case in the actual neuroses. As long as he maintained the correctness of the conclusion he had drawn from the data he had reported in 1895, as long as he maintained that there are adults—those with actual neuroses—whose anxiety is unanalyzable because it is a purely automatic response to excessive stimulation, Freud was obliged to maintain as well that unpleasure associated with the drive derivatives of infancy, though without ideational content, is not simply unpleasure, but is specifically anxiety. In 1926 he had to maintain the idea of contentless anxiety in infancy if he was to keep the idea of contentless anxiety in adult life in those patients whom he called actual neurotics.[2]

One can only speculate as to why Freud insisted to the very end of his career that actual neurosis is a valid diagnostic category, that anxiety can and does arise automatically on a purely

[1]The word actual is a poor translation of Freud's gallicism, *aktual*. By *aktual* Freud meant current, of the day, which is the meaning of *actuel* in French. His idea was that this was a neurosis caused by poor sexual hygiene in the present, not by repressed memories of sexual events or wishes, or both, in the past. Thus in the name "actual neurosis," actual must be understood to mean, "caused by events of the present, not by events of the past."

[2]For a more extensive discussion of this matter, see Brenner 1957b.

quantitative basis and without ideational content in vulnerable adults with unhygienic sexual practices. The diagnosis is one that has hardly ever been made by other analysts since the time when Freud first suggested it. Fenichel (1945b) claimed he had seen such a patient, but his report was a cursory one, a bare assertion without any detail to make it persuasive. Moreover, the data on which Freud originally relied were not psychoanalytic data by current criteria, since they date from before 1895, i.e., from a time when psychoanalysis barely existed as a method of investigation and therapy. This fact seems to me to be the one which is the most telling. It was Freud's assertion (1895a) that the anxiety of patients suffering from actual neuroses cannot be analyzed, a statement that is unacceptable at face value today. It is one thing to say it is impossible to analyze a particular patient who suffers from anxiety. No one doubts that that is often the case. It is quite a different thing to say, as Freud did (1895a), that a patient is analyzable, but that analysis shows his anxiety is not caused by or related to fears and memories from his past life. Unless substantiated by adequate psychoanalytic data, such a statement cannot command credence. To date, no such data have been presented.

To repeat, then, whenever satisfaction of a childhood drive derivative gives rise to unpleasure, the unpleasure is either anxiety, depressive affect, or a mixture or combination of the two. By anxiety is meant unpleasure plus ideas of danger, i.e., of an impending calamity. By depressive affect is meant unpleasure plus ideas of a calamity, not of the future, but of the past. In some cases the two affects are, for practical purposes, indistinguishable. However, when they can be distinguished, as they usually can be, it is important that the distinction be made.

Before proceeding with further discussion of some of the implications of this revision of Freud's theory of anxiety and conflict, it is appropriate to take note of divergent opinions that have appeared in the recent literature.

Rangell (1978) reiterated his contention (Rangell, 1955) that what Freud (1926) distinguished as automatic anxiety is really the same as what he called signal anxiety. According to Rangell, intense unpleasure due to an overwhelming influx of drive stimuli does not automatically produce anxiety, as Freud assumed. Rangell believes that what happens under such circumstances is the following. The unpleasure is itself a danger, the danger being that the unpleasure will get worse, or will never stop, or will recur. Since, according to Rangell, danger always begets anxiety and since unpleasure is a danger, therefore unpleasure gives rise to anxiety. Thus, he concludes (1978) it is incorrect to say that unpleasurable affects other than anxiety can initiate defense. The proper view, according to Rangell, is that unpleasure equals danger, danger begets anxiety, and it is the anxiety which, in fact, initiates defense in every instance.

What Rangell presented as a painstaking analysis of psychic events—his own term is microanalysis—seems in fact to involve an assumption that is by no means trivial. In truth, it begs the question at issue. Rangell assumes the ideational content of intense unpleasure—at least of the unpleasure that arises in connection with drive derivatives—necessarily involves the future. According to him, unpleasure must have, as part of its ideational content, an expectation that it will get worse, that it will never stop, that it will recur. In his view the ideational content of unpleasure cannot be that a calamity has occurred. It can only be that a calamity impends, which is the definition of danger. An intensely unpleasurable affect, according to Rangell's view, can never have the ideational content that one is abandoned, or unloved, or, for that matter, punished or castrated. It is only the prospect for the future that counts in psychic conflict, according to Rangell, never the past. Presumably Pollock would agree with this view, if one is to judge from his statement that anxiety is not like other affects, that it is, in fact, "a special category of response" (Pollock, 1978, p. 261). In my opinion this view is contradicted by abundant clinical data of the sort contained in the case material offered above.

Yorke and Wiseberg (1976) agree with the conclusion "that *any* unpleasant affect can mobilize defensive measures" (p. 127), but dismiss it as well-known. "Such a view has been implicit or explicit in psychoanalytic theory since the earliest formulations of the pleasure-unpleasure principle" (p. 127), which presumably means since the pleasure-unpleasure principle was adumbrated in Chapter 7 of *The Interpretation of Dreams* (Freud, 1900). Unfortunately, the authors did not document this assertion, which, as far as I know, is not supported by Freud's published works from 1900 onward. They also mistakenly attribute to me the view "that anxiety is only *one* affect which can assume a signal function" (p. 127). As I have tried to make clear, I believe that any affect that combines unpleasure and the expectation of calamity is by definition a form or variety of anxiety. Whenever an unpleasurable affect contains as part of its ideational content the idea of danger, whenever it signals calamity ahead, it is anxiety by definition.

Despite their agreement that anxiety is not the only trigger for defense, Yorke and Wiseberg focus their attention on "a developmental view" of anxiety, ignoring the role of other unpleasurable affects in conflict. Perhaps they are influenced in their presentation by the opinion of A. Freud (1976), who followed her statement that any unpleasant affect can give rise to defense with the assertion that "all defense activity, whether benign or pathogenic, is set in motion by token[3] anxiety" (A. Freud, 1977, p. 90). At any rate, they postulated for anxiety "a developmental advance . . . from diffuse panic states to adaptive token anxiety" (A. Freud, 1977, pp. 89-90).

As the quotation suggests, the developmental theory of Yorke and Wiseberg follows that of Freud (1926) in the main. There is, however, an important exception. As we have seen, Freud adduced as the principal support of his idea that anxiety can arise automatically his observations on patients suffering from what he called actual neuroses. Yorke and Wiseberg adduce as their principal support for the concept of automatic anxiety or, as they prefer to say, of diffuse panic states in adults, their observations on traumatic neuroses, including the neuroses of war. In their presentation they refer to Freud's (1920) attribution of the traumatic neuroses to an economic or quantitative factor, namely, to the flooding of the mental apparatus by an overwhelming inrush of stimuli, after rupture of the stimulus barrier. Traumatic neurosis, according to Yorke and Wiseberg, is caused by just such an overwhelming flood of stimuli. It is different, therefore, from what they call ordinary neurosis in its etiology and is diagnosable by its very symptomatology, i.e., on a purely descriptive basis. "The dazed appearance and

[3]"Token anxiety" is a synonym for signal anxiety.

inarticulateness of the patient, together with the absence of memory for this phase, bears clinical witness to the processes involved" (Yorke and Wiseberg, 1976, p. 131). In thus substituting a presumed pathogenesis of traumatic neurosis for Freud's theory of the pathogenesis of actual neurosis as a principal support for the concept that anxiety arises automatically when the mind is flooded with stimuli, Yorke and Wiseberg, it should be noted, overlook Freud's later (1926) reservation about the pathogenesis of traumatic neurosis. It is true that in 1920 Freud attributed traumatic neurosis simply to flooding of the mental apparatus, i.e., to a rupture of what he called the stimulus barrier. In 1926, however, he expressed doubt that this factor alone can cause a neurosis in adult life without "the participation of the deeper layers of the personality" (Freud, 1926, p. 129). As Fenichel (1945b, pp. 117ff.) said at greater length, stimuli are not traumatic for merely quantitative reasons. The unconscious *meaning* of an experience is always crucially important, whether the trauma be minor or overwhelming in its nature. A set of stimuli, i.e., an experience that is catastrophically traumatic for one person, may be of minor psychological significance to another. In adult life, at least, psychoanalytic evidence strongly favors the view that anxiety does not appear automatically as a consequence of an excessive influx of stimuli and, what follows from this, that it is never without ideational content. It may *appear* to do so and to be so if one relies on descriptive evidence, as Yorke and Wiseberg do, rather than on psychoanalytic evidence. To follow this course, however, seems hard to justify. Psychoanalytic data are, at present, by far the most reliable, relevant data. One is never on safe ground when one contradicts them on the basis of evidence that is necessarily less reliable.

So much for objections to the assertion (Brenner, 1975a) that either depressive affect or anxiety can initiate conflict and that the two are to be distinguished from one another both clinically and theoretically. What must now be added has to do with the similarities between the ideational content of each affect, similarities as important as the differences on which I have focused till now.

When he revised his theory of anxiety and conflict Freud

(1926) gave his views on the ideational content of anxiety associated with drive derivatives in early childhood. He asserted that the calamities that impend, i.e., the dangers that are feared, are object loss, loss of love, castration, and self-punishment. They appear in the order just given, he said, and they exert a profound influence on mental life thereafter. The correctness of Freud's formulation has become more and more apparent in the years since 1926. So have its great value and importance, both clinically and theoretically. To it I add the following: the ideational content of depressive affect associated with drive derivatives in childhood concerns the very same calamities, i.e., object loss, loss of love, castration, and self-punishment. It is only the temporal aspect of the ideational content of unpleasurable affects associated with drive derivatives that varies. The calamities are the same, whether they are feared as events in the future or perceived as having already happened.

One must bear in mind in this connection the fact that to a child there is often much less difference between "now" and "soon," between "is" and "may be," than there is to an adult. This is one aspect of the phenomenon in psychic life called the omnipotence of thought. To a child's mind, and often enough to an adult's mind as well, especially unconsciously, what is strongly wished or greatly feared seems already to have happened, so that anxiety and depressive affect can be coexistent and, for practical purposes, indistinguishable. This is of special importance, for example, in the case of guilt. When a person, whether consciously or unconsciously, fears punishment for wishes he or she feels are bad or wrong, we say that person feels guilty. When, instead of fearing punishment, a person feels that he or she is, in fact, being punished and/or must do penance or make amends in order to be forgiven for bad deeds or bad wishes, we also say that the person in question feels guilty. The two affects are clearly distinguishable despite the fact that both are called by the same name, guilt. The first is a variety of anxiety, the second is a variety of depressive affect. Yet in many instances they are indistinguishable for the reason mentioned above, namely, that bad wishes and bad deeds may be felt to be the same and that a future danger, in this case punishment, may become, psychologically, a present ill. Distinguishing between the two affects is often important clinically, but the distinction must be a real one, not one that is artificial and merely schematic.

I have already drawn attention to the incorrectness of assuming a fundamental antagonism between drive derivatives (id) and ego (Chapter 2). It is appropriate to allude to it again at this point for the following reason. An antagonism between id and ego is often referred to as a fear of the drives or as a fear of the intensity of the drives, by which are meant, of course, drive derivatives. Analysts who speak thus seem not to realize that in doing so they revise that part of the psychoanalytic theory of conflict which has to do with the typical danger situations, or calamities, of childhood. The same is true for analysts who speak of death, of ego dissolution, of loss of ego boundaries, of merging with mother, of loss of identity, of emptiness, etc. as the ideational content of the anxiety giving rise to conflict in the patients whom they treat.

The factual correctness of Freud's four, typical calamities and their consequent practical importance in clinical work has been established by the collective experience of several generations of analysts. It should not be added to lightly. Any addition, if it is to be taken seriously, must be documented by pertinent clinical, i.e., psychoanalytic evidence. It is especially important that a patient's conscious complaint not be offered as evidence of the ideational content of the anxiety and/or depressive affect which are involved in his or her pathogenic conflicts. A patient's complaint or report that he or she is empty, is merging with someone else, or is dissolving into nothing is not to be taken as a reliable report of the patient's psychopathology. It must not be taken at face value, as though it were a true, endopsychic perception of an aspect of the patient's psychic life. Such a report, such a complaint, is a symptom. It is a compromise formation among the drive derivatives, the anxiety and/or depressive affect, the defensive efforts, and the superego prohibitions and demands that constitute the patient's psychic conflict(s). It is not a description of part or all of the patient's psychopathology. Adequate analysis will reveal it to be a consequence of the patient's psychopathology rather than a description of it, a consequence that can be properly understood and evaluated only after such analysis has been done. In my own experience I have found no evidence to support the propriety of adding another to Freud's list of typical calamities. The four he listed account satisfactorily for the initiation of conflict in every case I have observed or personally treated to date. Until evidence to the contrary is available, the calamities which figure importantly in psychic conflicts originating from childhood drive derivatives should be limited to object loss, loss of love, castration, and, after superego formation, various aspects of superego functioning, such as fear of punishment, remorse, self-punishment, etc.

As Freud (1926) pointed out, these calamities assume positions of importance in psychic life in sequence rather than all together. Object loss begins to play a role before loss of love, while castration begins to play its role later than either of the other two. For this reason each calamity is sometimes considered to be phase-specific. Object loss is considered to be specific to the oral phase, loss of love to the anal phase, and castration to the phallic phase. This schema has value if it is understood to apply to the approximate stage of development at which each calamity first assumes importance. However, it must be kept clearly in mind that once it has become important, each calamity remains so throughout the remainder of childhood and, indeed, of adult life as well. Nor is each calamity kept separate from its fellows. On the contrary, all three become and remain intimately interrelated.

It is a serious mistake to suppose that the importance of object loss or loss of love as sources of unpleasure in connection with drive derivatives is limited to the first two and a half years of life, that is, to the prephallic or preoedipal stage of development. Nothing is further from the truth. Both play a major role throughout the phallic-oedipal phase and for the rest of life thereafter. Since I shall return to this in a later chapter, here I shall say only that every analyst knows what a catastrophe it is for a child in the phallic-oedipal phase to lose a parent or a parent's love for whatever reason.

As for the interrelationship of the calamities of childhood, that is something to which attention has been directed earlier (Brenner, 1959, p. 214), but to which due importance is rarely given, especially in theoretical discussions to which it is relevant. This is all the more surprising in view of the fact that the interrelationship is readily substantiated by everyday clinical experience.

It is no novelty to discover, for instance, that a boy in the phallic-oedipal phase fears losing his father's love because this means to him that the danger of castration is made greater and more immediate. I shall say more on this subject also in a later chapter, but its importance justifies repetition. Just as fear of loss of love and castration anxiety can be inseparable calamities in a child's mind, so too can depressive affect, whose ideational content is loss of love, be inseparable from depressive affect with the ideational content of phallic inferiority. As an example, a boy's depressive affect over the small size of his penis relative to his father's can be intensified by the conviction that, because of it, there is no hope his mother will ever love him best. Most common of all, perhaps, is the conviction of girls in the phallic-oedipal phase that their lack of a penis is proof that their mothers do not or did not love them. In short, analytic experience makes it quite clear that in the great majority of individuals, if not in every case, the calamities of childhood become intimately interwoven, so intimately that even to discuss each separately, as one must do in an exposition of this sort, does some injustice to the true state of affairs by offering a somewhat artificial scheme of the place of each in psychic life.

To anticipate yet again, one thing is apparent at the very start of any discussion of the implications for psychoanalytic theory and practice of the revision of Freud's (1926) theory of anxiety and conflict which I propose. Depressive affect is not related exclusively to object loss. It can have as its ideational content any or all of the calamities of childhood, just as anxiety can. The difference between the two affects is not defined by the nature of the calamity involved. The difference lies in a temporal factor. If a calamity is anticipated, if it lies in the future, the affect is anxiety. If the calamity has already happened, if it lies in the past, the affect is depressive affect.

This obvious consequence of the revision of Freud's conflict theory must be emphasized because ever since the publication of *Mourning and Melancholia* (Freud, 1917a) precisely the opposite view of the relation between depressive affect and the calamities of childhood has dominated psychoanalytic thinking. Among psychoanalysts the conviction is so generally accepted as to require no documentation that depressive affect, when it appears as a symptom of neurotic illness in adult life, derives from a similar affective response to object loss in early childhood. Depressive affect is linked exclusively and indissolubly with object loss in the psychoanalytic literature and in psychoanalytic thinking. The widespread belief among psychoanalysts in the correctness of this linkage is at odds with the facts. It is a belief, moreover, which seriously hampers psychoanalytic understanding of depressive illness (Brenner, 1974a, 1974b, 1975a; see also Chapter 10).

SUMMARY

1. Psychic conflict ensues whenever gratification of a drive derivative is associated with an unpleasurable affect that is sufficiently intense. The affect may be of two kinds, either anxiety or depressive affect.

2. Anxiety is unpleasure plus ideas of danger, i.e., ideas of impending calamity.

3. Depressive affect is unpleasure plus ideas of a calamity that has already occurred, a calamity that is a fact of life.

4. The calamities that are feared or experienced as having happened are the same for depressive affect as for anxiety. They are object loss, loss of love, castration, and superego demands and prohibitions (the last of these is discussed separately in Chapter 8).

5. Though object loss, loss of love, and castration appear in psychic life sequentially, each persists once it has appeared. None of them ever ceases to play an important role in psychic life once it has appeared. They are all, moreover, intimately intertwined with one another.

6. These generalizations concerning the roles of anxiety and depressive affect in psychic conflict have important implications for psychoanalytic theory and practice. Before discussing these implications in more detail, however, I shall turn to the subject of the response to anxiety and depressive affect

when these affects are aroused by drive derivatives—to the subject of defense.

CHAPTER 5

DEFENSE

In the course of every child's development, anxiety and/or depressive affect come to be associated with certain drive derivatives and, later, with aspects of superego functioning. When this happens, defenses are instituted to minimize or, if possible, to eliminate the unpleasurable affects in question. Such defenses, according to psychoanalytic theory, are specialized ego mechanisms. Every student of psychoanalysis is familiar with the list of defense mechanisms: regression, repression, reaction formation, turning from active to passive, turning against oneself, condensation, displacement, projection, identification, identification with an aggressor, denial, and negation. Without question the concept of specialized defense mechanisms and the list of them just given, perhaps with one or two additions, are among the best known and most widely accepted parts of the psychoanalytic theory of conflict.

Despite their familiarity and wide acceptance, the time has come for a major, even a radical revision of this part of conflict theory, a revision based on a reappraisal of the psychoanalytic data having to do with psychic conflict. As I shall show, those data substantiate the conclusion that there are no special mechanisms of defense. Whatever ensues in mental life which results in a diminution of anxiety or depressive affect—ideally in their disappearance—belongs under the heading of defense. Defenses are not special mechanisms of the ego, as they are customarily considered to be (A. Freud, 1936). Still less are they compromise formations (Schafer, 1968) or symptoms, as is implied by formulations like, "The patient's homosexuality is a defense against a paranoid psychosis." Defense is an aspect of mental functioning which is definable only in terms of its consequence: the reduction of anxiety and/or depressive affect associated with a drive derivative or with superego functioning.

To understand defense properly one must be clear about the relation between ego and id in general.

In situations of conflict the two are opposed. The function of opposing and checking drive derivatives to avoid or reduce anxiety and depressive affect is assigned to the ego. One can go further and say that the decisive reason for distinguishing ego from id is furnished by the fact of psychic conflict (Arlow and Brenner, 1964). As A. Freud (1936) pointed out, except in situations of conflict between id and ego, the two cannot be separated. It is true that Freud *defined* the ego as that part of the mental apparatus having to do with an individual's relation to his environment, but the *reason* for giving a separate name to that part of the mind is the opposition between id and ego in situations of conflict. In speaking of the relation between ego and id generally, however, it is quite as correct to say that ego functions serve the gratification of drive derivatives as it is to say that ego functions control, limit, and/or oppose the gratification of drive derivatives. Both statements are true. What determines which prevails in a particular case is the pleasure-unpleasure principle. Too much unpleasure results in defense, whether the unpleasure is anxiety, depressive affect, or both. If there is less or no unpleasure associated with gratification of a drive derivative, ego functions serve to promote and to achieve gratification.

These considerations may be amplified as follows. The usual relation of an adult to his environment—Freud's definition of the overall function of the ego—includes a very wide range of phenomena. Among them are desire for gratification of drive derivatives, habit, social pressures, intellectual curiosity, esthetic or artistic interest, and many others. In childhood, however, it seems likely that there is no such profusion of reasons for interest in the environment. As far as we know, a young child wishes only for the people and things in the environment to gratify his or her wishes fully and without delay. As Freud (1911b) said, in early childhood the demand for drive gratification holds full sway. The environment is interesting to an infant, psychologically speaking, as a possible source of gratification of drive derivatives. The parts or functions of the mind that have to do with exploiting the environment in this way are what develop gradually into the ego as Freud defined it. I would add to Freud's definition of the ego thus: the ego is that part of the mind which is concerned with the environment for the purpose of achieving a maximum of gratification of drive derivatives. In brief, the ego is the executant of the id. It exploits the environment to that end (Brenner, 1973b).

Control of drive derivatives and opposition to them begin early in life. They are an aspect of development whose cause, as Freud pointed out, can be traced to two factors. One factor is the long period of childhood dependence, due to man's physical immaturity at birth, especially the immaturity of the neuromuscular system. The other is the efflorescence of genital sexual desire long before pubescence. In the last analysis it is these factors, as far as is known at present, which are responsible for the fact that, in childhood, one or another drive derivative inevitably comes to be associated with affects sufficiently unpleasurable to result in defense. Anxiety, depressive affect, and conflict associated with drive derivatives are not mere accidents that might be avoided if parents were sufficiently loving, conscientious, and knowledgeable. To be sure, the intensity and consequences of childhood conflicts can be either fatally exacerbated by the environmental influences in a child's life or substantially mitigated by them, but conflict there is bound to be in any childhood milieu of which we know. The calamities of childhood are part of man's fate. They are part of the human condition,[1] perhaps the most important of its causes.

To return to the subject of defense, the significance of these considerations is this. The ego does not develop in isolation from the drives or in opposition to them. It develops as part of the means of drive satisfaction. The same aspects of psychic functioning one observes clinically in the psychoanalytic

[1]"The human condition, fickleness, ennui, unease," appears in Pascal's *Reflections*, VI, 46.

situation as defenses against drive derivatives, at other times further the gratification of other drive derivatives. There are no special ego functions used for defense and for defense alone. There are no specialized defense mechanisms.

Thus, to discuss defense in terms of defense *mechanisms*, as Freud and every analyst since has done, myself included, is wrong. To do so implies there are special ego mechanisms of defense, mechanisms which are used for defense and for nothing else. This is not the case. To do so also implies that only some ego functions—the defense mechanisms—are used for defense, while the rest of the range of ego functioning is not. This is also incorrect.

As to the first point, ego functions are all-purpose. There are no aspects of ego functioning that are used for defense alone. Ego functions mediate drive gratification, they are used to oppose drive derivatives and to prevent their satisfaction, they serve as means of enforcing or opposing superego demands and prohibitions, and they enable one to adapt, in the psychological sense of the word, to one's environment (Brenner, 1976).

As to the second point, the ego can use defensively whatever lies at hand that is useful for the purpose. It can use any ego attitude, any perception, or an alteration of attention or of awareness. It can use the promotion of another drive derivative which arouses less unpleasure than the derivative to be defended against, in which case the one drive derivative masks and supplants the other. It can use fantasy formation or identification. It can use a refusal to be serious, a lack of conviction, or an attitude of make-believe. In short, the ego can use for defense anything that comes under the heading of normal ego functioning or development. Modes of defense are as diverse as psychic life itself.

Despite their diverse nature, however, there is something that all modes of defense have in common. This is opposition either to one or more drive derivatives or superego trends which arouse anxiety and/or depressive affect or opposition to the affects of anxiety and depressive affect themselves. To say this is to do no more than to restate the definition of defense. But reiteration in this form calls attention to something that is often overlooked, which is that there is in defense, by definition, an element of denial or negation, in the colloquial meaning of those words. Every defense against a drive derivative arousing anxiety and/or depressive affect is a way of saying, "No," to some aspect of it. The same is true of defense against a superego demand or prohibition which gives rise to anxiety and/or depressive affect.

Take repression, for example. What does it mean to say that a typical oedipal fantasy, for instance, a young boy's wish to replace father in mother's bed and be her husband, is defended against by repression, in whole or in part? The wish, part of which can be expressed by the words, "I want to marry Mommy," does not disappear. It is, however, excluded from awareness. As far as the boy himself is concerned, he does not want to marry Mommy. What is more, he no longer remembers he ever did want to marry her. If asked in later life, "Do you want to marry your mother?" he would answer, quite sincerely, "No, I do not." If asked, "Did you ever want to marry her?" he would answer, "Never," just as sincerely, despite the fact that, as we know, the wish to marry her has persisted and is still present in a dynamically active form. In other words, repression is a way of saying, "No," to a wish and its associated memories.

So, also, is displacement, when used defensively. If the same boy, in addition to repressing his incestuous wishes for his mother, displaces them, or part of them, onto an aunt or a schoolteacher, his conscious conviction is, "I want to marry Aunt Jane [or Mrs. Smith], not Mommy."

The same is true of reaction formation. Should a young boy quarrel with his mother in order—at least in part—to defend against his incestuous wishes for her, the defensive function of his quarreling can be expressed by the words, "I do not love her; I *hate* her."

Similarly, if identification is used defensively by a boy who imagines himself to be his baby sibling in order to defend against incestuous wishes for his mother, the defensive aspect of his identification has the meaning, "I do not want to marry Mommy and make babies with her, like Daddy. I want to be her baby and have her hold me and pet me." In this illustration, drive derivatives, i.e., the wish to be held and petted, also serve a defensive function against phallic, incestuous drive derivatives, as they would if the defensive identification were with mother herself rather than with baby.

Repression, displacement, reaction formation, and identification are all familiar methods of defense. All appear in the list of defense mechanisms given above. To take a less familiar method of defense, Arlow (1959) called attention to the fact that in the experience of *déjà vu* a factually incorrect belief serves a defensive function. That is to say, he called attention to the fact that an individual who is convinced that he has already been through something which is, in fact, happening to him for the first time is avoiding anxiety by saying to himself, in effect, "Don't worry. The calamity you are always afraid will happen will not happen this time either."

In such cases a disturbance of reality testing serves a defensive function. In some dreams, however, the reverse is the case. It is an improvement in reality testing which is used for defensive purposes. When a dreamer reassures himself with the idea that he is dreaming, rather than awake, he is in effect avoiding anxiety and/or depressive affect by telling himself the calamitous fantasies he was experiencing as real in his dream are not real after all (Arlow and Brenner, 1964).

The examples I have just given are schematized and much simplified. They are, nevertheless, faithful to the facts of psychic life. Whatever example of defense one may choose will illustrate and support the correctness of the generalization that to defend against a drive derivative or a superego manifestation is to deny or negate it in some way. In defense, a person's ego is saying, "No," to whatever is the target of defense, i.e., to whatever is being defended against. Denial, in the colloquial sense of the word, is intrinsic to all defense.

It is important to specify that this is true in the colloquial sense for the reason that denial has also a sense that is technical, a sense that is strictly psychoanalytic. In this sense, the word denial refers to the defensive distortion of one's perception of some aspect of one's environment, of what is usually called external reality (A. Freud, 1936). It is misleading to extend the term, as Lewin (1950), Jacobson (1964), and others have done, to include defensive distortion or disavowal of one's own wishes, affects, memories, etc. since, as we have just seen, every defense denies something. Unless the term denial is limited to the usage A. Freud proposed, it has no special or technical meaning whatever. It is merely a synonym for defense (Brenner, 1973b).

To return to the first point made earlier, the assertion that no aspect of ego functioning is exclusively or specially defensive may be illustrated as follows. A child who "forgets" having been told not to masturbate has repressed the parental prohibition in the service of drive gratification, not as a means of defense. The same is true of an adult who "forgot" he had loaded a gun and who accidentally wounded someone with it. His action was a slip of the mind. It was one of the class of phenomena Freud (1901) subsumed under the heading, the psychopathology of everyday life (a topic to be considered at length in Chapter 12). Every such slip is a compromise formation. Every such phenomenon has many interacting determinants, and the slip in question was no exception. Repression played a significant defensive role as one of the determinants of that slip, but, in addition, repression played a role in the service of gratification of certain drive derivatives. The patient had repressed the childhood determinants of his murderous rage for defensive reasons, i.e., to avoid the guilt and anxiety they would have aroused had he not done so. As a result he was unaware he wished to kill the person at whom he pointed the gun. His conscious conviction when he pulled the trigger was that he was only pretending to shoot his victim. In addition, however, repressing (= forgetting) the memory of having loaded the gun the week before served the function of gratifying his murderous wishes of childhood origin. It was an instance of the ego using repression in its function as executant of the drives. In this respect it parallels the example given earlier of a child repressing the parents' prohibition of masturbation in the service of the wish to masturbate. There is no doubt that repression very often serves the purpose of defense. What I add here is that it often can and does serve as well the purpose of facilitating the gratification of a drive derivative.

The same is true of every other familiar mode of defense, as well as of those which are less familiar. Examples lie close to hand for the very reasons mentioned earlier. When unpleasure is aroused or threatens to be aroused, one does whatever one can do to avoid or to reduce it. When one desires gratification and pleasure, one does whatever one can to achieve it. What one can conceivably do—the range of ego functioning—is the same in either case. *It is the function served by what one does that determines whether it is properly called defense.* To repeat what was said earlier, defenses are not specialized ego functions. The same ego functions serve drive gratification, defense, superego demands, and adaptation either alternately or simultaneously. Properly speaking, a defense can be identified only by the purpose or function it serves in the psychic economy, i.e., the function of opposing or warding off some psychic impulse or tendency that has aroused or will arouse anxiety and/or depressive affect. It is a mistake to define or identify defense primarily by the method used to achieve the purpose of defense, which is the conventional and traditional way of identifying defense at present. To do so has the advantage of familiarity of usage, but it has the double disadvantage of being both ambiguous and misleading (Brenner, 1976, p. 78). Repression, reaction formation, regression, displacement, etc. are defenses only when they are used to ward off something that arouses anxiety and/or depressive affect.

As an example of the sort of ambiguity associated with the practice of identifying defense in the traditional way, it has been suggested that every defense "inherently provides libidinal and aggressive gratification at the same time as it serves counterdynamic purposes" (Schafer, 1968, p. 61). Such a suggestion blurs the concept of defense as a component of conflict by making defense indistinguishable from compromise formation.

When a paranoid man is convinced that another man wants to attack him, his conviction is a symptom, not a defense. It is not correct to say that "what we call the defence mechanism of projection is to be seen also as the expression of a wish to be penetrated" sexually (Schafer, 1968, p. 55). The symptom expresses both a wish for sexual penetration *and* an attempt to eliminate the unpleasure, i.e., the castration anxiety associated with that wish, by attributing it to someone else (projection) and by changing it from passive to active. If we model our formulation of such a paranoid patient's defense on Freud's well-known prototype (1911a, pp. 63ff.), it will be expressed as, "I do not want to be sexually penetrated. He wants to penetrate me and is trying to make me submit against my will." That the defensive effort involved in the formation of such a delusional symptom includes projection is clear, but to say that the defense of projection enacts a fantasy of being sexually penetrated blurs the necessary distinction between symptom and defense. In the case in point, projection is part of a defensive effort whose result—a delusion—is a mixture of warding off and gratifying a drive derivative. A delusion is not a defense. It is a compromise formation, of which, by definition, defense is but a part.

Another example may further clarify the points at issue. It is not rare for a love affair to start in the following way. One person sees another who is sexually attractive, under circumstances that preclude an immediate, direct approach. Instead, before actually approaching the future partner, he or she has a pleasurable daydream in which the two are already sexually united. Such a fantasy involves projection—in this case, attributing one's own sexual desire and excitement to another. The attribution enhances and facilitates gratification of drive derivatives through the fantasy of which it is a part. Here is an instance, then, where projection functions to further drive gratification rather than functioning defensively. At the same time it must be recognized that the fantasy itself, pleasurable though it is, is a compromise formation. It is compounded of childhood drive derivatives, of defenses to eliminate the unpleasure associated with them, and of superego demands and prohibitions. A fantasy, like a symptom, is a compromise formation. In some fantasies projection serves the function of defense. In others, as in the example just given, it furthers gratification of drive derivatives.

To repeat, then, no aspect of ego functioning, no ego function, is "a defense mechanism." All aspects of ego functioning are all-purpose. They can as well be used to further the gratification of a drive derivative or to enforce an aspect of superego functioning as to prevent or to minimize the unpleasure associated with either. Anything that comes under the heading of ego functions can be used in any one of several ways or in two or more ways at the same time.

A realization of the full import of these facts involves a reevaluation of two familiar concepts in psychoanalytic theory, concepts that have, till now, been accepted as correct generalizations that are applicable to clinical work. One of these is the concept that each patient has a characteristic repertory of defenses, a repertory broadly determined by the patient's diagnosis. The other is the concept that defenses disappear as a consequence of psychoanalytic work.

As for the first of these, it is an idea that applies only to particular symptoms, not to an individual's total mental functioning. As we have seen, everyone's defensive repertory includes every aspect of his or her ego functioning. The range of each person's repertory is as broad as his or her range of ego functions. Particular symptoms, however, do involve characteristic defensive patterns, sometimes by definition. It is only if attention is concentrated on one or more prominent symptoms or on a prominent aspect of the patient's transference reaction while the remainder of the patient's mental functioning is ignored that one can make out a case that he or she has a special repertory of defenses.

For example, displacement is involved in every phobia. So is avoidance, by definition. The defensive "repertory" of every phobic patient's *symptoms* therefore includes avoidance and displacement. If, as often happens, attention in the analytic situation is focused on the patient's phobic symptom(s), his or her defenses may seem to be limited to those and other, related defenses, since they are the ones that appear repeatedly and must be dealt with over and over again. Likewise, if a patient has many prominent somatic symptoms of psychic origin, by definition conversion of psychic conflicts into somatic manifestations plays a role in the dynamics of those symptoms. Again, there are patients with delusional symptomatology. It is not difficult to identify projection operating defensively in many such patients, since delusions so often involve attributing one's own wishes, fears, etc. to others in order to minimize the anxiety and/or depressive affect associated with one's wishes, etc.

Thus, to speak of a characteristic repertory of defenses is really to say only that prominent neurotic symptoms and/or character traits are apt to be persistent in any patient, are apt to be prominent in that patient's analytic material, and are apt to require repeated analysis and interpretation in the course of analysis. As a matter of practical necessity one focuses analytic attention principally on such troublesome features of a patient's psychic life and, by extension, on the defenses involved in their genesis and dynamics. However, if one includes in one's assessment of each patient's defenses not just those that are part of his or her major symptomatology, but those that are involved in the patient's dreams, fantasies, ambitions, plans—in a word, in the entire gamut of the patient's psychic life, normal as well as pathological, one sees immediately how inapplicable is the concept of a limited repertory of defenses. It is not patients who show a limited repertory of defensive methods, it is one or another symptom or compromise formation—one or another character trait, one or another transference manifestation—which is characterized by a special method of defense.

As for the idea that defenses disappear in the course of analysis, the following remarks are in order. In the course of a successful analysis, defensive patterns change. Of this there is no doubt. However, particular modes of defense neither disappear, nor do they change in any regular, uniform, or predictable way as a result of analysis. What happens as analysis proceeds is not that defenses change in a progressive way, but that the patient's compromise formations change in a progressive way. By this I mean that, as analysis progresses, the patient's compromise formations change in such a way that the drive derivatives in question are less disguised, less distorted, and can be gratified with pleasure to an increasing degree. One is referring to this progressive change in a patient's compromise formations when one speaks of an improvement in the general functioning of a patient's ego or in its integrative capacity.

As will be shown (Chapter 10), to speak of progressive changes of the sort just described in a patient's compromise formations is the same as saying that when analysis is successful, those compromise formations we call pathological give way to other compromise formations which are properly called normal (Brenner, 1975b, 1976). An example will be useful in clarifying these statements.

The patient was a twenty-nine-year-old woman who had

been in analysis for six years at the time of the episode to be reported. The relevant data concerning her preanalytic and analytic history are these. Prior to analysis she had had sexual relations only with women. Her behavior during these affairs was dominated by her unconscious need to deny (1) sexual feelings for her father, (2) jealous and hostile wishes towards her mother and her older, married sister, and (3) her rage and humiliation that she did not have a penis. Thus for example, when having sex with a woman, she had the fantasy, which was unconscious prior to analysis, that she herself had a penis, that she was a man in a sexual embrace with a woman.

In the course of the analysis, the patient had sexual intercourse with men for the first time. During intercourse she sometimes had conscious fantasies of controlling her partner's penis. At other times she imagined that his penis was part of her body rather than of his. These heterosexual affairs were interspersed with homosexual ones, each of which was initiated by her unconscious need to defend herself against sexual longings for her analyst. These she warded off by assuming the male role in a homosexual relationship, just as, before analysis, she had warded off her unconscious sexual wishes for her father.

At the time with which we are concerned, the patient was once more involved in a homosexual relationship. It had begun some months before, just after her analyst had left for his vacation. Though consciously struggling to give up her current girlfriend, she was obviously resentful of her analyst and was trying to provoke him. She complained with righteous indignation that he behaved unfairly toward her and that he never gave her her due. During one session, when she was arguing with herself that she should give up her girlfriend, she paused frequently, obviously waiting for her analyst to speak. He finally did intervene to say she was trying to get him to order her to give up her girlfriend so that she could rebel, just as she had so often tried to get her parents to take a position she could use as an excuse for rebelling against them. He did not add to this interpretation in words what the patient well understood, because it had been interpreted to her many times in the past, on appropriate occasions, that her anger at her parents throughout her life and at her analyst now was really because she had not been given a penis and because neither her father nor her analyst loved her as she was sure they would have if she had been the boy her father had hoped for before she was born. Thus this interpretation, as the patient understood it, had to do with her wish for love and for a penis in the transference situation and with the fact that it was the frustration of those wishes which made her feel anger toward her analyst, anger she attributed to him, via projection, lest she feel guilty, i.e., to avoid superego condemnation. This interpretation appeared to have a considerable effect on the patient. During the next week she showed the following changes:

1. She discontinued the homosexual affair.
2. She was more feminine in dress and manner.
3. She began to date a man.
4. She asked an older, male colleague, an obvious father figure, to accept her as a pupil, even though she said in advance that she was sure he would refuse.
5. She was much less angry at her analyst and was aware that she wished to be close to him.
6. She had a frightening dream, the associations to which led to thoughts of being sexually excited while on her analyst's couch. It should be noted that she did not actually feel sexually excited either in connection with those thoughts or at any other time when she was on the couch.
7. She became aware that she was angry at her mother, at her older sister, who was her lifelong rival, and at a married female friend.
8. She recalled longing to be close to her father when she was five years old.

Here is an example of analytic progress. The patient improved as a result of a correct interpretation, properly timed and preceded by much previous interpretive work along the same line. What were the changes in the patient's defenses in this particular instance?

It will be recalled that before the interpretation the patient was not conscious of love and sexual longing for her analyst. Instead, she was angry at him. In other words, her loving and sexual wishes were defended against, in part at least, by anger. The same sort of defense warded off her anger and jealousy toward women whom she saw as rivals. She was not aware of negative feelings toward such women. Instead, she was carrying on a love affair with a girl for whom she yearned and by whom she was sexually aroused.

She dealt with her castrative and vengeful wishes toward men in a different way. She felt mistreated by her analyst. She felt that he shortchanged her. In other words, she projected her anger onto him. Still another defense involved in her unconscious effort to deal with her castrative and vengeful wishes toward men was identification. She played the part of a man in the sexual affair she was having.

Finally, the memory that she longed for closeness with her father when she was five had long since succumbed to repression, a repression that lifted only after the interpretation was made.

This account of the patient's defenses is far from complete, but it will suffice for my present purpose. If the substitution of anger for love, and vice-versa, be called reaction formation, for convenience in describing it, we can say that before the interpretation in question the patient was using repression, reaction formation, projection, and identification as defenses against certain of her drive derivatives and superego demands. How were they changed by the interpretation?

First of all, the patient's pattern of reaction formation changed. That is, she gave up her homosexual affair and began dating men. She also expressed anger at female rivals on several occasions—her mother, her older sister, and her married friend—while she was less angry at her analyst than she had been and was aware of wishing to be close to him. In other words, the reaction formations of love for women in order to ward off anger at them and of anger at men in order to ward off love for them were both much diminished.

Second, repression of some memories of her oedipal wishes for her father was undone. At the same time we may safely assume that many other, related memories remained repressed. That is, repression was diminished rather than wholly undone.

Third, identification with the older, admired colleague who was her new teacher clearly played a role in her becoming his pupil.

Fourth, she defended against her sexual wishes for her analyst, which gave rise to anxiety in her dream, by experiencing them as ideas, as mere inferences from her associations to her dream. This sort of defense is usually called isolation of affect.

Finally, her anger at mother and sister was, in part, displaced to her married friend.

It will be recalled that prior to her improvement the patient was using repression, reaction formation, projection, and identification as defenses against certain drive derivatives and superego demands. She progressed analytically as a result of interpretation. What were the changes in her defensive pattern? How can one generalize about them? Can one say that pathogenic defenses disappeared, or that they were replaced by normal ones, or even that more infantile defenses were replaced by less infantile ones?

None of these questions can be answered in the affirmative. The patient's defenses neither disappeared, nor became normal, nor more mature.

For example, a defensive identification with men was present both before and after the interpretation. Before the interpretation this identification decisively influenced her sexual behavior. She had wooed a woman and was engaged in a sexual relationship with her, a relationship in which the patient played the part of a man. After the interpretation the same identification was expressed in her vocational behavior. She took steps to become the pupil of the man she admired in order to learn his skills and to be able to use the tools of his profession—tools, it may be added, which had for her a phallic significance. This is to say that both before and after the interpretation certain aspects of her behavior were motivated by identification with a man, an identification that served to defend against her feminine oedipal wishes, as well as gratifying her masculine ones. That there was a significant change in her behavior, no one can doubt. She became more mature. One can fairly say that she became more normal, since before the interpretation her masculine identification was expressed in a homosexual affair, while after the interpretation it was expressed in her relationship to an older man, her teacher, whom she planned to emulate vocationally in a realistically rewarding, socially desirable way. But what of the defense of identification itself? She still identified with a man. The tools of her teacher's profession were transparently phallic symbols, and to learn to use them expressed her unconscious fantasy that she had a penis. Can one say her use of identification as a defense was any less infantile or more normal after the interpretation than before it, even though the compromise formation of which it was a part was certainly more mature and normal?

Similarly, repression was lifted in one respect following the interpretation. Certain oedipal memories from age five emerged for the first time in her adult life. Yet repression intensified in another respect, since the patient's castrative wishes toward her analyst were repressed after the interpretation, whereas they had been warded off by projection before it. In this case, then, projection disappeared after the interpretation, but repression, a potentially pathogenic defense by any standard, appeared in its place.

If one looks at what I have called the patient's reaction formations, one is faced with similar data. The patient's use of love to defend against jealous anger was much less after the interpretation than it was before, but it was replaced, in part at least, by displacement. The reverse—the use of hate to ward off love—was partly replaced by isolation of affect, a defense so often found in patients with obsessional symptoms.

It is apparent, then, that in this example of analytic progress the patient's defenses neither disappeared nor became, in and of themselves, less pathogenic or more mature. What happened in fact, was this. There were certain drive derivatives the patient had to defend against to avoid or minimize anxiety and/or depressive affect. These included the following: affection for her analyst; longing for his love; memories of affection and longing for her father's love when she was a child; the wish to be closely associated with an older, admired man and to be his pupil; the wish to attract men and to have sexual intercourse with them; and anger at rival women. All of these were oedipal derivatives. Before the interpretation the derivatives I have just listed could not be tolerated or gratified. They aroused too much unpleasure. After the interpretation the patient's reaction to her oedipal wishes and jealousy was less defensive in the sense that the resulting compromise between drive derivative and defense allowed more in the way of gratification. The change was not so complete that no defenses were necessary—quite the contrary. The patient's reactions to her positive oedipal wishes after the interpretation were no less a compromise between drive derivative and defense than they had been before. Defenses against her oedipal drive derivatives were as easily identifiable after the interpretation as they had been before it. The new compromise formation represented analytic progress, but it was still a compromise formation for all that.

I hope that this rather lengthy illustration has served to persuade the reader of the fact that in the course of analysis defenses neither disappear nor become progressively more normal (less pathological) or more mature. As for the idea that repression, or reaction formation, or any other functional capacity of the ego which is used defensively at times can ever disappear, no illustration or further discussion should be necessary to demonstrate how incorrect and inapposite it is. A particular instance of the defensive use of any ego function may cease, but it is out of the question to imagine that the function as such can disappear as a result of analysis.

I have been concerned so far with defense as an aspect of ego functioning which is defined by its consequence, the consequence being the avoidance, disappearance, or mitigation of anxiety and/or depressive affect developing in association with drive derivatives that originated in childhood. I turn now to another topic, namely, the targets of defense, that is to say, to the question, "What is warded off or defended against to avoid or minimize these unpleasurable affects?"

Freud's answer was that when a drive derivative (or a need for punishment) arouses anxiety, the essence of defense is opposition to it. If an incestuous wish arouses anxiety, the wish is defended against, or warded off, in one way or another. If the defensive effort is successful, anxiety is avoided or disappears. One cannot dispute the correctness of Freud's formulation. Confirmation of it is available daily from the analysis of every patient. It is, however, but a partial answer, as the following discussion will show.

Defense proceeds in accordance with the pleasure-unpleasure principle. It is the unpleasure of anxiety and of depressive affect that triggers defense, and this unpleasure is tied to a particular ideational content, i.e., to one or more of the familiar calamities of childhood. It is the connection between a drive derivative and a calamity or calamities that gives rise to defense in accordance with the pleasure-unpleasure principle. Thus a childhood drive derivative does not give rise to unpleasure directly. It does so because it is associated in the child's mind with ideas of calamity.

Since the function of defense is to eliminate unpleasure or, at least, to reduce it to a minimum, one would expect that this could be accomplished in any of several ways. One way is the one Freud described, namely, to oppose the drive derivative—to say, "No," to it. Another possible way would be to oppose or ward off not the drive derivative *per se*, but the anxiety and/or depressive affect aroused by the drive derivative. This, one can imagine, might be accomplished in any of three ways. A defense might oppose, i.e., say, "No," to the unpleasure of the affect, to its ideational content, or to both at the same time. Clinical psychoanalytic data demonstrate that all these possibilities do, in fact, occur.

The most familiar target of defense, the one Freud described, is the drive derivative itself. Examples of this type of defense were given earlier in this chapter. The other possibilities are less familiar, though I have drawn attention to them in the past (Brenner, 1975b, 1979a). I believe that Fenichel's (1939) description of the counterphobic attitude is the first extensive exposition of the fact that defense can reduce or eliminate anxiety by taking as its target the anxiety associated with a drive derivative rather than the drive derivative itself.

Again, one must bear in mind that a symptom is a compromise formation. It is never merely a defense. For instance, being counterphobic by becoming a daredevil and delighting in doing what is realistically dangerous is a symptom. It is a compromise formation and, as such, it serves to gratify drive derivatives as well as to eliminate or to minimize anxiety. Being a daredevil may, for example, gratify an unconscious masochistic wish. However, turning anxiety into pleasure, which is the essence of the counterphobic attitude, is a way of eliminating unpleasure which is quite different from opposing, i.e., from defending against a dangerous drive derivative. Instead of the drive derivative being the target of defense, the affect itself is the target—in this case by denying the unpleasure altogether. Often the reversal of affect (pleasure instead of unpleasure) is buttressed by narcissistic, exhibitionistic gratification, as when a daredevil performs publicly for applause and approval. Often it is buttressed by identification, by a conscious or unconscious fantasy of being an admired and envied rival. Doubtless there are other ways, more subtle and more specifically individual, by which such a reversal of affect can be buttressed or reinforced. Whatever the means used, it is the affect associated with the calamity that is the target of defense, not the drive derivative.

When anxiety or depressive affect is itself the target of defense, as noted earlier, it is often the case that both the sensation of unpleasure and the ideational content which together constitute that affect are defended against. In the example just given, for instance, a daredevil's unconscious castration anxiety may be represented by parachute jumping, with its attendant mortal danger. In other words, the counterphobic person may become a sky-diver. If he does, part of his defense is to transform anxiety into pleasurable exhilaration. For him, to leap into space has become a source of joy and pleasure. Another part of his defense, however, is to disguise the ideational content of his infantile calamity by substituting body for penis and sky-diving for castration. The calamity a sky-diver consciously faces is not that of losing his penis, but that of smashing his body to bits, like Icarus, on the earth below. Still another part of his defense is likely to be to study the technique of sky-diving, to buy the best equipment, to fold his parachute himself, to jump only in fine weather, etc.

Daredevils are rarely seen as analytic patients. I recall but one such patient in my own practice. The defensive pattern they illustrate is by no means a rarity, however. It is common for patients and, for that matter, for many who are not patients, to do something to "prove" they need not be afraid or, indeed, that they *are* not afraid, when it is obvious that they are very afraid indeed. In other words, it is common for patients and others to diminish anxiety by repressing, or denying, or projecting, or otherwise warding off either the unpleasure, the ideational content, or both, associated with object loss, with loss of love, and/or with castration. A life-threatening example would be a patient with a myocardial infarct who refused to stay in bed. Another example, but one within the range of normality, would be a timid schoolboy who took up football or boxing. In fact, what is called courage is closely related to what Fenichel identified as the counterphobic attitude. Thus psychoanalytic data confirm the conventional wisdom of military personnel that courage in combat is the ability to ignore or overcome fear, an aphorism to which psychoanalytic data lend greater depth and a wider applicability than could otherwise have been suspected.

Like anxiety, depressive affect that has as its ideational content one or more of the calamities of childhood can be the target of defense. It, too, can be reduced or eliminated by defending against either its unpleasure, its ideational content, or both (Brenner, 1975a).

To deny that a calamity has occurred, when in fact one believes it has, by pretending that it is really a joy, to insist that one feels pleasure rather than unpleasure on account of it, is one of the basic features of pathological elation (mania or hypomania). In any case of pathological elation much more is involved than reversal of affect of the sort just described. Elation is a syndrome, not a defense. As such it is a compromise formation. It necessarily involves the (partial) gratification of drive derivatives and the satisfaction of superego trends as well as defense. Nor is a reversal of affect ever the whole of any patient's defensive effort. I do not believe that any instance of pathological elation can be fully or satisfactorily explained as merely a consequence of a patient denying that a calamity has occurred and thereby turning unpleasure into pleasure as a method of defense. I maintain only that this defensive maneuver is of fundamental importance in every case of pathological elation. It is by no means the whole explanation, but it is an essential element in the dynamics of elation.

SUMMARY

1. Defense must be defined in terms of its consequence or function, which is the reduction of the unpleasure aroused by a drive derivative or by some aspect of superego functioning.

2. Ego functions serve equally for defense, for drive satisfaction, and for superego functioning. The ego is both the executant or servant of the id and its opponent.

3. The term defense mechanism is incorrect and misleading, since (a) there are no aspects of ego functioning, no ego mechanisms, which are used for defense and for nothing else and (b) every aspect of ego functioning can be and, at times, is used for defense.

4. Every defense is a denial in the colloquial sense of the word. When its meaning is extended, as has been done, denial loses its specific psychoanalytic meaning and becomes a mere synonym for defense.

5. No one's repertory of defense is limited or repetitive. It is only the defenses in a particular (pathological) compromise formation that are characteristic and stereotyped.

6. Defenses do not disappear during analysis, nor do they become progressively more normal or more mature.

7. Defense is not directed only against drive derivatives or aspects of superego functioning. Defense may have as its target the anxiety or depressive affect aroused by drive derivative or superego. When this is the case, the defense may be directed at either the sensation of unpleasure, the ideational content of the affect, i.e., the real or fantasied calamity, or against both at the same time.

CHAPTER 6

THE CALAMITIES OF CHILDHOOD

In this chapter I return to the topic of the role of affects in psychic conflict in order to discuss a special aspect of the topic which is of unique importance in psychic development and functioning.

The phallic-oedipal phase or period of development lasts from approximately two-and-a-half to approximately five-and-a-half years of age. The psychic conflicts of this period, which I shall call the oedipal period for short, are inevitably severe. Their effects on psychic development are great and they are of major, often of crucial importance to later character structure and to mental health or illness in adult life. To take note of their intensity and importance is but to repeat what has been generally accepted and regularly confirmed by generations of analysts since Freud's original observations and conclusions on the subject.

I shall apply the concepts I have developed in the preceding chapters to the problem of furthering an understanding of the nature of oedipal conflicts. Of particular importance in this respect are the distinction between anxiety and depressive affect, and the role each plays in psychic conflict.

The role of anxiety in initiating oedipal conflicts was discovered and first described by Freud in 1926. The role of depressive affect remained largely unknown or unappreciated until I called attention to it (Brenner, 1975a, 1979a). As I shall explain in what follows, its role is comparable in extent and importance to that of anxiety. In consequence, an understanding of the role of depressive affect in oedipal conflicts is of great value for both the practice and the theory of psychoanalysis.

It will be recalled from what has gone before that anxiety and depressive affect are the same in two respects and different in a third. Both affects consist of sensations of unpleasure, which are more or less intense, plus ideas of calamity, by which I mean ideas having to do with object loss, with loss of love, and with castration.[1] In these respects, therefore, the two affects are the same. The difference between them is that anxiety has to do with an impending calamity, with danger, with a calamity in the near or distant future, while depressive affect has to do with a calamity that has occurred already, with a calamity that is a fact of life.

It must be kept in mind also that the three calamities just mentioned are always intimately, not to say inextricably interwoven. They appear in sequence in the course of psychic development, it is true, but, having once appeared, each persists as an important factor in psychic life from that time onward. By the time the oedipal period is well under way the three have become so closely associated with one another that they form but a single fabric. To isolate each from the others involves a certain schematization, a degree of artificiality for which the reader must compensate. In any single case, all three calamities will invariably play a part. Nevertheless, I shall treat each separately, to some extent, in the course of my exposition, in the hope that this sacrifice of verisimilitude will be offset by a gain in comprehensibility.

ANATOMY AND DESTINY

Unpleasure associated with the idea of castration appears for the first time during the oedipal period and is characteristic of that time of life. Psychoanalysts believe with good reason that

[1]See Chapter 8 for a discussion of guilt, the fourth calamity listed by Freud.

for most children in that stage of development the idea of castration is chiefly responsible for unpleasure associated with drive derivatives. In most cases it is the principal initiator of conflict, though it is never the sole one. It is, after all, in the oedipal phase that genital sensations assume such great importance in the psychic life of every child. It is then that the genitals themselves acquire their unique and overriding significance. It is then that nearly every drive derivative, whatever its origin, is woven into the pattern of the wishes, fears, and fantasies which are characteristic of that time of life. As far as can be judged from all of the available evidence—from the psychoanalysis of adults, from the psychoanalysis of children with neurotic disturbances, and from psychoanalytically informed observation of the behavior of normal children during the oedipal phase—children of that age are very concerned with the question of who does and who does not have a penis and, if one does have a penis, with the question of its size—with whether it is a small child's penis or a large adult's. Boys feel inferior to older boys and to men because older boys and men have larger penises. Girls feel inferior to boys and men because boys and men have penises.

The evidence for these statements is clear and indisputable. It derives from the combined data gathered by many analysts over many decades. Why the facts are as they are is by no means so clear, however, and there has been much dispute on this score, particularly in recent years. Whether anatomy is destiny, as Freud (1925a) put it, or whether social and cultural factors are decisive, as many others maintain, is a question that cannot be finally settled by the available evidence. All that can be said with assurance is that, on the one hand, children reared in our culture are intensely interested in sexual anatomy and profoundly affected by it and that, on the other hand, social and cultural factors, as represented by the attitudes and behavior of parents and siblings concerning sexual differences, are of profound importance to the severity and the consequences of the conflicts aroused by drive derivatives during the oedipal phase. Whether anatomy is the primary factory and cultural influences are secondary, or whether the reverse is the case, is a question no one can answer at this time, however hotly they may debate it. More than that, the answer to it is, in fact, unimportant for my present purpose. What is to the point as regards the population with whom we are concerned and the findings—psychoanalytic data—on which our understanding of the oedipal phase is chiefly based, is that anatomy and cultural influences are both important, that neither can safely be neglected or emphasized at the expense of the other, and that each interacts with the other in the course of the development of every child in ways so manifold and so complex as to make them inextricable from one another for practical purposes.

DEPRESSIVE AFFECT, ANXIETY, AND CASTRATION

The calamity of castration appears in the psychic lives of children in the oedipal phase in two ways. At times it appears as a danger, as a calamity that impends. At other times it appears as a fact of life, as a calamity that has already happened. In other words, the calamity of castration is at times the ideational content of anxiety and at times the ideational content of depressive affect.

Enough has been written about castration anxiety in boys in the oedipal phase of development to make unnecessary any additions to it here. It will suffice to summarize what is both familiar and generally accepted: in boys in the oedipal phase, both positive and negative oedipal wishes arouse intensely unpleasurable anxiety, the ideational content of which is impending castration. Defense ensues in an effort to eliminate or mitigate the anxiety. More simply, in oedipal boys castration anxiety initiates conflict (Freud, 1926).

There is less agreement as to the role of castration anxiety in the psychic conflicts of girls in the oedipal phase. On the one hand, psychoanalytic data leave no room for doubting that, in girls as in boys, anxiety plays an important role in connection with castration during the oedipal phase. The question is whether this anxiety is true castration anxiety, i.e., a young girl's fear of losing her penis. Is it possible for a girl, to whom it is obvious that she is without a penis, to fear castration?

Freud himself (1925a, 1931, 1933) was persuaded that it is not possible and that castration anxiety is not a significant factor in the conflicts of girls in the oedipal phase. He suggested that fear of loss of love plays the role in girls which is comparable to that of fear of castration in boys.[2]

The logic of this position seems incontrovertible. One cannot lose what one does not have. Yet it is contradicted by abundant clinical experience. There are women who show every sign of intense castration anxiety, as witness their reactions to bodily injury, to defloration, to menses, and to parturition. Indeed, all women show evidence of a considerable degree of castration anxiety, even though it is far more intense in some than it is in others. What is involved, as Rado (1933) was the first to point out, is the fear of losing a fantasied penis, not a real one.

Girls in the oedipal phase regularly fantasy that they are boys. They regularly imagine that they have a penis. This wish-fulfilling fantasy is responsible for the unconscious equations: stool = penis = baby (Freud, 1917b). In an oedipal girl's mind her stool becomes the penis she longs for. The same is true if she imagines her body is her penis, or a part of her body, e.g., an extremity or a deciduous tooth, or her cleverness, or her athletic ability, or whatever else she chooses to symbolize her penis for reasons determined by her experience and her situation. Her fantasied penis, the penis she longs for, is real to her. It is real enough so that anything symbolizing the idea that it may be injured or lost arouses anxiety which is comparable to the castration anxiety of a boy with respect both to intensity of unpleasure and to ideational content. One need not hesitate, therefore, to assign to castration anxiety an important role in the conflicts of the oedipal period in both girls and boys. To girls at that stage of life as well as to boys castration is a danger. It is the ideational content of anxiety which can be as intense as any in the life experience of both girls and boys.

What of the role of depressive affect whose ideational content is the calamity of castration? What role does it play in the psychic lives of girls and boys in the oedipal period?

It is simplest to begin with the reactions of girls to being without a penis. In his paper on the character type he called the exception, Freud (1916) noted that women unconsciously

[2]For an excellent summary of Freud's views on this subject, see Strachey, 1961.

consider themselves to be exceptions in his sense of the word. By this he meant that oedipal girls consider themselves to have been unfairly discriminated against by having been denied that part of the body which boys and men have. What Freud recognized as a belief which persists unconsciously (or, in many cases, consciously) in adult life, is of central concern to an oedipal girl.

As noted earlier, it is impossible to decide to what degree an oedipal girl's conviction that she is inferior because she has no penis is an inevitable consequence of the anatomical difference which is of such concern to both girls and boys, and to what degree it is determined by the attitudes of the persons who make up her social milieu. However much is due to each factor, the consequence of both together is that oedipal girls in our society—and in many others as well—do feel themselves to be inferior and to have been objects of unfair discrimination because they are without penises.

The unpleasurable affect they experience is a variety of depressive affect which, in this case, has the ideational content that they *have been* castrated. To this they react in various defensive ways, i.e., in ways that serve to eliminate or to mitigate the intense unpleasure which is part of the depressive affect they feel. One such reaction has already been noted, since it provides the basis for castration anxiety in girls and women. Oedipal girls deny what they believe to be a defect in their bodies by imagining that they *have* a penis.

In his paper on the exception, Freud illustrated a different reaction. It is one that is also common among oedipal girls and, like the fantasy of having a penis, serves a defensive function. The illustration Freud chose was a fictional character, Shakespeare's hunchbacked king, Richard III. Shakespeare depicted Richard as filled with rage and with a determination to be revenged on the world for having been born with his physical deformity, and Freud chose Shakespeare's portrayal of Richard to illustrate how a child who feels physically defective often reacts psychologically.

Such children, as we know from psychoanalytic data, blame their parents for having made them defective. They typically feel their defects as signs of lack of love and/or punishment for wrongdoing. When the child is an oedipal girl who is miserable because of what is, to her, a genital defect, she attributes her defect to the fact that her parents did not love her or punished her. If she reacts like Shakespeare's Richard, she rages against them and imagines making them suffer at her hands what she is convinced she has suffered at theirs. Castrative, murderous fantasies of revenge and triumph serve, in part, to mitigate her misery. As abundant analytic experience has shown, such vengeful fantasies arouse anxiety (fear of retribution) in turn, which must be defensively mitigated. Thus depressive affect and anxiety can become interwoven as parts of an oedipal girl's reaction to the calamity of castration. Her misery at being without a penis, her rage at the parents she loves, her triumphant fantasy of seizing a penis for herself, and her fear that she will lose it again are all inextricably combined in her efforts to satisfy the passionate drive derivatives which motivate her while avoiding as much as possible of the intense anxiety and depressive affect they arouse.

However, the fantasy of having a penis, a reaction of rage, or a thirst for vengeance are by no means the only reactions oedipal girls have to their mistaken conviction that they have been castrated. Another, which is often mixed with rage and a desire for revenge, is to seek to placate and to ingratiate, to woo rather than to wreak vengeance, to become more submissive and passive rather than active and violent. Nor does this complete the list of possible reactions. The truth is that no catalogue of such reactions can be complete. Whatever thought, whatever action, whatever fantasy a child is capable of, she can and does use. The possibilities are limited only by her ego's capacity and experience (see Chapter 5). Analytic data have made analysts familiar with the manifold consequences in later life of the defensive reactions occasioned in girls by what one may call castration depressive affect, by analogy with castration anxiety. Those aspects of the psychology of women that belong under the headings of penis envy, castrative impulses, masculine identification, and frigidity are all readily traceable to the psychic conflicts engendered during the oedipal phase of development by the depressive affect associated with the conviction all girls of that age share, that to be without a penis is a calamity, a calamity, moreover, that has been unfairly visited upon them.

What of castration depressive affect in oedipal boys? What part does it play in their conflicts if any?

The answer, based on psychoanalytic data, is that it plays an important part, a part not hitherto recognized.

The simplest illustrations of this fact are oedipal boys who are exceptions in Freud's sense of the word (Freud, 1916). These are boys with penile deformities, with testicular abnormalities, or with other physical defects which symbolize castration in their minds. Everything just said about castration depressive affect in oedipal girls applies with the same force to such boys. In their minds castration, symbolized by their physical defects, is a calamity that has already occurred. They suffer from the misery of depressive affect, with the result that they seethe with rage, seek vengeance, fear retribution, demand pity, deny the very fact of their defects, etc., just as oedipal girls do. The specific details are less important at the moment than the obvious fact that for these boys, as for Shakespeare's Richard, depressive affect plays a very large role in conflicts about the calamity of castration.

Another group of oedipal boys in whom the role of castration depressive affect is especially important are those with a strong feminine identification. In them the relation between castration anxiety and castration depressive affect is extremely intimate and difficult to disentangle. Often, in an individual case, one can see only that both are involved and that neither can be seen in isolation from the other. The reason for this lies in the fact that for such boys the fantasy of being a girl or woman typically serves an important defensive function. By this I mean that a boy may ward off the anxiety associated with his jealous, murderous, and incestuous wishes by the fantasy that he is a girl or woman. To the extent that this defense is successful, he is vulnerable to the conviction that the very calamity—castration—he so feared has actually befallen him. To that extent his unpleasure is depressive affect rather than anxiety. The psychological situation is then complicated by the fact that what follows is an attempt to mitigate the unpleasure of this depressive affect by violent sadistic wishes which emphasize phallic intactness and potency. The result is that feminine wishes and fantasies are used to defend against masculine wishes that arouse anxiety, while masculine wishes defend against feminine ones, expressed as a fantasy of being a girl or a woman, which give rise to depressive affect. To put the matter more succinctly, feminine wishes and masculine ones are used to defend against one another. If both give rise to intensely unpleasurable affects, as often happens, the resultant rapid fluctuations of gratification and defense constitute what can fairly be described as a kind of psychic chaos. Less severe consequences, with less disastrous effects on psychic stability, are also encountered. In analytic practice with adults one sees such an oscillation very clearly in many male homosexuals, for example.

More examples could be adduced, but the ones presented document well enough my assertion that castration depressive affect can play an important role in the psychic conflicts of oedipal boys. Anxiety is not the only unpleasurable affect that occasions defense in connection with the calamity of castration in oedipal boys. It is true that for boys in the oedipal phase castration is, in fantasy, a real and imminent danger (Hartmann and Kris, 1945), but it is not always only a danger, a thing of the future. There are instances when reality and fantasy combine to convince an oedipal boy that castration has actually happened, that it is a fact, not a danger. There are instances when a substantial share of the unpleasure that motivates defense is depressive affect in boys as it so often is in girls.

Granting, then, that both castration depressive affect and castration anxiety play important roles in the conflicts of oedipal boys and girls, what is the relative importance of each?

At present the answer to this question can be only impressionistic and, hence, provisional. Since the role of depressive affect in conflicts of any sort has been clearly recognized but recently, time must pass before enough information about its role accumulates to permit a satisfactory degree of consensus. My own impression is this.

Both anxiety and depressive affect play important parts in the castration conflicts of every oedipal child. Speaking very generally, and allowing for many exceptions, castration depressive affect plays a larger role in the conflicts of oedipal girls than does castration anxiety, while the reverse is true for boys. I must emphasize in connection with this opinion that the attempt to assess the relative importance of anxiety and depressive affect in any individual case is made more difficult by the fact that depressive affect so often gives rise to anxiety and vice versa. Each can lead to the other and back again. Matters are far from simple even in cases in which the one affect seems, at first glance, to be greatly overshadowed by the other. As noted above, the jealousy and rage which are often a consequence of depressive affect give rise in turn to anxiety, anxiety that appears as fear of retribution, of loss of love, and/or of object loss. Or, when the need to minimize castration anxiety results in a strong wish to be a woman, the latter wish, as has also been noted, can result in intense depressive affect. One must not imagine, therefore, that in any individual case there is a simple relationship between castration anxiety and castration depressive affect. The generalization that the one plays a more important role in most boys and the other in most girls is, to be sure, simply stated, but it does not refer to a simple state of affairs. On the contrary, simple though the statement is, it refers to a highly complex relation and mutual interaction which are correspondingly difficult to assess with accuracy, be it in a boy or a girl.

DEPRESSIVE AFFECT, ANXIETY, OBJECT LOSS, AND LOSS OF LOVE

I turn now from the subject of castration to a consideration of the other typical calamities of the oedipal phase, object loss and loss of love. What can be said with respect to each concerning the relative importance of anxiety and of depressive affect?

The intensity of a child's normal, jealous rivalry at the height of the oedipal phase has special consequences with respect to object loss, as psychoanalysts have long recognized. It is nearly universal at this stage of development for a child to wish both parents dead and gone, though at different times and for different reasons. Typically, such wishes are directed at the parent of the same sex who can then be replaced in sexual union with the parent of the opposite sex. Just as typically, boys turn on their faithless mothers and girls on their fathers for betraying or scorning their love, as witness their continued sexual union with the child's adult rival. That such death wishes are often intensified by primal-scene exposure or by the birth of a sibling is also well known. The relation of homosexual incestuous wishes to death wishes directed at both the rival and at the heterosexual love object is equally familiar. All of this means that the passionate sexual wishes characteristic of the oedipal phase are most intimately bound up in every child's mind with object loss, that is, with the disappearance of one or both parents, to say nothing of whichever siblings are seen as rivals for parental love.

The purpose of repeating facts as familiar as these is to call attention to the role of depressive affect in a child's reaction to real or fantasied object loss in the oedipal phase. Until now analysts have paid principal attention to the role of anxiety and of conflicts engendered by it in connection with oedipal death wishes. In many cases, however, it is important to recognize the role of depressive affect as well. One can be sure, for example, that when the principal love object of an oedipal child disappears from home for an extended period of time, the unpleasure that develops and must be warded off by whatever defenses can be mobilized is depressive affect in large measure. If a very young boy's mother is consistently away from home for business or pleasure, if she is in the hospital for several weeks, or, worst of all, if she dies or never returns for some other reason, the child's reaction is not merely one of anxiety. He is not merely terrified by the possibility of retribution for his death wishes. His reaction is, in large part, depressive affect, i.e., intense unpleasure at a calamity he perceives not as a danger, but as having happened. It has been noted earlier that depressive affect is often defended against or warded off more or less successfully by identification with the aggressor, as evidenced by rage and by a wish for retributive (talion) revenge. When this is the case in connection with real or fantasied object loss during the oedipal phase, the child's angry, vengeful wishes themselves generate anxiety which must in turn be warded off.

As a result, depressive affect and anxiety and the defenses designed to eliminate or to minimize both become intimately entwined in the psychic life of the child and, later, of the adult. The conflicts that ensue must be viewed in terms that include both varieties of unpleasure, not merely the one or the other, if they are to be correctly understood and usefully interpreted.

It should be obvious that although I have been speaking, for the purpose of illustration, of a boy losing his mother, the same considerations apply to children of either sex who have, whether in reality or in fantasy, lost a beloved parent. The point is that when oedipal children are convinced that they have lost an important love object, their unpleasure is depressive affect and their defenses are, in the first instance, directed at eliminating or minimizing depressive affect. This knowledge is as important for understanding the nature and origins of the conflicts, and of the symptoms and character traits or abnormalities which may result, as is the knowledge of the role of anxiety in the conflicts in which it plays the major role.

All that has been said about the importance of object loss in the oedipal stage can be applied, with suitable changes, to loss of love. The latter plays a major role in the psychic life of every child of this age, although in some children its role is greater than in others. However great its role may be, though, it is never a solitary one. On the contrary, loss of love is invariably associated with the two other calamities of this time of life, castration and object loss. Depending on the circumstances, moreover, loss of love may appear either as a danger or as a calamity that has happened: if the former, it gives rise to anxiety; if the latter, to depressive affect, but never exclusively to the one or the other. Finally, there is no evidence that depressive affect associated with loss of love is either more or less important in girls than it is in boys of the oedipal period. In this last respect loss of love resembles object loss, while both differ from castration, since, as I have said, castration anxiety is usually more important in the conflicts of oedipal boys than is castration depressive affect, and the reverse is true for oedipal girls.

DISCUSSION

A major defect in the psychoanalytic account of childhood sexual development has been the lack of clarity concerning the

Oedipus complex of girls, compared with what was known about the Oedipus complex of boys (A. Freud, 1975). This defect can now be remedied. Both girls and boys in the oedipal phase react to the discovery that to be a boy means to have a penis and to be a girl means not to have one in ways complexly determined by each child's previous development and current psychic state. In our society, which is the only one about which we have abundant and reliable analytic data, to be without a penis means to be castrated, as far as an oedipal child is concerned. Each child's reaction, which evolves with many vicissitudes over a period of many months, involves both castration anxiety and castration depressive affect. Both must be taken into account if one is to make sense of the similarities and the differences between the psychosexual development of girls and of boys in the oedipal period.

Essential as it is, however, for the solution of the riddle of psychosexual differences and similarities between the sexes, an understanding of the roles of castration anxiety and castration depressive affect does not by itself suffice for an adequate understanding of the Oedipus complex in any child. It is equally important to appreciate and to pay attention to three other facts, to each of which I have already alluded several times. (1) *Any* of the typical calamities of childhood can and does give rise to both anxiety and depressive affect. It is not only castration which is sometimes a danger and sometimes a calamity which has already happened. The same is true for object loss and for loss of love. Either can and does give rise to both anxiety and to depressive affect in every child at one time or another. (2) All three calamities are important in the psychic lives of oedipal children. There is reason to expect castration to be more important than either of the other two during the oedipal phase, but both object loss and loss of love remain factors of major importance in psychic life throughout the oedipal period. All three, for that matter, continue active throughout the rest of childhood and of adult life. (3) The calamities, and the affects whose ideational content they constitute, are always intimately interrelated. Anxiety can give rise to depressive affect and vice versa. Moreover, the same reciprocal relation exists among castration, object loss, and loss of love.

It is also true, I believe, that in an oedipal girl's conflicts castration depressive affect usually outweighs castration anxiety in importance, while in the conflicts of oedipal boys castration anxiety usually outweighs in importance castration depressive affect. In every other respect, the passionate storms of the oedipal phase and their effect on development are the same for girls as they are for boys. The oedipus complex is no more clear, nor any more obscure, in the one sex than in the other. When depressive affect is taken into account, psychosexual development in the oedipal phase is seen to be entirely parallel in the two sexes.

All of this deserves amplification. What, for example, is the reason for emphasizing at this point the fact that depressive affect, like anxiety, can be related to object loss, to loss of love, or to castration? To put the same idea in other words, what is the significance of the fact that the ideational content of depressive affect, like the ideational content of anxiety, can be either castration, object loss, or loss of love?

Ever since Freud's (1917a) discussion of the psychopathology of depression, psychoanalysts have attributed depressive affect, whether normal or pathological, to real or fantasied object loss. It is not widely recognized that to do so can lead one far astray in clinical work. It is essential when one is analyzing a patient to be aware that depressive affect is no more restricted to a single type of childhood calamity than is anxiety. It is true that depressive affect *can* have object loss as its ideational content. When it does, however, what makes it depressive affect is not that its ideational content is object loss. What makes it depressive affect is that its ideational content is that an object *has been* lost, in fact or in fantasy. If the ideational content of an unpleasurable affect is that an object *may be* lost, the affect is, by definition, not depressive affect; it is anxiety. *Any* calamity can give rise either to depressive affect or to anxiety, depending on whether it has occurred or it will occur. To assume that depressive affect must be due to a conscious and/or unconscious idea of object loss is to run counter to abundant psychoanalytic evidence. It is to misunderstand the dynamics and origins of many patients' psychic conflicts.

So much for the first of the three points mentioned above.

The reason for emphasizing the second point is this. When a conflict does hinge on object loss, i.e., when object loss plays the largest role in the ideational content of a patient's anxiety and/or depressive affect, it is often assumed that the conflict is oral (see Chapter 5). That is to say, it is often assumed either that the conflict dates from trauma and fixation during the first year of life, or that it is a consequence of defensive regression to oral wishes and conflicts, or both. Similarly, loss of love is not infrequently taken as a hallmark of the anal period. Often the separation between object loss and loss of love, between what is oral and what is anal, is not made explicitly. Instead, when a conflict hinges on either object loss or on loss of love, it is simply assumed to be of preoedipal origin. The conviction appears to be held fairly widely among analysts that for the origin of a conflict in later life to be attributed to the oedipal period, the theme of castration must appear in a patient's symptoms in an explicit, undisguised way. It must be, so to speak, on the surface. Consequently, the calamities of object loss and of loss of love are taken as hallmarks of a preoedipal origin when they appear in a patient's symptomatology so little disguised as to be clearly recognizable.

Common as it seems to be, this is an assumption that flies in the face of the available psychoanalytic data. As I pointed out earlier, conflicts triggered by anxiety or by depressive affect whose ideational content are object loss and/or loss of love can, and often do, have their origin in the oedipal period of development. Rivalrous incestuous and parenticidal drive derivatives have, as a part of their content, thoughts of object loss (= death wishes) and of loss of love (= fantasies of punishment and of retribution) as well as thoughts of castration. Psychoanalytic evidence shows that in every individual all three calamities participate in the anxiety and the depressive affect that initiate conflict in the oedipal period. There is no basis for attributing the origin of a conflict to the period of life before two-and-a-half years of age simply because anxiety and/or depressive affect whose ideational contents have to do with object loss and/or loss of love are prominently involved in the symptoms to which it has given rise. Only a reconstruction of the psychic events of childhood which is soundly based on all of the available facts, particularly on adequate psychoanalytic data, can suffice to decide the relative importance of preoedipal and oedipal factors in any individual case. An *a priori* assumption will not do.

As to the third point, one must keep in mind the complexities involved if one is to follow the full range of the analytic material of any patient. One must be prepared to see evidence of misery alternating with terror, of terror breeding misery, of loss of love implying castration, of castration depressive affect leading to object loss, and of all the other combinations of the ideational content of the calamities of childhood that characterize psychic life in the oedipal phase of development. It is only by being prepared for these complex interrelations that one can hope to catch the evidence for each of them as it appears in a given patient's analytic material. Unpreparedness in this respect will lead all too often to conjectures and interpretations in one's clinical work which are simplistic, incomplete, or both, as well as to theoretical formulations and generalizations which are similarly incomplete and misleading.

SUMMARY

The correct and most useful way in which to understand the psychosexual development of the oedipal period and its attendant conflicts is to take account of depressive affect as well as of anxiety, of the relation of each to the calamities of childhood, of the continuing, active presence of all three calamities throughout the oedipal period, and of the reciprocal interaction of affects and of calamities. Nothing less will do.

An approach that satisfies these criteria affords a vastly improved understanding of the conflicts of the oedipal period of development, of their consequences for psychic development then and later, and of their persistent role in psychic life throughout latency, adolescence, and adulthood. To mention but one feature of the improvement in one's understanding to which I refer, such an approach illuminates many features of the Oedipus complex of girls which were obscure till now. It permits equal understanding of the Oedipus complex and the oedipal conflicts of girls and boys. What obscurities remain are the same for both sexes. What can be understood is as clear for the one as for the other.

CHAPTER 7

COMPROMISE FORMATION

The essential components of psychic conflict are drive derivative, anxiety and/or depressive affect, and defense. Its consequence is a compromise among its several components (Brenner, 1979b). It is compromise formation one observes when one studies psychic functioning. Compromise formations are the data of observation when one applies the psychoanalytic method and observes and/or infers a patient's wishes, fantasies, moods, plans, dreams, and symptoms. Each of these is a compromise formation, as are, indeed, the entire range of psychic phenomena subsumed under the heading of material for analysis.

The components of compromise formations in adult life include various aspects of superego functioning in addition to drive derivatives, anxiety and depressive affect whose ideational content includes one or more of the calamities of childhood, and defense. All the components of adult compromise formations except the superego have been discussed (Chapters 2-6), and it would be logical to discuss the superego before examining the many consequences of conflict in more detail, were it not for the fact that the superego is itself a compromise formation. It is one of the most important of the many, fateful consequences of the stormy conflicts of the oedipal period of development—so much so, that Freud (1924c) referred to the superego as the heir to the Oedipus complex. Thus the superego is both a consequence of psychic conflict and, once it has come into being, a component of subsequent conflicts.

It will be recalled (Chapter 2) that ego functions serve both to gratify drive derivatives, i.e., id derivatives, and to oppose them. If there is too much unpleasure, the result is opposition, i.e., defense. If there is less unpleasure associated with drive satisfaction, or none at all, the ego promotes the achievement of satisfaction. More simply, if a wish arouses too much unpleasure, ego functions appear as defense; if not, they appear as mediators of satisfaction.

What I wish to add at this point is that the balance between defense and drive gratification is a mobile one, not a static one. For example, in a revery, a dream, or a slip of the tongue, a drive derivative often emerges into conscious awareness or is given verbal expression only to be forgotten, repudiated, or ignored moments later. The same happens in joking, as Freud himself noted (1915c, p. 151). Coprophagia, for instance, is not a source of pleasure to most adults in our society, either in action or in fantasy, yet coprophagic jokes are extremely popular and a great source of amusement and pleasure to many. This means that, under certain circumstances and for brief periods, coprophagic wishes give rise to pleasure, while shortly thereafter they are again ignored and repudiated or, if they do become conscious, give rise not to pleasure, but to indifference or disgust.

When one looks at such phenomena from the point of view of drive satisfaction, one can say that there are special techniques, as Freud called them, for temporary abrogation of repression, the word Freud (1915c) used for what he later called defense. There is no doubt that drive derivatives which are opposed, i.e., defended against, by the ego at one time can find satisfaction, often via fantasy, at another. Looked at from the other side, from the point of view of defense, one can say that such defenses as adopting an attitude that a wish is only make-believe, something not to be taken seriously, that one is not responsible because one is still a child, that anything goes at carnival time, etc., can at times suffice to reduce anxiety and/or depressive affect to such a degree that other defenses, e.g., repression or reaction formation, are temporarily unnecessary, with the result that a psychic element previously repressed or replaced by a contradictory element, as happens in reaction formation, emerges undisguised into consciousness.

However, this way of viewing conflict and its consequence, first from one side and then from another, gives too limited a picture of the psychic phenomena one is trying to describe and to understand. It is better to formulate the matter thus. Shifts like the one described above in the balance between defense and drive satisfaction demonstrate that the mind functions so as to afford to drive derivatives the fullest expression or satisfaction compatible with a tolerable degree of anxiety and/or depressive affect. When anxiety and/or depressive affect become too intensely unpleasurable, defense is heightened to mitigate them. When they grow less intensely unpleasurable, more drive satisfaction is achieved. It can even happen that full satisfaction and intolerable anxiety—orgasm and panic—coincide, as in the classic nightmare (Jones, 1931). Usually the results are less dramatic and less paradoxical. Nevertheless, the guiding principle is the same: as much satisfaction and as little unpleasure as it is possible to attain.

It is important to bear in mind that Freud did not conceive of defense as shifting in the way I have described under normal circumstances. His view was that the balance between defense and what is defended against is normally static and that shifts are to be reckoned as signs of pathology. He expressed this most clearly with respect to repression, the defense he discussed most often and at greatest length. Since the formulation I offer does differ significantly from Freud's views on repression (see Brenner, 1957a), I shall summarize the aspects of Freud's concept of repression which I propose to alter. Although my discussion will refer explicitly to repression, it is equally applicable, with suitable and necessary changes, to what Freud, after 1926, recognized as defense in general.

Freud believed the effects of repression to be twofold. In the first place, he thought, repressed drive derivatives are excluded from the ego and consigned to the id. This meant, to Freud, that as long as the repression is maintained, a repressed drive derivative has no access to consciousness, produces no emotional consequences, and does not give rise to any motor activity aimed at drive satisfaction. However, the repressed drive derivative, according to Freud, persists in the id and exerts pressure in the direction of emergence into consciousness and of gratification. Consequently, there is a tendency for offshoots of the repressed drive derivative to intrude into the functions of the ego and to reach consciousness in dreams, jokes, fantasies, slips, neurotic symptoms, and other, similar psychic manifestations, which may, in general, be described as compromise formations.

Freud referred to such phenomena as instances of a *return of the repressed.* By this he meant to indicate that each is a result of a failure of repression. The failure, according to Freud, may be either temporary or prolonged, it may be either so direct as to be unmistakable or so disguised as to be hardly perceptible, it may be either of such slight practical importance in the life of an individual as to pass quite unnoticed or of such great importance as to be decisive for the whole future course of a person's life. Whatever its characteristics in any of these respects, however, it is still a failure of repression, according to Freud, which gives rise to a compromise formation in psychic life.

Still according to Freud, there are three general conditions under which a return of the repressed may occur: (1) a weakening of the defenses of the ego, as by illness or during sleep; (2) a strengthening of the drives, as in puberty or as the result of long-continued frustration and/or abstinence; (3) a correspondence between the content of current experience and of the repressed drive derivative. To these should be added the influence of current seduction, which presumably corresponds in part to each of the three conditions just mentioned.

The main point I wish to make is that in Freud's view compromise formations in which repressed drive derivatives reach consciousness and influence behavior are failures of repression. His view was that, insofar as repression is successful, whatever mental elements have been repressed are effectively barred from access to consciousness, which means the conscious recall of memories and emotional expression, and from access to conscious behavior. It is only when there is a return of the repressed, i.e., when there is a failure of repression, that, according to Freud, disguised and distorted derivatives of what has been repressed appear in conscious psychic life.

My view differs from that of Freud as follows (Brenner, 1966). The available psychoanalytic evidence indicates that what has been and is repressed does have access to consciousness, even when repression is successfully maintained. It is not true that what has been repressed gains access to consciousness only if repression fails. A strongly cathected drive derivative, even though it is repressed, does not simply press for discharge or satisfaction, as Freud said. It regularly gains access to consciousness and influences conscious mental life and behavior while it is repressed. Put in another way, the phenomena of our daily mental life, our fantasies, our thoughts, our plans, and our actions, are compromises among the forces and tendencies of id and ego and, later, of the superego as well. This means that the parts of the id Freud called the repressed are among the determinants of the phenomena of daily psychic life. I wish to emphasize that this holds true of psychic functioning in general. It is not true only for those relatively atypical phenomena called neurotic symptoms. Compromise formation is a general tendency of the mind, not an exceptional one. Id impulses, including repressed ones, exert an influence on conscious psychic functioning and on behavior, although their tendency to do so is opposed by the ego's defensive activity.

What evidence is available for this revision of Freud's theory of repression and, more generally, of defense? What are the data that support it?

The evidence which is most readily available, most abundant, and, therefore, most convincing comes from the everyday experiences of psychoanalytic practice. What makes analysis possible, what accounts for the efficacy of the psychoanalytic method, is the fact that what is defended against, lest it arouse intolerable anxiety and/or depressive affect, nevertheless contributes a substantial share to those compromise formations which are called conscious thought, speech, wishes, plans, fantasies, dreams, and behavior. Psychoanalysts rely on the fact that when a patient in analysis speaks, the conflictful drive derivatives and superego manifestations being warded off or defended against constantly find expression in what the patient is thinking and talking about. Depending on the extent to which individual patients are able to refrain from editing their thoughts, they will be giving more or less recognizable expression to strivings that arouse unpleasure and defense as they talk. Were this not the case, the psychoanalytic method would be useless and analysis itself, impossible.

By speaking freely, a patient reveals to the analyst evidence of childhood drive derivatives. Although the drive derivatives are defended against or warded off in various ways, they constantly influence every patient's thoughts enough so that they can be inferred with some certainty by the listening analyst. The psychoanalytic method depends on the fact that, even when they are strenuously warded off, drive derivatives play a determinative role in conscious psychic life. They are not the only determinants. Anxiety and depressive affect, defense, and superego functioning all play their parts as well, but drive derivatives, no less than the other components of psychic conflict, find constant expression in conscious adult psychic life. Analytic material, so-called free associations, afford readily available, abundant, convincing support for revising Freud's theory of defense as I have done.

One can say the same about that other pillar of psychoanalytic technique, the transference. The positive value of recognizing and analyzing transference manifestations lies in the fact that they are compromise formations determined in part by the childhood mental strivings against which each patient has defended for his or her entire life after childhood, in order to eliminate or to mitigate anxiety and/or depressive affect. Every transference reaction reveals something of those childhood strivings or wishes.

No analyst will dispute that, in an analytic situation, a patient's associations and transference reactions always reveal something of the childhood drive derivatives which are repressed or otherwise defended against. The objection may be raised, however, that they do so because they are examples not of successful defense against drive derivatives warded off to avoid unpleasure, but of unsuccessful defense. It might be argued, therefore, that they support Freud's idea of the fate of the repressed rather than the idea I have advanced. It might be argued that they illustrate the consequence of a failure of defense, as Freud believed, rather than a balance between defense and drive derivative, as I have described.

The difficulty with this objection is that, if one accepts it, one is forced to include under the heading of failure of defense a very wide range of psychic phenomena ordinarily thought of as normal. Freud himself called attention to what he described as a temporary failure of defense in the psychogenesis of certain normal phenomena: dreams, jokes, and the slips and errors of everyday life (Freud, 1900, 1901, 1905c). In connection with the last of these, he went a step further and attributed to repressed complexes a determinative influence on seemingly casual or chance ideas. He presented examples to support the idea of psychic determinism in normal psychic life as, for instance, when one chooses a number seemingly at random. Shall one maintain that the random choice of numbers represents a failure of repression, i.e., of defense, in everyone, sick or well, or is it more reasonable to recognize that no defense prevents the drive derivative that occasioned it from exerting a substantial influence on conscious thought and behavior, albeit an influence that is disguised, distorted, or even vehemently disavowed?

Moreover, the normal phenomena to which Freud referred as instances of a failure of repression are but a beginning. Kris (1935) called attention to a great variety of normal psychic phenomena and activities that afford pleasurable expression in adult life for drive derivatives against which strong defenses have operated ever since childhood. These he called examples of regression in the service of the ego. They include intellectual and artistic creativity, the enjoyment of works of art or of mere entertainment by the members of an audience to whom they are directed, religious activities, etc. One may add, as further examples sports and recreational games. If all of these are to be considered instances of failure of defense, one must wonder whether the idea of a successful defense as Freud defined it is real or chimerical.

To put the matter simply, conflict and compromise formation are not hallmarks of pathological mental functioning. They are equally important in normal functioning, as we shall see in more detail in the chapters that follow. Conflict is always dynamic, always mobile. A successful defense does not fetter and immobilize a drive derivative. It does not render ineffective the psychic striving to be warded off. The ego's function is to oppose id derivatives to the extent necessary to eliminate or to mitigate unpleasure. In their role as executants of the drives and, later, of the superego, ego functions will grant to both the fullest expression compatible with a tolerable degree of unpleasure. When anxiety and/or depressive affect become too intensely unpleasurable, defense is heightened to mitigate them. When there is less intense unpleasure, more satisfaction is achieved.

At this point some explanation is in order about terminology. Compromise formation was at first synonymous with neurotic symptom. One of Freud's earliest discoveries was that obsessional and hysterical symptoms express or represent simultaneously the gratification of a drive derivative, an attempt to ward it off, and moral condemnation or self-punishment (Freud, 1896, 1898). Another early discovery was that more than one drive derivative, or unconscious wish, can be expressed simultaneously by a single conscious phenomenon, e.g., a dream. This Freud called overdetermination. Since both overdetermination and compromise formation refer to multiple unconscious determinants of conscious phenomena, the two have often been equated, though Freud's original usage, at least, suggests a distinction between them.

Waelder (1930) introduced, as a special case of overdetermination or compromise formation, what he called the principle of multiple function. He proposed that the ego be thought of as a central steering agency, i.e., an agency that solves problems and/or performs tasks set for it by id, superego, external reality, and the repetition compulsion (see Chapter 2). According to Waelder, each sets two tasks for the ego: (1) to obey its demands or wishes and (2) to master or control them. By this Waelder meant that the ego must attempt, at one and the same time, to gratify id wishes and to defend against or control them, to carry out the superego's demands and prohibitions and to oppose or mitigate them, to submit to reality and to exploit or modify it, and to submit to the compulsion to repeat as well as to use it actively for the ego's own ends. As Waelder pointed out, it is impossible to accomplish all eight of these tasks in equal degree; the ego can only try.

The most serious weakness of this formulation is Waelder's assumption that the ego is a steering agency—that it is like a little man, a homunculus, in a sort of driver's seat of the psychic apparatus. Waelder did not attempt to support this assumption, he simply stated it as fact. The ego has its own interests, he said, and manipulates id, superego, external reality, and repetition compulsion as best it can, now yielding, now opposing, to achieve its aims. Though he referred in his paper explicitly to "Inhibitions, Symptoms and Anxiety" (Freud, 1926), Waelder made no special reference either to anxiety or to psychic conflict. His idea of multiple function was not that it is a result of conflict. He believed it to be a result of a problem-solving activity of the ego. The ego is a steerer, a problem solver, he thought, and multiple function or overdetermination results from the eight-fold nature of the problems which the mind sets the ego to solve.

As a result, Waelder's picture of mental functioning impresses the reader as passionless, intellectual, almost mechanical. The ego he depicted could easily be replaced by a computer. It is little wonder, therefore, that the principle of multiple function, as Waelder presented it, attracted little interest and found almost no clinical application in its original form. Nevertheless, it has the great merit of clearly enunciating the idea that ". . . every psychic act has a multiple meaning," so that, for example, ". . . every act of man, including all his purposeful reactions directed toward reality, must also yield to overinterpretation in regard to its content of instinctual satisfaction," or, more generally, "Each individual act or fantasy has its ego side, its id side, its superego side . . ." (Waelder, 1930, pp. 73-82, *passim*). Waelder sensed clearly enough, despite the faults in his formulation, that id, ego, and superego combine to shape thought and action, both normal and pathological.

Brenman (1952) referred to Waelder's paper when she pointed to the many functions served by masochistic character formation. She noted that it serves the id as a source of satisfaction for drive derivatives; the superego as a means of punishment, of expiation, or of restriction of pleasure; and the ego as a defense or as a means of adaptation to external reality. At the same time she suggested that masochistic character formation has specific determinants as well. She asserted, in other words, that something more than compromise among id, ego, and superego is involved in the genesis of a masochistic character. She identified certain "underlying drives and defenses" (p. 273) specific for characterological masochism. These are, (1) from the side of the drives, an unusually strong need for love, the aggression resulting from the frustration of the need for love, and "an unusual disposition to anxiety" and (2) on the side of the ego defenses, the large-scale operation of four mechanisms of defense, namely, denial, reaction formation, introjection, and projection. Brenman thus took back, in her final summation, much of what would otherwise have followed from her application of Waelder's principle. She began by emphasizing the multiple function of masochistic character formation. She finished by suggesting that it is due principally to an excessive fear of loss of love associated with aggressive wishes.

My own interest in the psychopathology of moral masochism originated in my experience with analytic patients in whom masochistic character traits were of considerable importance. Stimulated by Brenman's paper, I gradually came to recognize, first, that my patients' masochistic character traits and/or behavior were compromises among drive derivatives, defenses, and superego trends and, second, that "masochistic character formation is in no way unique in this respect. On the contrary . . . *every* psychic act may be viewed as a compromise among the various parts of the psychic apparatus," i.e., among id, ego, and superego (Brenner, 1959, p. 211).

At that time I mistakenly attributed this formulation to Waelder (1930), and used the term he had introduced, the principle of multiple function, to refer to the consequences of psychic conflict in psychic life. As a result, Waelder's term has, since 1959, come to be rather widely used in both clinical and theoretical discussions in referring to those consequences, a meaning Waelder never intended his term to have, as a reading of his original paper makes clear.[1]

In what follows, as in what has gone before, I have used the term compromise formation to designate the outcome of conflict and have avoided both the term multiple function and the term overdetermination in describing that outcome or in referring to it. There are several advantages to doing so. For one thing it avoids ambiguity. What I call compromise formation is not the same as Waelder's concept of multiple function or overdetermination. Multiple function, as Waelder defined it, is not a consequence of psychic conflict. Compromise formation, as I define it, is a consequence of psychic conflict. Compromise formation is a term, moreover, which does not clash with common usage in psychoanalysis, since Freud introduced it to refer to neurotic symptoms, phenomena attributed to psychic conflict. Most important, by using a term which, though not new, is at least novel in the context in which I use it, I call attention to what is new in my evaluation of the role conflict plays in psychic life, namely, that, wherever we look, what we see is a compromise formation.

SUMMARY

In addition to explaining my use of the term, I have, in this chapter, called attention to the following points regarding compromise formation.

1. The balance between defense and drive gratification is normally a shifting or mobile one.

2. The balance is not, as Freud believed, mobile only when defense has failed—when there is a return of the repressed, as he put it—and static or steady when repression is normally successful.

3. The mind functions in such a way as to afford to drive derivatives the fullest degree of satisfaction compatible with a tolerable degree of anxiety and/or depressive affect.

[1]My attention was called to my error by a colleague, Dr. Guttman, who was Waelder's literary executor and who edited a volume of his papers (see Guttman, 1976), In fact, my ideas concerning the ubiquitous consequences of psychic conflict in mental life do not derive from Waelder, though I am indebted both to him and to Brenman for the stimulus their papers gave me.

CHAPTER 8

THE SUPEREGO

As noted in Chapter 7, the superego is both a consequence of psychic conflict and a component of it. Analysts have recognized the role of the superego as a component of psychic conflict ever since Freud introduced the concept of the superego as an agency of the mind in 1923. The fact that it is in large part a consequence of oedipal conflicts is also well known. Freud (1924c) called it "the heir of the Oedipus complex" (p. 59). What I wish to add is this. *The superego is a compromise formation or, to be more precise, a group of compromise formations originating largely in the conflicts of the oedipal phase.* It is not "the heir" of the Oedipus complex. It is one of the many compromise formations that arise from the conflicts of the oedipal period of development.

One of the most striking features of superego functioning when it is viewed as a component of psychic conflict is the diverse nature of its role. On the one hand it is closely allied to defense—so much so that even as late as 1933 Freud attributed defense as much to the superego as to the ego (Freud, 1933, p. 69). On the other hand, one of Freud's principal reasons for introducing the structural theory was to account for the fact that a need to punish oneself can play the same role in psychic conflict that a drive derivative does. A need to punish oneself, Freud noted, can be defended against by being repressed and may thus become unconscious. Finally, as Freud (1926) also pointed out, superego disapproval, i.e., guilt, by which Freud meant fear of punishment, is the last of the typical danger situations of childhood. It appears later in the course of development than the other three calamities of childhood—object loss, loss of love, and castration—and, in a sense, once it has developed, it subsumes them all.

No satisfactory explanation has been offered till now of the diversity of the role of superego functioning as a component of psychic conflict. How can it be defense at one time, the equivalent of a drive derivative arousing unpleasure at another time, and a calamitous unpleasure to be avoided or mitigated at still another?

This question can be answered only by tracing the process of superego formation. As I shall show, it is a process that has not, till now, been correctly understood. The superego is a compromise formation. Like every compromise formation it is the result of an interaction among and a blending of drive derivatives, anxiety, depressive affect, and defense. It is for this reason that defense, impulses to be defended against, and unpleasurable affects whose ideational content concerns the typical calamities of childhood all play a part in its functioning. They are what formed it in the beginning. They are the stuff of which it is composed. In genetic terms, the superego is definable as one of the consequences of psychic conflict as well as a component of all later conflicts.

Freud recognized that some explanation is due of the complex nature of superego functioning in psychic life, but he gave the problem only passing attention. He said the origin of the superego in the Oedipus complex accounts for the fact that after superego formation oedipal conflicts continue in a figuratively higher region of the mind, adding that such a continuation means that "the ego has not succeeded in properly mastering the oedipus complex" (Freud, 1923, p. 39). He thus implied that, normally, superego formation puts an end to oedipal conflicts, an idea he developed at length in a subsequent paper (Freud, 1924b). In any case, Freud's treatment of the complex nature of the role of the superego in psychic conflict is unsatisfactory, partly because it is so terse, but, more importantly, because at the time Freud wrote it he had not yet clearly identified the role of anxiety in psychic conflict. An up-to-date exposition based on currently available data and current concepts is long overdue.

Superego formation can be described as follows. Directly and indirectly, standards and rules of conduct are imposed on children by parents or parent substitutes. In our society, at least, the imposition of such rules and standards begins very early and continues for many years. Thus, in most cases superego formation begins at least as early as toilet training (Ferenczi, 1925) and continues through adolescence (Hartmann et al., 1946). Despite its early beginnings and its later development, however, one must agree with Freud (1923, 1924b) that the conflicts of the oedipal period play by far the largest role in superego formation.

To repeat what has been stated in Chapter 6, the passionate desires of the oedipal period regularly give rise to intensely unpleasurable affects—anxiety and depressive affect—whose ideational content includes the typical calamities of childhood. Of these, ideas of castration are most disturbing in the majority of children, but object loss and loss of love never lose their importance in the mind of any child and one or the other may rival castration on occasion.

The resulting conflicts rage acutely, though with fluctuating severity, for many months. Eventually, they subside. That is to say, relatively stable compromise formations appear which allow for as much gratification of incestuous and parenticidal drive derivatives as is possible without intolerable anxiety and depressive affect. Some of these compromise formations, though by no means all of them, have to do with morality. They have to do with being "good" or "bad" in the sense of conforming to or transgressing real and fantasied parental prescriptions for behavior. They have to do with feeling virtuous or the reverse, with remorse, with self-punishment, with penance, with atonement, and with forgiveness, reconciliation, and love.

By no means all oedipal compromise formations have to do with morality. Some are ambitious fantasies of success in life. These fantasies have so profound an influence in later years on such matters as the choice of vocation, the choice of avocations, and the choice of sexual partners that it is hardly an exaggeration to say that the oedipal fantasies determine adult goals and ambitions in these areas. Other compromise formations of the oedipal period are more like neurotic symptoms than they are like normal ambitions and character traits. Examples of these are food preferences and dislikes, bowel and urinary habits, bedtime rituals, masturbatory fantasies and practices, and patterns of muscular activity such as habitual gestures, facial expressions, and the like. But among the host of compromise formations that result from oedipal conflicts, the ones concerning morality make up the superego. Moreover, like other oedipal compromise formations, they persist throughout life. The compromise formations that make up the superego form the basis of the moral aspect of psychic functioning.

Hartmann et al. (1946) gave the simplest and most concise definition of the superego. They defined it as the aspect of psychic functioning that has to do with morality. To apply this excellent definition correctly, however, one must know how a young child thinks and feels at the time of life when superego formation is at its height, i.e., in the oedipal and immediately postoedipal periods. To a young child, morality is something very different from what it is, at least consciously, to an intellectually sophisticated adult. A knowledge of developmental psychology is essential to a proper understanding of the consequence of oedipal conflicts which we call the superego, just as it is to a proper understanding of any other consequence of the conflicts of that fateful period.

For a young child, morality means, essentially, feeling, thinking, and behaving in such a way as to avoid the calamity of being punished. By this is meant the calamity of having to endure or to face the danger of enduring any or all of the calamities of childhood, viz. object loss, loss of love, and castration. The crucial questions are, "What will win or forfeit parental approval?" and, "What will rouse or dissipate parental wrath?"

These two questions are the touchstone that decides whether a thought, a wish, an action, an affect, or a physical sensation is good or bad in the sense of being moral or immoral.

In all of this, as analysts well know, it is not only a child's experiences of punishment that are important. Superego formation depends only in part on parental discipline. What a child believes is punishable is not wholly determined by whether its parents are forbidding or indulgent in their treatment of the child. A child's own fantasy is always the decisive factor.

The example most often offered to illustrate this fact is that of a patient with great guilt and consequent inhibition about sexual matters despite the fact that the patient's parents were unusually permissive sexually during the patient's childhood, were often nude in the patient's presence, left bathroom and bedroom doors open, answered sexual questions freely, etc. As we have learned from analyzing such patients, it was the child's reaction to its sexually stimulating, yet frustrating home environment that resulted in the formation of an unusually severe superego. It is the undue intensity of its incestuous, murderous, sadomasochistic wishes that make such a child expect punishment for wishes and actions, e.g., masturbation, no matter how nonpunishing the parents try to be.

Another example of the role of fantasy in this regard is afforded by the frequency with which children believe they are being or will be punished by something, e.g., by illness, by temporary separation, or by physical injury, which is not intended as punishment by their parents and which may be, for that matter, quite beyond their parents' control. One can say, in fact, that a child's belief that it is being punished or that punishment is in the offing is never congruent with the parents' intent; rather, it is a child's fantasy that decides what is and what is not seen as punishment.

This is not to disregard the importance of how punishing a child's parents actually are in speech and action. It clearly makes a great difference whether parents are reasonably accepting of a young child's drive-determined behavior or whether they harshly oppose it. One must realize that parental discipline is but one factor in superego formation. It is not the only one.

To repeat, morality and avoiding punishment are synonymous in the oedipal period. To be moral means to take measures to eliminate or to minimize the anxiety and/or depressive affect aroused by oedipal drive derivatives, which include in their ideational content that one's parents are or will be angry, disapproving, and punishing.

What measures do children usually take to accomplish this end? How do superego compromise formations arise?

The most familiar, because it is the one Freud (1923, 1933) emphasized, is identification with real or fantasied parental prohibitions, i.e., identification with the parental superego. This means that the child becomes like the disapproving, forbidding parent and is strict, disciplinary, and punitive with itself. The result of such an identification is to increase or strengthen a child's ability to oppose drive derivatives that arouse anxiety and/or depressive affect. The child's defensive capacity is enhanced. Incidentally, as Freud (1923, 1933) also pointed out, from having been rebellious, castrating, and murderous, the child becomes punitive and angry with itself. The child's aggression, according to Freud, has been turned back against the child.

There is no doubt that identification with a parent whose retributive anger is feared plays a large defensive role in the oedipal conflicts that form the superego. In this connection, A. Freud (1936) called special attention to what she termed identification with an aggressor as a first or pre-stage of superego formation. However, identification, whether with parental superegos or with the aggressor, are not the only important defensive maneuvers that contribute to superego formation. There are other modes or areas of ego functioning which are often used defensively and which are, therefore, frequently identifiable as important in superego formation. One of these is an intensification of loving wishes toward the child's rival or rivals—a kind of reaction formation. Another is the inhibition of competitive wishes or their repudiation. Still another, the substitution of oral or anal wishes for genital ones, i.e., the displacement of drive derivatives from genital to oral and anal modes and aims, while still another is the adoption of attitudes and behavior characterized by submissiveness.

As already noted, the common thread which runs through all these otherwise diverse defensive maneuvers is the belief that it is of vital importance to be approved of and loved by one's parents. Any aspect of ego functioning that furthers parental approval and/or avoids disapproval and punishment can and does participate in superego formation. Thus, identification with an aggressor or with the parental superego are not the only paths that lead to superego formation—something which is often erroneously assumed to be the case. They are the most familiar paths, but not the only ones.

Just as identification is not the sole aspect of ego functioning that contributes to superego formation, aggression is not the only drive involved. Analysts generally have followed Freud (1933) and Hartmann et al. (1946) in viewing superego formation solely in terms of aggression. Even those who have considered the role of libidinal drive derivatives in superego formation, e.g., Kramer (1958) and Schafer (1960), have concurred with the majority view at least to the extent that they also assigned to aggression an exclusive role in superego formation during the period of oedipal conflicts, asserting that the benign or loving aspects of superego functioning have their origins during the preoedipal phase of development. The fact is, however, that the vicissitudes of the drives involved in superego formation are far more complex than the turning of aggression against oneself, important as that aspect of the process is. Superego formation also involves an alliance with one's parents and a submission to them, both of which are libidinally gratifying.

The neglect of the role of libidinal drive derivatives of the oedipal phase in superego formation is all the more remarkable when one considers that Freud's first extensive discussion of superego formation, in the final section of *Totem and Taboo* (1912-1913), was framed exclusively in terms of libidinal, oedipal strivings. Perhaps the reason for the neglect is to be found in historical circumstances, i.e., in the history of the development of psychoanalytic theory. *Totem And Taboo* was written as a contribution to sociology and religion. One must translate what Freud wrote in his final chapter about social morality into the language and the concepts of the psychology of the individual in order to apply it to superego formation. In addition, Freud did not consider aggression to be a drive, on a par with libido, until 1920. Moreover, when this reformulation of drive theory did finally emerge, Freud's decision to consider aggression a drive probably rested to a great extent on his study of unconscious guilt, i.e., on superego functioning (see Chapter

2). Aggression as a drive and superego as an agency of the mind appeared closely linked in psychoanalytic theory both in time and conceptually. It is, therefore, plausible to attribute to historical circumstances a share in the neglect of the role of libido in superego formation and functioning.

It may be, however, that other factors are involved as well. To give due weight to the importance of libidinal wishes from the oedipal phase in superego formation and functioning is to make explicit the role of masochism in both. Superego formation and functioning furnish the most important as well as the most readily accessible examples of the role of masochism in normal mental life (Brenner, 1959). If one is committed to the opinion that masochism plays no part in normal superego functioning (Loewenstein, 1957) and that any evidence of it is, by definition, pathological, one must, to maintain this position, ignore any evidence of the role of libidinal gratification in the compromise formations that constitute the superego.

Psychoanalytic data currently available speak against such a one-sided view. Masochism plays an important role in normal superego formation and functioning. It is to this role that I now address myself.

Masochism is best defined as an acceptance of pain and suffering as a condition of libidinal gratification, conscious, unconscious, or both (see Brenner, 1959). Now self-imposed unpleasure, a word that includes pain, suffering, and diminished gratification, is, clearly, a part of most conflicts which stem from drive derivatives. By this I mean that every defensive effort that interferes with drive satisfaction is an instance of self-imposed unpleasure, greater or less in degree. In the case of the conflicts which lead to superego formation, the feature of self-imposed unpleasure has a special characteristic, however. It is modeled on real or fantasied experiences of punishment and/or retribution for misdeeds, a term that, in this case, includes wishes as well as actions. Self-imposed unpleasure is, in a child's mind, a way of avoiding object loss, loss of love, or castration by appeasing the parents, or it is a way of winning their love, or it is both at once.

Insofar as superego demands and prohibitions serve the function of appeasement, i.e., of avoiding punishment in the form of one or more of the calamities just mentioned, there is nothing about it that one can properly call masochistic. One does not ordinarily think of a person who bows to superior forces as a masochist. One's inclination is rather to think of such a person as a realist—one who accepts a certain degree of unpleasure to save him- or herself far greater unpleasure. Even if one goes a step beyond and recognizes that part of normal superego functioning is a *need* to punish oneself for bad wishes or deeds, this too can be attributed to the persistence in unconscious psychic life of the childish conviction that, if one does not propitiate one's forbidding parents, if one does not win back parental love after having forfeited it by bad wishes or deeds, one is in danger of being punished. The pain and frustration of penance and renunciation would then be, not masochistic, but realistic acceptance of a minor discomfort in order to forestall the possibility of a major calamity. In other words, appeasement is not, in itself, unequivocally masochistic.

As Freud (1912-1913) was the first to observe, however, there are other motives involved than mere appeasement in the compromise formations we are discussing. A child's attitude toward its parents during the oedipal phase of development is invariably ambivalent and basically bisexual. The degree of ambivalence as well as the degree of bisexuality varies from child to child, depending both on constitutional factors, of which we have little knowledge, and on the particular environmental factors that make up the special circumstances of each child's family setting. Normally, for example, a boy in the oedipal phase has not only rivalrous and murderous wishes toward his father, but feminine ones as well. When, in the course of his psychological development, he attempts to control his rivalrous wishes toward his father and the accompanying murderous feelings by identifying with his father's moral prohibitions against such wishes, his passive feminine wishes will be gratified simultaneously. The unconscious fantasy of being close to and of merging with his envied and beloved father gives rise to libidinal gratification at the same time that it relieves anxiety. It satisfies a wish to be castrated, i.e., to be turned into a girl, as a condition for love. By definition, then, it satisfies a masochistic wish.

In his discussion of superego formation and functioning,

Freud (1933) gave as the motive for submissively identifying with parental authority the need to gain support against instinctual impulses which arouse anxiety. As Freud noted, a child thus insures against the enmity feared from the parent. It must be added that this is not the only motive. Another motive is involved than the need to avoid or to dissipate anxiety and/or depressive affect. That motive, as Freud (1912-1913) also observed, is to be united with the parent, in fantasy, for the sake of the libidinal gratification such a union can bring. Though the example I gave, following Freud, has to do with an oedipal boy, I have made clear (Chapter 6) that the acceptance of castration, loss of love, and object loss as a condition for love plays no less important a role in oedipal girls than it does in oedipal boys.

Thus remorse and self-punishment are unconsciously gratifying in a masochistic way, as well as having a defensive value in a child's struggle to control dangerous and unwanted drive derivatives. Moreover, the degree to which a masochistic element participates in superego formation and functioning may be presumed to vary from one person to another, depending both on constitutional endowment and on the vicissitudes of childhood development. This is illustrated by the following clinical vignettes.

An analytic patient in his late twenties had an extremely ambivalent attitude toward his father, whose behavior toward the patient throughout the patient's childhood had shown a mixture of neglect and disinterest on the one hand and physical seductiveness on the other. The seductiveness, though not overtly sexual on the father's part, had been very stimulating sexually to the patient. In adult life, whenever the patient was angry or rebellious toward an older man, he became conscious of thoughts of submitting to him sexually. He either ignored these or brushed them aside as stupid and crazy. He viewed them as intrusive, i.e., obsessional thoughts rather than as his own. Other aspects of his behavior showed similar characteristics. He was not overtly homosexual. However, if he felt slighted or disappointed by an older man, in addition to becoming angry, he would find it necessary to behave in a way calculated to ingratiate himself to the older man or, at the very least, to attract some sort of friendly attention, despite his annoyance with himself for being such a boot licker.

In terms of superego functioning, therefore, this patient demonstrated an exaggerated degree of masochism. Whenever his unconscious, parricidal wishes were stirred up, he reacted not only with signs of guilt and remorse, but also with unmistakable signs of a wish for feminine sexual gratification by his feared and beloved father. That this wish served the purpose of defense as well makes it no less masochistic (see Brenner, 1959).

The case of a female patient who suffered from episodes of depression marked by tormenting self-recriminations also provides a clear illustration of the relation between superego functioning and masochistic gratification. After much analysis, the patient gradually became aware of something neither she nor her analyst had suspected previously. The episodes of self-accusation and self-torment, episodes which were both defensive in their function and expressive of guilt caused by her ambivalent and violent oedipal wishes, were at the same time sensually pleasurable to her. They were accompanied by genital sensations which were part of a half-conscious mood of sexual excitement.

Once alerted by such clinical material, in which the masochistic aspect of superego functioning is unusually prominent, to a degree which warrants calling it pathological, it is not difficult to perceive the role of masochism in a wide variety of other instances which are clearly within the range of normality.

In our society, one of the traditional ways morality is institutionalized is via religion. Religious beliefs and practices in general satisfy a variety of unconscious needs. Religion is by no means simply a moral code. However, morality is a part of every religion—inescapably so, for psychological reasons, as Freud (1912-1913) maintained—and the moral code of each religion is an expression of the morality of the individual members of that religious group. The compromise formations that make up each member's superego must have some place in the code of the group if the code is to remain viable. Once a religion, or its moral code, has lost its psychological value for too large a number of its believers, they will of necessity change or replace it.

Since the usual way of looking at the relation between—in current terms—God's moral code and that of his believers is just the reverse of what I have said it to be, a word of explanation is in order.

It is accepted belief among religionists that religion makes people moral rather than the reverse. Proponents of religion argue that, even though the truth of religion cannot be logically proved, still religion is necessary if for no other reason than to keep man from being amoral and, consequently, asocial. Man, they say, would have no moral standards whatever, but would be guided wholly by his selfish passions, were it not for the promise of God's love as a reward for being moral and of the threat of God's wrath and punishment for transgressing.

In fact, however, no mere creed can make a person moral. Superego formation does not derive from Sunday school, the catechism, and their equivalents in other religions. It derives from the violent passions and the intolerable fears and depressive affects of the oedipal period. What has been institutionalized by past generations into an accepted moral code undoubtedly has some effect on subsequent generations. For any one person, however, this effect is less important by far than the effect of his own oedipal conflicts. The truth is, as Freud (1912-1913) surmised, that societal and religious moral codes reflect this aspect of childhood psychological development—that the outcome of the oedipal conflicts of the individual is what gives rise to moral codes, rather than the reverse.

It is in consequence of this that aspects of morality which are unconscious or otherwise disguised in normal persons are explicit, with only slight disguise, or with none at all, in religious moral codes and practices. For example, the connection between masochism, i.e., between suffering and libidinal gratification, on the one hand and obedience to moral demands and prohibitions on the other, is quite clear in the case of the beliefs that center about the rite of communion in the Roman Catholic church. The communicant identifies with Jesus in his or her submission to God's commandments. Being like Jesus means being pure and moral like him and resisting all temptation to sin in the future as one has sinned in the past. Failure to refrain from sin will result in punishment by God. All of this has to do with defense against drive derivatives which arouse anxiety and/or depressive affect. However, by the same act of communion, a communicant identifies with Christ crucified. Identified with Jesus in this sense, the communicant welcomes physical torture and mutilation as the necessary condition for libidinal gratification. The communicant believes that as a consequence of submitting to mutilation, even if only in fantasy, he or she will be loved by God and will be united with him in bliss.

One has only to take this much of the rite of communion literally to recognize in it an expression of the two principal unconscious motives for superego formation: first, the fear of punishment by one's parent and, second, the wish for sexual union with one's parent. Clearly there is much more that can be said about the psychology of communion. I restrict myself to what I have just said about it because my purpose is only to show that the rite of communion provides evidence to substantiate the fact that there is in normal persons a connection between morality and masochism, that self-punishment, penance, and remorse gratify libidinal wishes as well as serving an essential, defensive purpose.

Another religious practice of great antiquity is circumcision. According to Herodotus, it can be traced back to ancient Egypt, but there is no doubt that its origins reach far back into prehistoric times. Like communion, circumcision and other forms of penile mutilation, e.g., subincision, serve the defensive purpose of reducing anxiety and/or depressive affect associated with drive derivatives. Both give the promise that the rest of the penis will be spared and that heterosexual activity will be permitted if the prepuce is sacrificed or the urethra is incised. At the same time, however, like communion, circumcision and subincision offer libidinal gratification as well. According to Róheim (1950), Australian aborigines have the same name for the opening of a penile subincision as they have for the vagina. Moreover, the subincision opening is offered to other men and is used by them for sexual purposes. Malev (1966), pointed to the expression of a similar homosexual wish to be united with one's father in the orthodox Jewish rite of circumcision. A very important part of the ritual is that the first drop of blood from the infant's circumcised penis be sucked up by one of the men present. According to Malev, this represents an unconscious fantasy of abjuring sex with women and finding libidinal satisfaction instead with other men, a conclusion he supported by reference to the Hebrew words of the ceremony. Additional support for his conclusion can be drawn from the fact that, for a Jew, being circumcised means more than a precondition for God's permission to be a man among men and women, i.e., to gratify wishes of oedipal origin without fear of castration by father. It means, in addition, to become one of God's chosen people, one of his beloved, one of those whom he specially favors, not merely with his protection, but with his love.

Thus penile mutilation, like communion, combines morality and masochism. Among the motives for submission to and identification with parental moral demands, wishes for libidinal gratification play a significant role in both circumcision and subincision.

Still another example of the connection between morality and masochism is offered by certain funeral customs. The aspect of funeral rites most often discussed in psychoanalytic literature has to do with the defense against feelings of triumph and hostility toward a dead friend or relative. In general, any show of pleasure or satisfaction over someone's death is strictly forbidden. It is one's moral duty to say only good things about the deceased and to demonstrate grief by word and deed. In addition, it is customary in many cultures for mourners at a funeral to rend their clothing and to lacerate or bruise themselves as part of the ritual of mourning. Such behavior is additional evidence to the mourner as well as to fellow mourners that the death causes the mourner only grief. It is offered as proof that his or her (unconscious) rival's death gives rise to no pleasure or satisfaction. At the same time, this self-injurious behavior, which is unconsciously self-destructive and self-castrating, is a way for the mourner to experience self-inflicted retribution for the unconscious satisfaction occasioned by the gratification of murderous wishes. Briefly, these funeral customs all serve the purpose of defense against drive derivatives whose ideational content includes a wish to kill the deceased and pleasure at his or her death and, at the same time, they atone for the satisfaction of those wishes.

In addition to all this, however, a mourner's self-injurious behavior fulfills another function. It is a way for the mourner to feel united with the departed, ambivalently loved and hated friend or relative in a close and loving relationship which is, at least unconsciously, a sexual one as well. Self-injury during mourning is partly masochistic. It is partly a condition for libidinal gratification.

A mourner's wish for loving closeness with the dead is usually conscious. A wish for sexual union is less often conscious, though it is by no means rare for sexual wishes to be conscious as well. Funeral services are conducted with the consciously expressed hope that the dead person will be made happy by what the mourners are doing. The sentiment, "It's what he or she would have wanted," is one that is frequently expressed, as is the companion thought, "What we are doing must make him or her happy." Nor is it rare, in many funerals in our culture, for mourners to embrace and to kiss the dead and to long, consciously, to be embraced, kissed, and made love to in return.

In other words, mourners pretend that the dead person is still alive, is pleased by what they are doing, and will love them for it. We all know from personal experience that it is very hard to part from someone who is taken from us by death and that one continues to cherish the fantasy, even though one knows it is only a fantasy, that the dead person is still alive, rather than dead and gone.

The overtly loving behavior mourners show a corpse with the conscious wish to be loved in return is certainly not masochistic. However, mourners also woo the dead by their own suffering and by physically injuring themselves. Such self-injurious, even self-destructive and self-castrating behavior during a funeral is not only defensive and self-punitive, i.e., intended as atonement, it is, unconsciously, intended to lead to libidinal gratification as well. It is an example of pain that is sought as a condition of libidinal gratification. Thus masochism is one aspect of the complicated psychological reaction to death that has achieved an institutionalized form in funeral rites. In these, morality and masochism are also seen to be related.

My next example has to do with a psychological aspect of

artistic creativity. In our own society man's inner conflicts over artistic creation do not find institutionalized expression, as far as I know. In other societies, especially in earlier times, they have found such expression.

In classical antiquity, for example, it was immoral for poets to claim personal responsibility for their artistic achievements. The morally accepted behavior, the proper form, as it came to be in later classical times, was for a poet to attribute the act of artistic creation to inspiration by divine powers. The belief to which all subscribed or to which, as time went on, they pretended to subscribe, was that one could write a good poem only if a god or goddess entered one's body and fertilized one's imagination.

Psychoanalytic authors in the past have pointed out that many fantasies of inspiration have, as one of their unconscious roots, feminine, sexual wishes (Kris, 1939; Arlow, 1951). The unconscious wish is to be penetrated and impregnated by one's father.

Among the Greeks, to write a great and popular poem was to compete for fame, fortune, and immortality—to become as a god. In other words, to be a successful poet meant to gratify the unconscious, oedipal wish to triumph over one's parent and to fulfill one's childhood incestuous and murderous wishes. A protestation that one did not write the poem oneself, that one was inspired by a divinity, was a way of denying that one had triumphed over one's rival by emphasizing instead one's sexual submission to that rival. Thus the fantasy of inspiration served a double function. It gratified a sexual wish and served the purpose of defense, which is to say that the institutionalized moral requirement that the origin of a poem be attributed to divine inspiration represents, among other things, an unconscious masochistic reaction to a moral transgression.

Though the fantasy of inspiration no longer has the moral imperative for a writer that it did in ancient days, it still has rather widespread appeal. It is one of many examples of the persistence of religious practices which are no longer consciously thought of as sacred and obligatory, but merely as charming and attractive. If, however, as seems likely, its attraction derives from an unconscious moral imperative, in whatever way it may be consciously rationalized, it exemplifies the role of masochism in morality today no less than in classical antiquity.

To sum up, it is frequent enough to be called universal that loving, submissive, libidinally gratifying wishes play a significant part in superego formation. In other words, such wishes are gratified in a disguised, often unconscious way by those compromise formations stemming from the conflicts of the oedipal period which we call the superego because they have to do with morality. The libidinal wishes in question serve a dual purpose, that of drive satisfaction and that of defense, in this case, of defense against competitive, parenticidal drive derivatives. It should be noted, by the way, that the use of a drive derivative as a defense is a commonplace in psychic conflict. Freud (1911a) recognized it in connection with his discussion of the psychopathology of Schreber's psychosis and, to mention but one other example, it is part and parcel of every reaction formation.

It follows from what I have said about the role of masochism in superego formation and functioning that the participation of masochistic wishes in moral functioning is not a sign of pathology in and of itself. It is part of normal functioning in most cases. When moral functioning is dominated by masochistic wishes to the extent that it is in patients Freud referred to as moral masochists, superego pathology is doubtless present. Some degree of masochism, however, is normal.

This brings me to the question of superego pathology and normality. An understanding of what is and what is not pathological in superego functioning depends on the broadened perspective of superego formation and functioning presented in this chapter. It depends on the recognition that the superego is composed principally of compromise formations which are results of oedipal conflicts.

At present superego pathology is usually described and explained by analysts in terms of defects in the superego—superego lacunae, as they are often called. This usage follows Freud (1923), who remarked, in passing, that well or fully formed superegos are probably exceptional and that most persons have but scanty, ill-formed ones. Current usage, like Freud's remark, derives from the inadequate theory that superego formation is due to identification with the superegos of one's parents. It supposes this identification has been incomplete and that consequently the superego has been incompletely constituted or, alternatively, that the identification was complete, but the parents' superegos were defective. Thus, behavior that deviates considerably from socially accepted ethical standards is customarily explained as a result of defects or lacunae in the superego; the same explanation is frequently offered for "immoral" fantasies as well. Such explanations and the concepts they embody are at odds with the facts of superego formation as I have set them down. These facts require quite a different concept of superego pathology.

It should be recalled, first of all, that all superego compromise formations are ways in which a child tells its parents, "Approve of me!"—"Love me!"

One way to win someone's love and approval, as children see it, is to be as like that person as one can be. Another is to avoid wishing or doing what that person would disapprove of or would punish, especially anything incestuous, castrating, or parenticidal. Another is to do what that person wants, or seems to want—to be polite, sociable, clever, athletic, or whatever else is demanded and rewarded. Still another is to be remorseful—to promise to be good and never again to do what is bad. Another, closely associated to remorse, is to accept punishment in the hope of being forgiven. Still another is to be sexually desirable and gratifying to the person whose love and approval must be won.

Obviously, these many ways of winning love and approval are not mutually exclusive. They reinforce one another with the aim of reducing the unpleasure aroused by oedipal drive derivatives in the form of anxiety and depressive affect. Identification (especially with parental demands and prohibitions), remorse, self-punishment (which includes physical illness and injury), atonement, penance, and sexual submissiveness all participate in the oedipal compromise formations that have to do with morality. The relative importance of each is different in different persons, but all are present in virtually everyone, inextricably intertwined. As with every compromise formation, those that constitute the superego are a balance between pleasure and unpleasure, between gratification and frustration of drive derivatives, between what is tolerable and what is intolerable in the way of anxiety and of depressive affect.

It is for these reasons that morality takes such different forms in different persons. In one person, impulsive, rebellious behavior is associated with self-injury which has the unconscious significance of penance. In another, such behavior is unconsciously reassuring against the calamities associated with being sexually submissive in order to win love and forgiveness. In another, rebellious behavior is interdicted, or it is permitted only under special circumstances, e.g., during a carnival, or when one is away from home, or during wartime, or if one has become a member of a group with an adored leader (Freud, 1921). In still another, rebellious behavior is (unconsciously) intended to provoke punishment for the real or fantasied gratification of childhood drive derivatives (Freud, 1923).

The list of variations and of combinations of variations is endless. The few just outlined, though much oversimplified and separated from one another in schematic fashion, will at least serve to indicate how much, and in what ways, superego functioning can vary from one person to another, while still qualifying as normal. Variations in superego functioning are not to be attributed out of hand to pathology. Normal superego functioning is far from being as uniform, as consistent, or as logically coherent as Freud thought. Everyone's superego is a conglomerate of diverse compromise formations, all of which have to do with morality. Like social morality, individual morality is a patchwork affair. It is always more or less internally inconsistent.

It cannot be repeated too often that what we call the superego is, in fact, a set of relatively stable compromise formations which have only two things in common: (1) they originate principally from conflicts related to oedipal drive derivatives and (2) they have to do with morality. With the exception of mental defectives—idiots and imbeciles—everyone has a superego. Everyone must deal with oedipal drive derivatives somehow, which is to say that the conflicts over oedipal drive derivatives must lead to compromise formations, some of which have to do with morality. Whether an adult be a criminal or an ascetic, whether he be acclaimed and admired or treated as a social outcast, whether he be liar or truth-teller, saint or sinner, he cannot be without a superego.

It is of very great importance, both to the person and to society, just what compromise formations make up his or her superego, and one can justifiably classify each person's superego as normal or pathological on the same basis as one judges the normality or pathology of any compromise formation. If a person's superego functions in such a way as to create too much unpleasure and permit too little pleasure, if self-injurious and self-destructive tendencies are too strong, or if superego function leads to too much conflict with the environment, it is justifiable and appropriate to call that person's superego pathological. What one cannot justify is the concept that any person's superego is missing in whole or in part. The idea that a superego can be small, absent, or show lacunae does not correspond with what we know about the origins and the formation of the superego.

Sachs (1942) defined the essential, universal nucleus of the superego as the prohibitions against incest and parenticide. In one sense this is correct. In another, it is incorrect and misleading, because implicit in Sachs' definition is the generally accepted formulation that the superego is a set of internalized (in Freud's terminology, introjected) prohibitions and demands. This is a formulation that describes only a part of superego functioning. It cannot account for the part concerned with drive gratification, whether it be the sorts of masochistic gratification described earlier, or the sadistic gratification so apparent in the behavior of those reformers and would-be reformers of society's morals who, like Savonarola and Calvin, delight in punishing and torturing others in the name of morality. Both what we know of superego formation and what we know of its functioning once it has been formed require that it be understood as a set of compromise formations and not simply as a set of internalized prohibitions aiming to interdict gratification of oedipal drive derivatives. Internalized prohibitions play a large part in superego formation and functioning, but they are far from the whole story. Drive derivatives, both libidinal and aggressive, as well as anxiety, depressive affect, and many defenses other than identification with the superegos of one's parents are all importantly involved in superego formation and functioning.

To avoid a possible misunderstanding I add this. In presenting my views on superego formation, I have given more space to the role of masochism, i.e., to the role of libidinal gratification than I have to the role of aggression. I did so not because I think that the role of the one drive is so much more important than that of the other. The disparity was dictated solely by the fact that the role of libidinal gratification, hence of masochism, has been largely unrecognized in the past. I do not believe that masochism is, in general, the most important factor in superego formation. I do maintain, however, that it is an important factor in that process in every individual. In some persons, e.g., in those whom Freud called moral masochists, it is especially prominent. In others, who do not fall into the same category, it is less prominent, but it is never insignificant.

SUMMARY

Under the heading superego are included those aspects of psychic functioning that have to do with morality. The superego is, for the most part, a conglomerate of compromise formations that have resulted from the conflicts of the oedipal period of development.

When one views superego formation and functioning from the side of the ego, one sees that much more is involved than an identification with parental superegos, important as that is. There are, in fact, many aspects of ego functioning other than such identifications which are involved in the formation and functioning of the superego.

Similarly, from the side of the drives, much more is involved than aggression turned against oneself. What I have emphasized particularly is the role of libido and, hence, of masochism in superego formation and functioning. I have done so because this aspect has been so generally neglected.

Superego pathology is not to be understood, as it has been

generally understood by analysts till now, in terms of defective or incomplete development. Everyone, whether saint or sinner, has a fully formed superego. Superego pathology must be understood on the same basis as the pathology of any compromise formation.

CHAPTER 9

PATHOLOGICAL COMPROMISE FORMATIONS

Under this heading I shall pay principal attention to psychoneurotic symptoms and neurotic character traits. However, a word of introduction will be useful before I proceed to the main business of the chapter.

Chapters 1–7 have to do with the several components of psychic conflict. Chapter 8 deals with the superego, which is both a component of psychic conflict and a consequence of it. Chapters 9–13 are concerned with the consequence of conflict in psychic life, i.e., with the subject of compromise formation.

Compromise formations fall into two groups, normal and pathological. The pathological ones, called neurotic symptoms and neurotic character traits, are the compromise formations most familiar to psychoanalysts, since they were the ones that were first recognized. My beginning with two chapters on pathological compromise formations is, therefore, determined, at least in part, by historical considerations.

Next comes a chapter on dreams and on the slips and errors of daily life. Freud used his discoveries concerning the psychology of these psychic phenomena to demonstrate the similarities between what is pathological in psychic functioning and what is not (Freud, 1916-1917). My discussion of them as compromise formations serves the same purpose. It furnishes a bridge between the consideration of pathological compromise formations and the consideration of normal ones. The chapter that follows, on transference and countertransference, does the same. All three topics—dreams, slips, and transference—have the great virtue of having been exhaustively studied by generations of analysts because of their practical importance in the analytic situation. They are phenomena about which there is a wealth of reliable analytic data.

Finally comes a chapter on normal compromise formations and their role in psychic life. In it I have tried to convey how nearly ubiquitous compromise formation is in every aspect of psychic functioning and how important its role.

Psychoneurotic or, for short, neurotic symptoms were the first examples of compromise formations Freud recognized as such. As early as 1894, in "The Neuro-psychoses of Defence," he demonstrated that an obsessional symptom is a compromise among an unacceptable sexual wish, a defense against satisfying that wish, and remorse or self-punishment. Within a few years he recognized that the same formula applies to all psychoneurotic symptoms; later, he and other analysts extended it to the understanding of neurotic character traits as well. Whether the result of conflict over a drive derivative of childhood origin is a somatic symptom, a phobia, an obsessional symptom, or a neurotic character trait, it is a compromise formation in which drive derivative, anxiety or depressive affect, or both, associated with the calamities of childhood, defense, and superego manifestations all play a role that can be recognized and identified when adequate psychoanalytic data are available, i.e., when the psychoanalytic method can be successfully applied.

The first question I shall consider has to do with the observations on which these statements are based. Granted that the statements themselves are true, as analysts are generally agreed that they are, what does it really mean to say that every symptom and every neurotic character trait is a compromise formation? What sort of data does one observe which support that view? How can those theoretical generalizations be applied and used in one's day-to-day work with a patient?

My first example, taken from an earlier publication (Brenner, 1976), is the following.

A thirty-four-year-old woman was anxious while flying in

airplanes. She complained particularly of the fact that she was "just a passenger" and that, should anything go wrong, it was impossible for her to get to the controls and try to save the situation. She added, quite seriously, that she did not know what good it would do for her to get to the controls anyhow, since she knew nothing about flying and had had no experience as a pilot. However, the feeling of being unable to get to the controls was associated with great anxiety whenever she let herself dwell on it.

The patient went on to say that on one occasion, when she flew in a small private plane, she experienced no anxiety whatever. On that occasion she sat next to the pilot, in the cockpit of the plane, facing a set of duplicate controls and instruments. She attributed her calm on that occasion to the fact that there was at least a possibility for her to "do something" should necessity arise. Though she did not say so in so many words, it was clear the patient's fantasy was that the pilot, a man, would die or become incapacitated, that she would then take his place, and that the controls would be hers to operate.

It is relevant to an understanding of the patient's fear of flying that what disturbed her most in life was the fact that she was a woman. Consciously, she accepted with philosophical calm her conviction that she lived in what she was convinced is a man's world. When she began her analysis she had no idea that her principal symptoms, which were depression and an inability to marry, were related to her conflicts over being female. Unconsciously, she was, as she had been all her life, simultaneously jealously enraged, hopeless and dejected, and constantly guilty in consequence of what she considered to be her castrated, inferior, unloved state. It was of great importance in this connection that she had a brother who was four years her junior, who bore their father's name, and who succeeded him as head of the family business as a matter of course. Anything that reminded the patient of the fact she was female exacerbated the pathological consequences of her conflicts, and it is apparent from her associations that her reactions to flying as a passenger in a commercial aircraft was just such a pathological compromise formation. What were its components as far as they can be identified from the available data?

First, the drive derivatives. The one of chief importance is the patient's wish to have a penis. Since she believed her father would love her best if she were a boy, her longing for her father's love is likewise identifiable as an important drive derivative, which was one of the components of the conflict of which her fear of flying was the resulting compromise formation. Still another was her wish to castrate and to be rid of her brother, both in order to have his penis for herself and to avenge herself on him and on their parents for having given him the penis they had denied her and for loving him more than they loved her, as she was sure was the case. It may be mentioned that she had castrative and murderous wishes toward her father, who, she felt, had been faithless to her, as well as toward her brother.

The calamities associated with the drive derivatives just listed were manifold as well. The dominant affect was anxiety. She was consciously fearful that a calamity would indeed happen during flight. Unconsciously she was frightened that her castrative wishes would result in loss of love, which was represented in her symptom by being ignored and excluded from the cockpit, and in castration, which was represented in her symptom by her feeling inferior, incompetent, just a passenger, and, probably, by thoughts of physical injury, of death, or of both. Depressive affect was present also as a conscious feeling of hopelessness and of inevitable, irremediable calamity. In other words, both depressive affect and anxiety, whose ideational content included castration and loss of love, were components of the patient's conflict and both appeared, in different measure, in consciousness in the resulting compromise formation, despite the patient's defensive effort to avoid them.

Among the patient's defenses, repression is readily identifiable. She was wholly unaware of wishing she had a penis at the time she first told of her symptom. Her rage at her father and brother were also unconscious at the time. Much analytic work had to be done before she was consciously aware of either. Since her conscious feelings for her brother were affectionate solicitude, while those for her father were love and adoration—he could do no wrong, she thought—one can add a defensive reaction formation to the list. Also, she avoided flying whenever possible, i.e., she suffered from a phobia, which, by definition, implies a defensive avoidance. Still another aspect of her defense involved displacement. Instead of envying her brother and coveting his penis, she thought of the pilot, of his controls, and of his superior position and competence. She also countered her feeling of irremediable inferiority by an omniscient or omnipotent fantasy: if she could only have the use of the controls, she would fly the plane to safety. Moreover, to the extent to which she believed parts of her fantasy, e.g., that something catastrophic would *really* happen, she used that conviction as a defense: it was not that she *wished* for something which gave rise to unpleasure and to conflict; something was going to happen over which she had no control and for which she had no responsibility to bear. Thus both defense and drive gratification were involved in the disturbance of the patient's ability to test reality, i.e., to distinguish fact from fancy in her omniscient-omnipotent fantasy.

The same fantasy, it should be noted, involved ideas that served to defend against her murderous, castrative wishes, since in her fantasy she appeared as a savior, not as a castrating destroyer. It should be noted as well that her fantasy of being a savior served a defensive function against the catastrophes of loss of love and castration. A savior is loved and rewarded, not unloved, banished, and deprived of the penis she longs for. A savior is good, not bad.

And, indeed, aspects of superego functioning are easily identifiable as components of the patient's conflict. In addition to her wish to be good, it is evident that, for her, being unloved and castrated were punishments she both dreaded and accepted as necessary for atonement and happiness. Her suffering, her tears, her unhappiness, and her feeling of helpless incompetence all had in them an element of appeal for forgiveness, for pity, and for love.

The list just given of the components of the conflict which resulted in this patient's symptom is by no means complete. I have not striven for completeness. Rather, I have limited myself to two tasks only. The first is to show that there are drive derivatives, anxiety and depressive affect related to the calamities of childhood, defensive efforts, and superego manifestations among the components of the patient's conflict. The second, as important as the first, is to illustrate how the various components of conflict appear in an actual case, i.e., to illustrate what sort of data support the theory or generalization that every neurotic symptom results from a conflict with just those components.

In the following illustration I shall attempt to fulfill the same two tasks for a neurotic character trait. I have chosen a commonplace example for the same reason that I chose a commonplace symptom for my first example. My illustrations aim at demonstrating universal aspects of psychic functioning, aspects that characterize every symptom and every neurotic character trait.

The character trait I have chosen is that of compliant obedience. The patient, a thirty-one-year-old man, felt compelled to do what he was supposed to do, always and unhesitatingly. He deplored this feature of his character, he sometimes castigated himself bitterly for it, but he could not change it. Despite every effort to behave otherwise, he remained obediently compliant.

From as far back as he could remember, he was well behaved, was a good student, combed his hair, brushed his teeth, and washed his hands without too much prodding, never got into fights or other scrapes, and was, generally speaking, a credit to his parents. In college he likewise did what was expected of him. He joined the right clubs, he went out for some sports that he did well in and worked hard at, he did reasonably well academically in most of his courses and very well in the important ones, he went out with girls of good family, and so on. He chose his clothes on the basis of what was proper, he went to work after college at a job that was proper, he even went to church occasionally to please his mother. Many of his associations and dreams demonstrated something of which he himself became aware in the course of his analysis, namely, that to please his parents, particularly to please his mother, was a lifelong desire. It was a desire that appeared in his character as obedient compliance to every person and to every social requirement or demand to which his mother subscribed.

Clearly, then, the patient's neurotic character trait satisfied a wish for his mother's love and approval. He was obedient and compliant to win mother's love—a childhood drive derivative. Just as clearly, being obedient and compliant to mother's wishes also served a defensive purpose. It kept him from being aware of his rage at her and from expressing it directly. In truth, he could not remember having ever quarreled openly with his mother before he began analysis. In fact, the patient was an unusually gentle person altogether. It was only on the rarest occasions that he felt consciously angry.

In course of time it became apparent that the patient's obedient compliance was more complex than it would seem to be from the description of it I have given so far. He was compliant and obedient for all the world, including his mother, to see. In addition, he shared the world's opinion of him in this respect, to his regret, as I have already noted. In fact, however, he was not merely compliant. In his school work, for example, throughout his boyhood and young manhood, he forgot everything he had learned as soon as he had no need to remember it in order to get a good grade. In his social and sexual life, he went to nice parties and went out with girls of families his mother knew and approved of, but he cared for none of them. He preferred bars and prostitutes, though he frequented them only in secret. In his work, he never enjoyed what he did, he never became very proficient or successful at it, and he unconsciously worked constantly to fail at it. In other words, his neurotic character trait must be described in detail in order to be properly classified. It is true that he exhibited in a conspicuous way compliant obedience to his mother's every wish, but his neurotic character trait included as well a secret defiance of his mother, a determination to displease her and to be a discredit to her, i.e., to revenge himself on her by disappointing her. His lifelong attitude—the character trait under consideration—can be adequately described only by saying that, while he would do and be what his mother wanted him to be in order to please her, he would never enjoy it and would never really succeed at it, so that, in the long run, he would disappoint and disgrace her.

Another feature of the patient's compliance was the feeling that, try as he might, he could never succeed in what he hoped for, i.e., he never could be his mother's favorite. This conviction appeared in consciousness as a feeling of indifference about whatever he was doing. He was compliant and obedient with the conscious feeling that what he was doing at the time in a compliant way was useless and uninteresting anyway. Among the childhood determinants of this conviction was the fact that his mother did favor his two sisters, one of whom was a year his senior and the other, three and one half years his junior. He unconsciously wished he were both a baby, like his younger sister, and a girl, like both the siblings whom his mother preferred to him. As is to be expected, this wish, from early childhood on, was associated with intense castration anxiety and depressive affect.

From this abbreviated account one can identify a number of childhood drive derivatives as components of the patient's pathogenic conflict. He wished to be his mother's favorite, he wished to be a girl and a baby to accomplish this end, and he wished to avenge himself on his mother for not loving him best. These drive derivatives aroused both anxiety and depressive affect associated with the calamities of object loss, loss of love, and castration. Obedient compliance, gentleness, and good deportment served an important defensive function as well as the function of gratifying his wish for love, both in fantasy and in reality. Repression also played a dual role: he forgot what he learned in order to spite his mother, i.e., for purposes of drive gratification, while he repressed many painful memories of childhood to avoid unpleasure. As for superego manifestations, the very essence of his character trait was to be good. Good deportment, desirable, socially acceptable interests, conformity to parental standards of morality—all were part of his character trait of obedient compliance.

As in the case of the first example, it must be understood that what I have presented is far from a complete analysis of the patient's pathogenic conflicts. Only enough data have been given to document the existence of the various components of the conflict of which obedient compliance was the consequence and to illustrate how those components appear in actual, clinical material, i.e., to show what sort of data support the theory of conflict which is the subject of my exposition. As can be seen from the illustrative material of both examples, similar data are part of every psychoanalysis. Every situation in which analysis progresses satisfactorily will furnish material in abundance to support what I have said about the components of conflict that give rise to neurotic symptoms or to neurotic character traits and how these components blend and interact with one another to produce pathological compromise formations.

The next question to be considered has to do with the term pathological as applied to a compromise formation. On what basis is one to decide whether a given compromise formation is pathological or normal? It is clear that one cannot define a neurotic symptom or character trait simply as a compromise formation. Certainly the superego is not necessarily pathological, yet it is, as demonstrated in Chapter 8, a compromise formation and, moreover, a compromise formation that is dynamically and genetically very similar to the pathological compromise formations which were just used as illustrations.

As I have indicated (Chapter 8), a compromise formation is pathological when it is characterized by any combination of the following features: too much restriction of gratification of drive derivatives, too much inhibition of functional capacity, too much unpleasure—i.e., too much conscious anxiety, depressive affect, or both—too great a tendency to injure or to destroy oneself, or too great conflict with one's environment—i.e., usually, with the people one comes into contact with. When any combination of these features of a compromise formation exceeds a certain limit, the compromise formation in question is properly classified as pathological (Brenner, 1973b, p. 200).

It must be obvious that the matter of setting the limits just referred to is an arbitrary one. There is no sharp line that separates what is normal from what is pathological in psychic life. The two shade into one another by imperceptible degrees, just as is the case with illnesses or diseases of the sort commonly called physical or organic. Infectious diseases, each of which is caused by a specific organism, offer a useful parallel, precisely because they seem, at first glance, to be so very different.

Take tuberculosis, for example. How does one draw the line between what is normal and what is pathological where tuberculosis is concerned? How does one define tuberculosis as an illness?

Can one say that anyone whose body contains live, pathogenic organisms—live *mycobacteria tuberculosis*—is ill with tuberculosis?

To do so would be to advance a definition of illness that is not merely useless, but positively misleading and potentially mischievous in its consequences. Millions of adults harbor live mycobacteria over periods of many years without any evidence of harm to themselves. It is true that no one can have tuberculosis whose body contains no live tubercle organisms. It is true, in other words, that absence of the organism is proof that an individual does not have the disease, tuberculosis. The converse, however, is not true. Presence of the tubercle organism does not prove the presence of the disease, tuberculosis, in any useful or sensible meaning of the word. The organisms must be present in sufficient numbers and they must have damaged tissues and organs to a sufficient degree to have caused, or to be causing, or to be likely to cause substantial deleterious effects if one is to label the condition as pathological, i.e., if one is to call a person ill with tuberculosis. Nor are these considerations unique for that disease. They apply to any disease caused by a microorganism. That is to say, even in the case of infectious diseases, in which etiology and diagnosis are relatively simple, certain, and disease-specific, there is no sharp line between what is normal and what is pathological, between health and illness. There is always a gradient from the one to the other, whether the gradient be gentle or steep. There is never a discontinuity.

To return to psychopathology, it must be understood that to say there is no sharp line between what is normal and what is pathological is not to belittle the difference between mental health and mental illness. Even moderately severe mental illness is very different from mental health or normality. Mental illness is not the trivial matter that many ill-informed, though well-intentioned persons assume it to be. The difference between illness and health is the difference between suffering and pleasure, between terror and confidence, between failure and success, between death or mutilation and life. There is no difficulty in distinguishing a substantial degree of psychopathology from what is, by general agreement, psychically normal. My point is that the difference is one of degree only, however great the difference may be and however great its practical significance to the individual.

Freud recognized something of this very early, when he asserted that psychopathology does not consist in a disruption or fragmentation of psychic functioning, that it consists instead in disturbances in the balance among its several elements, disturbances he characterized as quantitative rather than as qualitative ones (Freud, 1900, p. 608). As he put it then, it is the balance among the systems Ucs., Pcs., and Pcpt.-Cs. that is disturbed in mental illness, just as it is, he thought, in dreams and in parapraxes (Freud, 1900, p. 569).

At the same time, it must be realized that Freud's understanding of psychopathology in 1900, and for many years thereafter, was substantially different from the one he eventually arrived at (see Chapter 1). Until 1926 he equated psychic conflict with psychopathology. Conflict, he said, is a consequence of a failure of repression, which was his word, at that time, for defense. As long as, or to the extent that one's defenses hold fast, one is free from conflict and is psychically normal, he thought. It is the failure of repression, according to Freud's views before 1926, which gives rise to neurotic anxiety and to conflict. Thus, prior to 1926, Freud and his colleagues made a sharp distinction, at least in principle, between psychic normality, which was believed to be synonymous with no psychic conflict, and psychopathology, which was synonymous with psychic conflict due to failure of repression.

It is pertinent to note, in this connection, that even after Freud (1926) had revised his theory of anxiety and conflict, there remained a tendency among analysts to maintain Freud's earlier view, at least with respect to the distinction between normality, or health, and pathology, or illness. Analysts persisted in the belief that what is normal is free from conflict and that, conversely, conflict is a sign of pathology, even if only a premonitory one.

To repeat, every neurotic symptom and every neurotic character trait is a compromise formation. Each is a consequence of psychic conflict, originating in childhood, the components of which include drive derivatives, anxiety and depressive affect connected with the calamities of childhood, defense, and superego mainfestations. Each is characterized by an excessive degree of inhibition, unpleasure, lack of gratification, self-destructiveness, and/or social disharmony. Certain consequences follow from this definition which are worth emphasizing because they are frequently neglected or overlooked.

For one thing, when one says that a symptom is a compromise formation it follows that it is never just one component of the conflict of which it is a consequence. For example, an obsessional ritual is never properly described as a masturbation equivalent. An impulse to masturbate can never be more than one of the components of a ritual. The symptom itself is always a compromise among an impulse to masturbate (= drive derivative), defense, superego manifestations, and anxiety and depressive affect. Any generalization about such rituals must take this fact into account. So must one's practical, clinical work with any patient who suffers from such a symptom.

Precisely the same is true for defense. A symptom is never a defense. Defense is only one component of a symptom. Masochism is not a defense against object loss, any more than obsessional neurotic symptoms are a defense against something worse, e.g., a psychosis. One must never overlook the role of defense in symptom formation, but a symptom is never a defense and nothing else (see Chapter 5). Neither is a symptom ever just self-punishment, just remorse, or just atonement. It is always a combination of elements that includes all the components of conflict which go to make up every compromise formation.

For another thing, a symptom is never the cause of anxiety or depressive affect (Arlow and Brenner, 1964; Brenner, 1976, 1979b). For example, if a patient complains of thoughts of going insane and is, at the same time, anxious, it is just as mistaken to take at face value the patient's statement that it is the idea of insanity that makes him or her anxious as it would be to take at face value another patient's assertion that it is the idea that an airplane may crash which accounts for his or her anxiety about flying, or the idea that an elevator may become disabled that accounts for a fear of elevators. In each case both the ideas of catastrophe and the conscious anxiety are symptomatic. Both are parts of a compromise formation whose components determine the feeling of impending danger, i.e., the anxiety, and the ideational content consciously associated with it. In fact, one of the most important features of psychic conflict is that conscious anxiety as part of a symptom is an indication that a patient's defensive efforts are insufficient or inadequate to the task of avoiding unpleasure in connection with whatever drive derivatives are the instigators of conflict. Both anxiety and depressive affect are always related to drive derivatives of childhood origin when they appear in consciousness as part of a pathological compromise formation. Unpleasurable affects must be analyzed into their component determinants in every case, by applying the psychoanalytic method, for their true nature and origin to be known. This is something to which I shall return in more detail (Chapter 10).

As another corollary, neither symptomatic anxiety nor symptomatic depressive affect is ever without ideational content (Brenner, 1974c, 1975a). The terms free-floating anxiety and contentless anxiety are misnomers. They can refer only to situations in which the ideational content of the affect has been completely or nearly completely repressed or to situations in which it has been dissociated from the sensation of unpleasure. The same is true of depressive affect. Like anxiety, it has always an ideational content. Freud's (1895a) assertion that anxiety without content is clinically observable in some patients is a statement derived from early clinical experiences from which he drew conclusions that have been subsequently discredited (see Chapter 4). He thought at that time that in some individuals unhygienic sexual practices can give rise to attacks of anxiety which have no psychic determinants and hence no psychological or ideational content. This explanation of his patients' anxiety attacks has since proved to be unsubstantiated by available data. A symptom can no more be just unpleasure than it can be just drive derivative or just defense.

I have so far treated psychoneurotic symptoms and neurotic character traits as essentially equivalent psychic phenomena. To do so deviates from the customary practice of most psychoanalysts. While agreeing that symptom and character trait resemble one another in being compromise formations, most analysts put emphasis on the differences between the two classes of phenomena. That they consider these differences important is indicated by such diagnostic terms as symptom neurosis and character neurosis. What are the distinctions that can, in fact, be made between neurotic symptoms and neurotic character traits? How useful and how valid are they?

In extreme cases the distinction between the two seems easy to make. If a patient complains that he or she dare not fly for fear of being overwhelmed by anxiety and that the difficulty began three months before, one has no hesitation in labeling it a neurotic symptom. The same is true if a patient must check every gas jet, faucet, and electric light before leaving home. If, on the other hand, one hears from or learns about a person who is invariably or customarily provocative, quarrelsome, or both with superiors at work, one is equally prompt and unequivocal about using the label neurotic character trait.

Not all cases are so easy, however. There are persons whose refusal to fly is lifelong, is not accompanied by conscious dread, and is instead experienced by the individual in question as a preference based on sensible, logical reasons. It may be clear to an observer that unconsciously such a person is as afraid of flying as the hypothetical phobic patient, yet here one is dealing with something imbedded in character and thoroughly ego-syntonic. Should one call it a symptom nevertheless, or is it more correct to view it as a consequence of a characteristic timidity, i.e., as part of a neurotic character trait?

Or consider the following possibility, which is no more unusual than the one just presented. How should one classify this pathological compromise formation? A patient was characteristically hostile toward people viewed as superior, without actually provoking quarrels with them. His hostile, provocative wishes were expressed instead in a sarcastic, critical attitude, not toward his individual superiors, with whom he was characteristically on good terms, but toward the more distant, the more impersonal, social, economic, and political establishment. Yet on a few occasions, specifically when he had made a new sexual conquest, he was just as provocative and quarrelsome with his superiors as the patient in the example above was habitually. Is such an episodic compromise formation symptomatic or characterologic?

To add to the difficulty in distinguishing neurotic symptom from neurotic character trait, many of the latter are not ego-syntonic, as one might suppose a character trait should be. One frequently encounters persons who wish they were less stubborn, or less submissively compliant, or less subject to unhappy moods, for example. Such persons may feel as helpless in relation to the neurotic character trait of which they complain and as much at odds with it as are those who fear flying or enclosed spaces.

In fact, neurotic symptom and neurotic character trait are often as indistinguishable descriptively as they are dynamically. The most one can say is, in general, if a pathological compromise formation persists for many years and if it is not strikingly different from ways of thinking and behaving classed as normal, it will usually be called a neurotic character trait. Conversely, if a pathological compromise formation is of brief duration, or if it is of abrupt or recent onset, and if it strikes one as strange, bizarre, or quite out of keeping with the usual run of normal behavior, it will be called a neurotic symptom.

My own conclusion from all these considerations is that it is a fruitless task to try to distinguish between neurotic symptoms and neurotic character traits. The similarities between them are much more far-reaching and significant than are the differences. Whatever distinguishing criteria one uses, the two will always overlap to such an extent that a satisfactory delineation of one from the other will be impossible at least as often as it seems possible. In addition, I do not see much value in making the distinction when one can do so. The differences are not ones of any real importance. Often they express value judgments of those who propose the distinguishing criteria, rather than valid inferences from clinical data. Every patient who enters analysis suffers from some pathological compromise formations which may plausibly be classified as neurotic symptoms and others which arguably fit better under the heading of neurotic character traits. To try to decide in each case whether a pathological compromise formation is best given the one label or the other seems to me to serve no useful purpose for either analyst or patient.

Still another consequence of the fact that every neurotic

symptom is a compromise formation has to do with the distinction between an individual symptom and a class or type of symptoms. To illustrate the distinction I have in mind, I shall return to the first case cited in this chapter, the case of the young woman with a fear of flying.

Her symptom was of the type called a phobia. More narrowly, it is classifiable as an airplane phobia. To say this much about it, however, is to say very little. It will be recalled that the patient was anxious only on commercial flights. On the one occasion when she flew in the copilot's seat of a small, private plane, she felt fine. If one knows what the controls of such an aircraft look like, it is easy to guess that, for her, to sit at the controls of a plane with the control stick—colloquially known to pilots as the joy stick, i.e., as the penis—between her legs unconsciously gratified her wish to have a penis of her own. At any rate, one would give a much fuller and more precise statement of her symptom if, instead of referring to it as an airplane or flying phobia, one described it as follows. Whenever she had to fly with nothing between her legs, while a young man with whom she had no personal contact sat with a big stick between his legs and was in charge of the whole venture, she became anxious, she imagined that something would happen to the pilot, to the plane, or to both which she would be prevented from remedying despite her urgent desire to do so. When, however, she sat next to the man in charge, with just the same thing between her legs as he had between his, she felt perfectly comfortable.

In other words, a symptom is never adequately described as merely a phobia, as an obsessional thought, etc. A symptom or, for that matter, a neurotic character trait, is a *particular* compromise formation. The more precisely and the more fully one describes it, the more likely one is to get some idea of the components of the conflict whose consequence it is. The more cursory and general the characterization, the less informative and the less useful it will be.

A second, closely related point is this. If all phobias, for example, were dynamically or genetically similar in many important ways, calling a symptom a phobia would be useful. In fact, however, the reverse is the case. The only thing all phobias have in common is the defensive use of avoidance. They share nothing else, either dynamically or genetically, which distinguishes them from any other class of symptoms. It is true that, in addition to avoidance, repression and displacement play defensive roles in every phobia, but one can say the same of very many other neurotic symptoms. Repression and displacement, like many other aspects of ego functioning, serve the purpose of defense in the vast majority of symptoms and neurotic character traits. It is also true that castration anxiety and castration depressive affect are to be found among the determinants of every phobia; but one can say the same of every symptom and of every neurotic character trait. One can go even further and say that among the determinants of every symptom and neurotic character trait, anxiety and depressive affect involving not only castration, but object loss and loss of love as well are present.

The more thoroughly one studies pathological compromise formations on the basis of psychoanalytic data, the more evidence one has to support the view that there is little to be gained, either practically or theoretically, from classifying pathological compromise formations under the customary, traditional headings. There is, however, much to be gained from describing each such symptom or character trait as fully and in as much detail as possible with an idea to indications of the nature and origin of the components of the conflict of which it is the consequence.

What, then, is the advantage in grouping together under one heading compromise formations that have in common the defensive use of avoidance and calling them all phobias? I cannot see any except the dubious one of familiarity. Freud (1926) called such compromise formations symptoms of anxiety hysteria, i.e., he suggested that the common element of avoidance points to other similarities of both dynamic and genetic nature which are so far-reaching that they justify classifying all such symptoms under the one heading, phobia. It was Freud's theory that when a patient habitually avoids, or has recently begun to avoid certain situations, which were not previously avoided and which most other people do not avoid, one can conclude, on the basis of the accumulated psychoanalytic data relevant to the topic, that the patient suffers from a particular illness or, at the least, from a particular syndrome called hysteria.

There is no doubt that many patients whom Freud classified as hysterics have, among other pathological compromise formations, ones in which avoidance plays a conspicuous role. However, the same is true of many patients whom neither Freud nor any other analyst would class as hysterics. For example, most patients with a compulsive need to wash their hands have associated phobias. They may avoid touching other people's bare skins, for example, or they avoid public toilets. In such cases, phobias are part of what Freud called, not hysteria, but obsessional neurosis. Arlow and I (1964, p. 161) noted that avoidance as a means of defense is also common among psychotic patients. In fact, therefore, it is no longer appropriate to follow Freud's theories or generalizations about the value of grouping together under a single heading those pathological compromise formations in which defensive avoidance is apparent. The label phobia, when applied to a neurotic symptom, has no such diagnostic significance as Freud originally assumed it had.

With suitable modifications, the same conclusion holds true for every other, commonly used symptomatic label or classification of symptoms. For example, what is commonly called isolation of affect, i.e., an absence of conscious pleasure or unpleasure in connection with a thought or memory to which pleasure, unpleasure, or both are in fact connected, was given its special name for the same reason phobia was. Isolation of affect is believed to be of diagnostic significance. To state the matter more explicitly, analysts, following Freud (1926) and A. Freud (1936), believe pathological compromise formations in which isolation of affect plays a conspicuous role have many other dynamic and genetic features in common and that patients who manifest such compromise formations suffer from the illness or syndrome called obsessional or compulsive neurosis.

As in the case of phobic avoidance and hysteria, there is no doubt that patients whom Freud would have diagnosed as obsessional neurotics characteristically exhibit compromise formations in which isolation of affect plays an easily discernible role. Again, however, the same is true of many patients who clearly do not belong in that diagnostic category. For example, some patients with physical symptoms of somatic origin are consciously indifferent to them. They show what Charcot was the first to call *une belle indifférence*. Diagnostically, patients with psychogenic physical symptoms are hysterics, not obsessionals. It is an unforgettably dramatic experience to be informed by such a patient in a casual, conversational tone of voice and in a manner devoid of perceptible unpleasure, that he or she is blind or paralyzed. One cannot imagine a more extreme example of isolation of affect, yet no analyst would call such a patient an obsessional.

To complete the analogy between isolation of affect and avoidance, isolation of affect may also be conspicuous in the symptomatology of psychotic patients. The very term schizophrenia was intended by Bleuler, who coined it, to refer to the lack of an appropriate or usual connection between ideation and affect in a whole class of psychotic patients.

Thus, no single feature of a particular pathological compromise formation is unambiguous or decisive in its meaning and its import. Whether it be called a symptom or a neurotic character trait, the importance of a pathological compromise formation and its significance in an individual's psychic life can be judged only in terms of the nature and origin of the components of the conflict of which it is the consequence. The fact is that a neurotic symptom is not a foreign body of the mind. It is not something separate and apart from a normal or healthy part of the mind. It is not a discrete entity implanted by some external, noxious agency. On the contrary, it is as much a part of an individual's psychic functioning as are the compromise formations we rightly call normal. A pathological compromise formation is one of the consequences of a person's conflicts, conflicts that arise from childhood drive derivatives. Its origins reach back into early childhood; its determinants are to be found in each of the psychic agencies: id, ego, and superego. It is an integral part of psychic life, not a stranger to it, and it must be judged accordingly. It is part of a larger whole.

SUMMARY

1. Examples have been offered to illustrate how drive derivatives, anxiety, depressive affect, defense, and superego

functioning combine to produce a pathological compromise formation.

2. A compromise formation is pathological when it is characterized by any combination of the following features: too much restriction of gratification of drive derivatives, too much anxiety or depressive affect, too much inhibition of functional capacity, too great a tendency to injure or destroy oneself, or too great conflict with one's environment.

3. A pathological compromise formation is never just defensive, just instinctually gratifying, or just self-punitive. It is always a mixture of all the components of the conflict of which it is the consequence.

4. Pathological compromise formations never cause anxiety or depressive affect. These affects are among the determinants of a pathological compromise formation. They do not result from it.

5. Questions have been raised concerning either the theoretical or the practical value of classifying pathological compromise formations under the diagnostic headings commonly used.

CHAPTER 10

ANXIETY AND DEPRESSIVE AFFECT IN PATHOLOGICAL COMPROMISE FORMATIONS

In this chapter I shall discuss anxiety and depressive affect in their roles as conscious features of pathological compromise formations in adult life. As noted in Chapter 9, either affect or both may play such a role. Either may be part of what a patient complains of or, at least, of what he or she is conscious of. However, neither is invariably or necessarily part of a pathological compromise formation.

Obviously, both affects are always represented in some way in a compromise formation, be it normal or pathological, since anxiety and depressive affect are among the components of every conflict and always participate in the blending together of the other components of conflict. However, even in clearly pathological compromise formations, a patient is not always conscious of either unpleasurable affect.

For example, a patient with a crippling psychogenic paralysis who is indifferent to his or her physical disability—a hysteric with *belle indifférence*—has no conscious experience of either anxiety or depressive affect, despite the fact that one or both are determinants of the disability. Counterphobic and elated patients likewise afford striking examples of the fact that conscious unpleasure in the form of anxiety, depressive affect, or both is not necessarily a feature of a pathological compromise formation.

There are many less dramatic examples, more commonly seen in psychoanalytic practice. One frequently encounters patients who are consciously indifferent to symptoms that obviously interfere to a major degree with their ability to find satisfaction in their lives or even to avoid misery. It is also commonplace to encounter persons, whether they are patients or not, who, as far as they are consciously aware, take pride in their eccentricities, their foibles, and their incapacities and inhibitions, even when these are serious enough in their consequences to warrant being classified as pathological compromise formations (see Chapter 9).

Even more frequent are patients whose pathological compromise formations involve only a minor degree of conscious anxiety or depressive affect, or only occasional awareness of either. For instance, most patients who shun flying or who avoid elevators, or bridges, or public toilets, etc. are relatively free of conscious anxiety as long as they are able to avoid the particular situation they find disturbing. Similarly, if a pathological compromise formation consists of stereotyped thoughts or ritualized behavior, it is common for anxiety or depressive affect to become conscious only if something interferes with carrying out the stereotype in the usual way. For example, a patient who avoided speaking or thinking of death when he parted from anyone, became worried and gloomy whenever I interrupted his speaking of death or of dying to tell him that his analytic session was over. If he was not interrupted until he had finished talking about death or dying, he was not consciously anxious or gloomy. If he was interrupted, he was both.

Clearly, then, some pathological compromise formations are characterized by conscious anxiety and depressive affect, while others are not. How is one to account for this variation? What is the significance of the difference, if any?

The anxiety and depressive affect which are components of every conflict are closely related, as I have had many occasions to note. Each is composed of unpleasure plus ideas of one or more of the typical calamities of childhood: object loss, loss of love, castration, and the various aspects of superego functioning subsumed under the headings of punishment, guilt, remorse, self-injury, and penance. By definition, the difference between the two affects is a temporal one. Depressive affect has as its ideational content a calamity or calamities that exist in the present, in the child's view, while anxiety has as its ideational content a future calamity, i.e., a danger (see Chapter 4).

As Freud (1926) pointed out, when unpleasure associated with drive derivatives is sufficiently intense, defenses are instituted that prevent or limit the gratification of those drive derivatives. However, as I noted earlier (Chapter 5) drive derivatives are not the only targets of defense. Some defensive maneuvers are directed against the unpleasurable affects themselves which served to trigger defense in the first place. Both modes or aspects of defense operate in such a way as to avoid or reduce to a minimum the unpleasure which is one part of anxiety and of depressive affect. What is important to add at this point is that defense can also be directed at the ideational content of either anxiety or depressive affect, or both. Defense opposes and wards off not only drive derivatives, (Freud, 1926), but both the unpleasure and the ideational content of anxiety and of depressive affect.

It is for these reasons that sometimes a pathological compromise formation is characterized by no unpleasure whatever, as far as conscious awareness goes. In such cases, defense has been successful in avoiding any conscious sensation of unpleasure even though the capacity of the individual to enjoy gratification of drive derivatives has been seriously impaired, or there is serious impairment of functional capacity, or there are serious tendencies toward self-punishment, self-injury, or both, or there are serious difficulties in adjusting to one's environment—in a word, even though the compromise formation is pathological (see Chapter 9).

In other cases, the resulting compromise formation, while pathological for any or all of the reasons just listed, is characterized by slight or transient unpleasure in the form of anxiety and depressive affect, while in still others, it is characterized by a very considerable degree of unpleasure of either or both kinds. What determines the result in every case, as far as conscious unpleasure is concerned, is the nature and the adequacy of the defensive effort. The same is true of the ideational content of both affects.

To repeat, whenever one observes a pathological compromise formation, one can be sure that anxiety and depressive affect are components of the conflict which gave rise to it. That is to say, one can be sure that unpleasurable affects played a role in the conflict which resulted in the compromise formation one observes and hopes to understand. Unpleasure must play a part in every conflict. Without unpleasure associated with a pleasure-seeking drive derivative, there would be no conflict. As to the ideational content of the anxiety and depressive affect involved in any particular conflict, one can discover it only by analysis. Only application of the psychoanalytic method will yield data adequate to the task of learning which calamities are involved, what their individual features are, what memories and fantasies are associated with them, and what parts they played in the patient's psychic development and functioning. The following examples will illustrate these points.

A man in his early thirties had symptoms of anxiety when he was in a bus. In such circumstances the degree of his discomfort at times led him to get off the bus and proceed by taxi or on foot. The patient was conscious of a considerable degree of unpleasure, with very little by way of ideational content. He knew he was anxious, that he feared something, but what he feared he did not exactly know. The most he could say was that he was afraid something physical would happen to him, to his body.

Analytic data in the form of associations, dreams, etc., gathered over a period of several weeks, eventually led to an understanding of the patient's symptomatic anxiety. Whenever, in a bus, his wish to be a girl and to have a man make love to him became active, he was afraid that, if one of the men in the bus whom he unconsciously found sexually attractive tried to seduce him, he would succumb. He was unconsciously afraid of castration, i.e., of turning into a girl and thus losing his penis. When his feminine wishes were strong, he could relieve his anxiety only by removing himself from the tempting situation. Being in a bus reminded him unconsciously of an experience in early adolescence when a man seated next to him in a bus caressed the patient's leg in an obvious attempt to seduce him. The patient had become frightened and ran off the bus. Only in the course of analysis did he recall that what had frightened him most was that he responded to the older man's caress with an immediate erection and conscious, sexual excitement of brief duration.

Another patient, a woman in her twenties, was also anxious when traveling in a bus, especially if the bus was stalled in traffic. Like the first patient, she knew she feared something, but she was no more able to say what she feared than he had been. In this case analysis revealed a quite different ideational content. Being in a bus that would not do what she wanted it to do, that stood still instead of taking her where she wanted to go, intensified her rage at her mother. Like the stalled bus, which made her angry and anxious as a grown woman, her mother had failed her when the patient was a child. For one thing, she had deprived the patient of a penis by making her a girl. For another, closely related to the first, she had given the penis to a younger brother. The consequences of the patient's jealous rage at her mother and brother were intense castration depressive affect and castration anxiety as well as anxiety and depressive affect related both to losing mother altogether and to losing mother's love. When a bus disappointed her as mother had, especially when it took on extra passengers, the intensification of her conflict over her phallic, murderous drive derivatives resulted in conscious anxiety.

The fact that the patient in the first example attributed his anxiety to the idea that something might happen to him if he stayed in the bus is not to be taken as an explanation of his anxiety. No more is the explanation offered by the second patient that what she feared was that there might not be enough air for all the people in the bus to breathe. Neither idea was the cause of either patient's anxiety, though each believed it to be. In each case the patient's anxiety had, in fact, one or more of the calamities of childhood as its ideational content. In the case of the first example, it was castration, in the case of the second, it was object loss, loss of love, and castration. In each case, moreover, the ideational content of the calamity was altered by the patient's defensive efforts so that, in the resultant compromise formation, the patient's conscious reason for anxiety bore only slight resemblance to the original childhood calamity.

To repeat, with respect to the unpleasure of anxiety and of depressive affect, a patient's defensive efforts may be conspicuously unsuccessful in other respects and yet be successful in avoiding or mitigating anxiety and depressive affect as conscious phenomena. Contrariwise, defense may be successful in other respects and yet be rather unsuccessful with respect to avoiding or mitigating unpleasure in consciousness. With respect to the ideational content of anxiety and of depressive affect, what appears as a conscious part of the compromise formation has been disguised, distorted, altered, opposed, ignored, denied, or shrugged off, in the patient's defensive effort to reduce unpleasure to a minimum. The ideational content of the component affects of the conflict can be discovered or correctly inferred only by analysis.

Patients may insist they fear appendicitis, or being trapped in an elevator, or insanity, or death, or starvation, or disintegration. They may be consciously convinced that the misery they feel so keenly is due to the pain inflicted on a loved one by neglect or mistreatment, or to their own irreparable, professional inadequacy, or to abandonment. In every instance, however, analysis will show that the conscious ideational content of the patient's unpleasurable affect is a defensively altered version of one or all of the calamities of childhood, calamities which, psychoanalytic experience has shown, invariably fall under the familiar headings of object loss, loss of love, castration, and one or another manifestation of superego functioning.

In fine, *depressive affect or anxiety as a feature of a pathological compromise formation is a defensively altered version of the depressive affect and anxiety which are among the components of the conflict of which the pathological compromise formation is a consequence.*

One must keep in mind that this statement applies to *every* pathological compromise formation, not merely to the familiar ones used just now as illustrations. For example, perceptual disturbances, such as experiences of depersonalization, or feelings of unreality, or a sensation of *déjà vu* may be accompanied by anxiety or depressive affect. When they are, the anxiety or depressive affect is not a consequence of the perceptual disturbance, no matter how sincerely the patient may insist that it is. Both the perceptual disturbance and the unpleasurable affect are consequences of conflict. That is to say, that both are part of the compromise formation, the affect no less so than the perceptual disturbance (Arlow, 1959; Arlow and Brenner, 1964). The following vignette will serve as an illustration.

A physician in his thirties, in the midst of an analytic session, suddenly remarked that everything looked yellow. At the same time he felt unaccountably sad. He thought immediately of the fact that yellow vision can occasionally be caused by a cardiac stimulant, digitalis, and he remembered a patient with cardiac disease for whom he had cared several years before and who had finally died of his illness. Still, the patient could not understand why *he* should have seen yellow. He had never had heart disease and had certainly never taken digitalis in any form. It then occurred to him that his brother, three years his junior, had not only had heart disease, but had died of it at the age of seven. For nearly two years before her second son's death the patient's mother had devoted herself totally to caring for him, leaving the patient miserably lonely and very guilty at being both angry and jealous. His brother's eventual death understandably made him feel more guilty than ever. One way in which he could get some share of his mother's attention during his brother's long illness was to sit beside her and listen while she read aloud to the invalid. The latter's favorite story book was bound in bright yellow and was referred to by both boys as the yellow book.

To return to the onset of the patient's perceptual disturbance during his analytic session so many years later, it appeared from other analytic data that my having told him when I would leave for vacation had stirred up all the drive derivatives and the unpleasurable affects associated in his mind with his mother neglecting him, as he had felt, to care for his dying brother. It had stirred up his longing for her love, his depressive affect in the form of loneliness and jealousy, his rage, his fear of punishment, and his remorse. A fantasy of himself as the invalid who got all of mother's attention, the memory of his unhappiness, and memories of the yellow book are all easily discernible as determinants of the resultant compromise formation. It is not, however, my intention to give a comprehensive survey of the dynamics or of the genesis of this example of pathological compromise formation. I wish only to illustrate the thesis that when an unpleasurable affect appears in consciousness it is as one part of a pathological compromise formation, not as a reaction to it. Despite the unusual nature of his perceptual disturbance, my patient felt no anxiety. Instead, he felt sad, though not intensely so, an affect which, like his yellow vision, could be understood only after the components of the conflict in question had been explicated with the help of the analytic method.

The symptomatology of patients who are classified as overtly psychotic offers further illustration of my thesis. Analytic data about such patients are, understandably, much less abundant and less reliable than are data about patients who are less sick and who are more often amenable to analysis. However, the following vignette will serve.

The patient was a man in his early fifties. His marriage of many years' standing seemed on the verge of breaking up, but it was not this fact that consciously disturbed him. What he complained of was anxiety that he might lose control of his temper and strike a man on the street. He explained that, as he walked along, strange men offended him by the way they looked at him. It was not easy for him to be more explicit, but in the course of time he was able to put into words what it was that so infuriated him: By the way they looked at him, it was clear to the patient that strange men were thinking to themselves that he was not a real man. By dint of further, careful analytic work it was possible for the patient to say that he was aware, from time to time, of an impulse to kiss a man. Analysis of his symptom never went further than this, but even on the basis of such incomplete data it is evident that the conscious anxiety which was part of the patient's symptom was not caused, as the patient himself believed when he first consulted me, by his impulse to attack men on the street. On the contrary, one of the functions served by his desire to knock a man down was defensive. It did not intensify his anxiety, it tended to alleviate his anxiety by assuring him he was very much a man. It was the castration anxiety associated with his wish to make love to a man which, though unconscious when he first came to see me, was the important cause of his anxiety, as far as the available analytic data show. His defensive efforts were not adequate to the task of eliminating his anxiety, and it appeared in consciousness as part of his symptom.

To repeat what the clinical excerpts just given are intended to illustrate, when either anxiety or depressive affect is a feature of a pathological compromise formation, it is a defensively altered version of the anxiety or depressive affect which is a component of the conflict of which the compromise formation in question is a consequence.

Psychoanalysts have long taken cognizance of the fact that this is the case with respect to anxiety, though it must be added that even here the cognizance has been only a partial one (Brenner, 1976, pp. 12ff.). However, since 1926 it has come to be generally recognized that every pathogenic conflict involves anxiety and, as a result, anxiety may appear as part of any sort of pathological compromise formation, that is, of any symptom.

Psychoanalysts have taken quite a different view of the significance of depressive affect that appears as part of a pathological compromise formation. The difference is no doubt a consequence of the fact that it was not until 1975 that the role of depressive affect as a component of conflict was identified (Brenner, 1975a). Before that time depressive affect as part of a pathological compromise formation was believed, mistakenly, to have special dynamic and genetic implications, just as anxiety was believed to be transformed libido prior to the publication of *Inhibitions, Symptoms and Anxiety* (Freud, 1926).

This is a matter worth discussing at some length because of its considerable practical and theoretical importance. As I have indicated, depressive affect is frequently present as part of a pathological compromise formation in patients seen in analysis. The better one understands the dynamics and the genesis of depressive affect and the better acquainted one is with the consequences of that understanding, the better able one is to work analytically with such patients.

To reiterate what has been said more than once already, depressive affect is unpleasure plus the idea that a calamity has already occurred and is a present fact of life. When depressive affect is part of a pathological compromise formation, it is a defensively altered version of the depressive affect which is a component of the conflict of which the pathological compromise formation is a consequence. The unpleasure has been defensively mitigated and the ideas of childhood calamity have been defensively altered and distorted (see the case of the physician who "saw yellow," above).

There are certain corollaries to this understanding which must be kept in mind. One has to do with the relation between depressive affect and orality. As will be discussed in more detail below, the psychoanalytic view of depressive affect which has been generally accepted until now posits a close, causal relation between the two. In fact, however, depressive affect is or, at the very least, can be a component of every conflict caused by drive derivatives, whether the drive derivatives are oral, anal, or phallic (see Chapter 6). To be sure, one can always find oral wishes in a conflict that has as its consequence a compromise formation of which conscious depressive affect is a feature. The reason for this, however, is not that oral wishes specially characterize such conflicts and their consequences. It is, on the contrary, because oral wishes play some part in every conflict associated with childhood drive derivatives. Oral wishes of childhood origin are components of every pathogenic conflict, just as anal and phallic wishes are. It is as true that anal and phallic drive derivatives are causally related to depressive affect as part of a pathological compromise formation as it is that oral drive derivatives are.

Another corollary has to do with the relation between depressive affect and the calamity of object loss. Any of the calamities of childhood can be and often are part of the ideational content of the depressive affect which is a component of a conflict that has as its consequence a pathological compromise formation of which depressive affect is part. More than that, all of the childhood calamities usually figure in the ideational content of every major conflict. Thus, if one looks for fantasies or memories of object loss, one will find them in every or nearly every case. However, one will as often find fantasies or memories of each of the other typical childhood calamities. In some cases object loss does seem to have been the most important of the determinants responsible for depressive affect associated with drive derivatives in childhood; in other cases it seems not to have been. One can reach a reliable decision in the matter only if one is successful in reconstructing the psychically traumatic events and influences of the patient's childhood on the basis of reliable analytic data. One cannot, as analysts often do, assume *a priori* that when depressive affect is part of a pathological compromise formation, object loss is its principal ideational content. Still less can one assume, as many analysts do, that the principal trauma responsible for the symptom of depressive affect in later life was the real or fantasied loss of mother or of mother's attention and care.

The following clinical material will serve to illustrate that there are patients in whom ideas of castration are the principal ideational content of depressive affect which is part of a pathological compromise formation.

The patient was a woman of thirty who was chronically depressed. She spoke slowly, wept frequently, constantly felt miserable, could find no happiness in any love affair, and reacted adversely to every slight improvement in her life situation. She was truly in a slough of despond. It gradually became evident that she had been overwhelmed by penis envy since childhood. As evidence of the strength of her feelings, she remarked on one occasion that she had never felt comfortable with her body since the age of twelve. She had no idea why that should be so. Her body had just never felt right since that age. As one might guess, she first menstruated when she was twelve—irrefutable proof to her that her body was female.

As another illustration of how she felt about being without a penis, she came into my office one day indignant because, when she had gone to use the lavatory just before, she had found the toilet seat up.

"No one," she said, "has any right to leave a toilet seat in that position!"

"Why not?" I asked.

"Because," she said, "it looks so ugly that way!"

She explained that she had always felt one of the ugliest things in the world is a toilet with the seat up. If the lid or the seat were down, it looked presentable, but she could never stand the way it looked with the seat up.

The patient's envy of men and her unconscious anger at every man for having the penis she so envied and wished for did not prevent her from having sexual relations with men. It did, however, make it impossible for her to be happy with a man or to marry one. Marriage had the same significance for her as her menarche had had. It meant to be irrevocably a woman. To remain unmarried meant, unconsciously, to be a man—a gay blade with a stable of sexual partners to pick from. To marry meant to be castrated, as numerous dreams and associations made clear.

My own clinical experience underlines the importance of castration depressive affect in childhood as a determinant of depressive affect later in life as a feature of a pathological compromise formation. All of the childhood calamities play a part in every case, in my experience, and either object loss or loss of love may be the principal ideational content. In the majority of cases, however, castration seemed to be most prominent (Brenner, 1974b). My experience in this respect is consonant with some of the cases reported in the literature, e.g., Fenichel (1945b, p. 404), Rochlin, (1953). The latter reported four cases in each of which recurrent depressions, i.e., the repeated appearance of depressive affect as part of a pathological compromise formation, corresponded on each occasion to an unconscious fantasy of having been castrated. In Fenichel's case, the patient had become profoundly depressed by the birth of a brother when she was three years old, in a way which was the prototype of her later neurotic symptoms, in which depressive affect was a prominent feature. It is interesting to note that, despite these analytic data, neither Fenichel nor Rochlin relinquished the accepted psychoanalytic view that depressive affect as a feature of a pathological compromise formation in later life is principally associated with oral drive derivatives and is primarily determined by object loss.

A third corollary has to do with the relation between aggression and depressive affect. This relation is anything but simple (see Chapter 6). On the one hand, depressive affect often gives rise to aggressive drive derivatives in the form of rage and a desire for revenge. This relation between aggression and depressive affect is particularly well known in connection with what Freud (1916) identified as a special character type—the exception. On the other hand, the real or fantasied gratification of aggressive drive derivatives, e.g., of death wishes, can lead to depressive affect of which the ideational content often is that one has killed, lost, or forever forfeited the love of someone who is loved and longed for as well as hated and envied. The intensely ambivalent nature of object ties in childhood, especially during the oedipal period, inevitably leads to great complexity in the relation between aggression and depressive affect and, one should add, between aggression and anxiety as well. That the latter is the case, is well known and generally recognized. That the former is the case is equally obvious and easily documented by analytic data, once the relation between depressive affect and psychic conflict is understood.

To cite a commonplace example, if a child, furious at mother for withholding her love, wishes her dead and gone or imagines inflicting some injury on her or torturing her in revenge, the child reacts (or, at least, those children who are later seen as analytic patients react) with both depressive affect and anxiety to these murderous, vengeful, aggressive drive derivatives. The depressive affect whose ideational content is loss of love gives rise to aggression; the aggression in turn gives rise to depressive affect whose ideational content usually includes object loss, loss of love, and castration, as well as ideas of punishment and of atonement, i.e., to superego derivatives.

A fourth corollary has to do with defense. Like anxiety, depressive affect is a component of every psychic conflict. Like anxiety, it can appear in attenuated and disguised form in every sort of pathological compromise formation. Whether or not it does so depends on the nature and the adequacy of the defensive constellation. Depressive affect is not a result of a particular defense. More specifically, it is not a result of identification. Genetically and dynamically, depressive affect precedes defense. It triggers defense. It is not a consequence of defense any more than anxiety is.

At this point I shall summarize the view of the dynamics and genesis of depressive affect as a part of a pathological compromise formation that has been accepted by psychoanalysts until now (see Freud, 1917b; Fenichel, 1945b; Lewin, 1950; Rochlin, 1953; Jacobson, 1971). I do so in order to demonstrate how greatly it differs from the view I have just given, a view based on a correct appreciation of the role of depressive affect in psychic conflict. As far as one can judge from the literature, all analysts subscribed to the view I am about to summarize prior to the publication of my first papers on the subject (Brenner, 1974a, 1974b, 1975a).

Depressive affect as a conscious feature of a pathological compromise formation has been thought to be a kind of pathological mourning, i.e., to be due invariably to real or fantasied object loss. Moreover, the loss has been assumed to relate to the oral phase of development, either directly, by regression, or by a combination of the two. Thus the prevalent view among psychoanalysts has been that real or fantasied object loss of one's mother in the earliest months of life is an essential precondition of pathological depressive affect. Loss was thought to result in ingestion of the lost object in fantasy, i.e., to result in a fantasy of oral incorporation of the (ambivalently) loved and hated lost object. Thus, it was believed, what was originally an ambivalent object tie to the mental representation of an object is replaced by identification with the mental representation of an object. As a result, the aggression originally directed toward the object became directed against oneself, it was believed, since the object of aggression had become part of oneself via identification. The consequence of this was believed to be self-hate, i.e., depressive affect. In pathological mourning, as a result of ambivalence and regression, an individual was thought to identify with a lost object, resulting in self-hate and depression. In slightly different words, pathological depressive affect was thought to be aggression turned against oneself by identification with an object lost either really or in fantasy.

The differences between the view of the dynamics and genesis of depressive affect as part of a pathological compromise formation which I have just summarized and the view based on a correct understanding of the role of depressive affect as a component of psychic conflict are obvious. Also obvious is the relevance of the differences to clinical analytic practice.

Pathological depressive affect is not always related *specially* to oral drive derivatives; it is not always a form of mourning, since it is not always specially related to object loss; it is not a consequence of aggression turned against oneself; and it is not specially related to identification, much less caused by it. On the contrary, it is as true of depressive affect as it is of anxiety that when it is present as a feature of a pathological compromise formation it is a defensively altered version of the unpleasurable component affect of the conflict of which the pathological compromise formation is a consequence. Its genesis and its dynamics cannot be known *a priori* because they are different in all the respects noted above from one patient to the next. The ideational content of pathological depressive affect in any given case is but a derivative of the depressive affect of childhood origin which is a component of the conflict of which pathological depressive affect is one part of the consequence. Like pathological anxiety, pathological depressive affect is part of a symptom and, as such, it must be analyzed to be understood correctly.

In addition to its relevance to psychoanalytic technique, a proper understanding of the dynamics and genesis of both pathological depressive affect and pathological anxiety has relevance to nosology. For reasons that will become evident it is desirable to discuss this point separately for each affect.

It was in *Inhibitions, Symptoms and Anxiety* that Freud (1926) first correctly explicated the relation of anxiety to psychic conflict. As a result of that explication and of such sequels to it as *The Ego and the Mechanisms of Defense* (A. Freud, 1936) and *Problems of Psychoanalytic Technique* (Fenichel, 1941), psychoanalysts came to accept that anxiety is a component of every pathogenic conflict, that it can appear as part of any sort of pathological compromise formation, and, therefore, that its presence or absence has no diagnostic significance. By now it is agreed, though largely tacitly, that anxiety as part of a pathological compromise formation is not diagnostically significant and reveals nothing about the dynamics or the pathogenesis of a compromise formation except that the patient's defensive effort was such that the unpleasure of anxiety was not eliminated or avoided—that it was at best mitigated. For example, the term anxiety hysteria, which was introduced by Freud at a time when he had yet to discover the true relation of anxiety to conflict and to symptom formation, has largely disappeared from psychoanalytic parlance to be replaced for the most part by a synonym, phobia, a term that refers to what was considered to be a characteristic aspect of defense, rather than to the presence of anxiety in a pathological compromise formation, as the term anxiety hysteria does.

Now that the role of depressive affect in conflict has also been correctly explicated (Brenner, 1975a), it is apparent that it, too, is a component of every pathogenic conflict and that its presence in a pathological compromise formation of whatever sort has no more diagnostic significance than does the presence of anxiety.

It is not consonant with this understanding to base a psychiatric diagnosis on the presence of depressive affect as a feature, however prominent, of a pathological compromise formation any more than it would be to do the same for anxiety.

The major authority for doing so derived originally from Kraepelin. It was he who focused attention on the diagnostic significance of conscious depressive affect and who accordingly labeled a major diagnostic category manic-depressive psychosis. Later, with the introduction of therapies such as artificially induced convulsive seizures, monoamine oxidase inhibitors, tricyclic antidepressants, and ionic lithium, it has been alleged that each of these forms of treatment is specific for depression, or for depression and elation, thus supporting, in this view, the correctness of Kraepelin's diagnostic classification. To put the matter somewhat differently, it has been asserted that first convulsive therapy and later pharmacotherapy support Kraepelin's assertion that when depressive affect is a conscious part of a pathological compromise formation, it does indeed have diagnostic significance.

On the basis of the psychoanalytic evidence adduced in this chapter, one must raise questions about this assertion. All psychotic patients, like all neurotic ones, suffer from conflicts in which both depressive affect and anxiety play major roles. Moreover, in all mentally ill patients, whether they are psychotic or neurotic, it is the nature and the adequacy of the defensive effort that determine the amount and nature of unpleasurable conscious affect in the final compromise formation. For these reasons, it is impossible to decide about the relative importance of depressive affect and of anxiety as components of any patient's pathogenic conflicts without much psychoanalytic data—and the sicker a patient, the less likely it is that reliable psychoanalytic data will be forthcoming in sufficient measure to permit one to make such a decision. It may be that a diagnosis based on the presence of depressive affect as a feature of a pathological compromise formation is sound. Psychoanalytic data presently available speak against that possibility.

There are those who justify making the diagnosis of depression, depressive illness, and the like on the basis that such a diagnosis refers to patients who are treated successfully by antidepressant drugs or electrically induced convulsions. One can plausibly argue that it is useful to give a special label, i.e., a diagnosis, to a group of mentally ill patients whose symptoms respond favorably to a particular drug, or to electroconvulsive therapy, if that favorable response distinguishes such a group from the rest of the population who are mentally ill. One can justify labeling one group the monoamine oxidase inhibitors responsive group, another, the tricyclic responsive group, and so on. It is easy to justify studying each group separately in an effort to discover, for example, common etiologic factors for one group, not to be found in the others. What is implausible, in the light of available psychoanalytic data, is to base a diagnostic grouping on the presence of depressive affect as a major feature of the symptomatology. Depressive affect is an important determinant of the symptomatology of every patient. In other words, it is an important component of every pathogenic conflict. Its appearance as a feature of a pathological compromise formation is simply a consequence of the nature and the adequacy of the defensive effort, which is also a component of every conflict. It is for these reasons that its use, widespread at present, as a basis for diagnosis, is of dubious validity. As a diagnosis, depression or depressive illness is on a par with anxiety or anxiety illness.

SUMMARY

1. Some pathological compromise formations are characterized by conscious anxiety and/or depressive affect, while others are not.

2. *When either affect is a feature of a pathological compromise formation it is a defensively altered version of the anxiety and/or depressive affect, which are among the components of the conflict of which the pathological compromise formation is a consequence.*

3. Like anxiety, depressive affect can be related to oral, anal, or phallic drive derivatives. It is not exclusively related to oral drive derivatives.

4. Like anxiety, depressive affect can be related to object loss, to loss of love, to castration, and/or to manifestations of superego functioning. It is not exclusively related to object loss.

5. As is the case with anxiety, depressive affect and aggression are related in complex ways in each patient, and vary considerably from patient to patient.

6. As is the case with anxiety, depressive affect is not a result of a particular defense. Specifically, it is not a result of identification.

7. It appears as unlikely that a valid and useful classification of mental illness can be based on the presence (or absence) of depressive affect as a feature of a patient's symptomatology as that a valid and useful classification can be based on the presence (or absence) of anxiety.

CHAPTER 11

DREAMS, SLIPS, AND ERRORS

Freud's interest in these phenomena of mental life was twofold. The one was practical. He discovered early in the development of the psychoanalytic method that dreams and parapraxes, as the German *Fehlleistungen* (literally, faulty actions or performances) is most conveniently translated, can be analyzed. When a patient reported a dream or a parapraxis or, for that matter, exhibited a parapraxis during an analytic session, Freud found he could gain useful information about the patient's unconscious wishes, fears, and memories. Of the two, he prized dreams more highly as sources of information in analysis. Dreams, he wrote (1900), are a *via regia* to the unconscious. This is usually rendered into English as "the royal road," although a more idiomatic translation would be "the king's highway" or, today, a freeway or superhighway. Freud meant that the interpretation of dreams affords the swiftest, most direct access to a patient's unconscious mental life, that it is the easiest and surest route to follow.

These encomia are still subscribed to by many analysts, though it is no longer true, as it was for many years, that the psychoanalytic method is descriptively defined as the form of therapy that relies on dream analysis. Analysis of the transference and analysis of resistance and of defense are more often mentioned in epitomes of psychoanalysis today than is dream analysis. Nevertheless, dream analysis has retained a large measure of its original importance in psychoanalytic technique, and the same is true of the analysis of parapraxes. They are as much parts of psychoanalytic technique at present as they were when Freud was pioneering in the field.

The other reason for Freud's interest in dreams and in parapraxes has to do with psychoanalytic theory. By presenting analyses of dreams and of parapraxes, Freud felt he could best demonstrate two of the fundamentals of psychoanalytic psychology: psychic determinism and the existence and importance of unconscious mental processes. This consideration led him to organize his series of *Introductory Lectures* (Freud, 1916-1917) as he did, dividing it into a section on parapraxes, a section on dreams, and a final section on the theory of the neuroses, in which he included the whole of libido theory as he had developed it at that time. Dreams and parapraxes were important to Freud not only because they are part of the material of analysis and must be dealt with as such. They were also important to him because they illustrate in a convincing way that what he had learned about the nature of unconscious psychic processes and about their importance in the psychic lives of neurotic patients holds good for the dreams and parapraxes of normal persons as well (Freud, 1900, p. 608). Dreams and parapraxes demonstrated that psychoanalytic psychology has at least some applicability to what is normal. Freud used them to show that psychoanalytic psychology is not merely a psychopathology.

I have discussed the practical aspects of dream analysis and of the analysis of parapraxes elsewhere (Brenner, 1976). I need not repeat here what I have already written on the subject. It is equally unnecessary, in the present context, to adduce evidence from these or other sources as support for the concept of psychic determinism or for the concept that unconscious psychic processes are dynamically active and of major importance in the psychic lives of all individuals. Both concepts have been abundantly confirmed and generally accepted long since (Brenner, 1973b). My present purpose is to use psychoanalytic data concerning dreams and parapraxes as an additional means of supporting and illustrating the observation that compromise formation is part of normal mental life. I shall begin with the psychology of parapraxes because, as a rule, their structure is simpler than that of dreams. The following is a typical example.

A male patient, in speaking of his marriage, which had taken place some years before the start of his analysis, recalled the following incident. Shortly before the marriage ceremony, while he was driving through familiar city streets, he came to a traffic light at a major intersection. Though the streets at that hour were empty of cars, he obediently halted his own at the signal and waited for the light to change. Not until it had done so did he realize he had stopped at a green light, not a red one.

He and his fiancée had both been eager to marry. Neither had conscious reservations, nor were there objections to the match from either family. The young couple would have to struggle a bit financially, but neither felt intimidated by the prospect. If anything, they welcomed it as a challenge to be met and overcome. The groom's hesitation, so obvious from the incident just described, arose from sources that were unknown to him before his analysis. He had been introduced to his fiancée by his sister, who had been her college roommate. The two young women, who had met in college, had become best friends, and the patient remarked that they were similar not only in temperament and in interests, but physically as well. He went on to say that his sister welcomed his marriage to her friend. She expressed pleasure at the prospect that it would foster and strengthen the closeness she had always felt with him.

The patient went on to talk of his father, who had died several years before the patient's marriage. The patient, it appeared, had always felt preferred by his father over his brothers and had responded with conscious affection for him. With his father's death the family ceased to exist as a unit. Mother and the younger children went to live with relatives, while the older ones, himself included, lived independently. He recalled that his father had counseled him against marrying too early, i.e., against marrying before he was financially secure, as his father felt that he himself had unwisely done. "Don't be in a hurry," and, "Better a little late than too early," were words of his father that came to the patient's mind.

In addition to these immediate associations, the subsequent course of the patient's analysis revealed that his fiancée unconsciously represented for him not only his sister, but his mother as well. To marry meant to gratify his childhood wish to be rid of his father and to take his father's place with his mother, a wish that was associated with ideas of being punished by being castrated, deserted, and unloved and that was countered, in part, by affection for his father and a desire to please him and stay close to him.

Thus, the patient's behavior at the traffic light was a compromise among many determinants, all of which, in this example, were related to conflicts over libidinal and aggressive wishes whose origins could be traced back to childhood. To drive ahead, to marry, meant to kill or castrate father and to possess mother and sister. To stop meant to be "good," to avoid the guilt and anxiety associated with loss of love, abandonment, or castration and, at the same time, to feel close to father and loved by him. It should be added that while he was associating to his parapraxis, the patient remembered something that had at first escaped his memory. He recalled that when the light had changed to red his first impulse had been to drive forward, i.e., to break the law and run the risk of being involved in an accident in which he would have been at fault and would have suffered punishment—even, perhaps, physical injury. It is clear, therefore, that a wish to be punished, though successfully warded off as far as any practical consequences were concerned, was also one of the determinants of the patient's parapraxis. To sum up, the parapraxis was a compromise formation in which drive derivatives, anxiety, depressive affect, defense, and superego manifestations each played a part.

Another patient, also a man, reported the following experience. At a social gathering the evening before, the patient had been unable to remember the name of an acquaintance, A. He was embarassed by his lapse of memory at the time and felt unhappy about it both then and later, since it was obvious to him he had hurt A.'s feelings. He rather liked A., though he knew him only casually. He particularly reproached himself because A. was obviously just recovering from a recent neurological illness. His face was still somewhat distorted and one arm was nearly useless. "How cruel," said the patient, "to do such a thing to a man who has been through so much!"

At first the patient could not understand what the reason for his parapraxis could possibly be. How could he have wished to do something of which he was so ashamed, something he so much regretted having done? His associations went first to the forgotten name. It reminded him of the name of a rival of younger days, a man with whom he had competed unsuccessfully for a girl to whom they were both attracted. She had preferred his rival, which had made the patient unhappy and jealous for a time, but it was nothing serious. He had not thought of either the girl or of his successful rival for years. He did not see how that memory could have much to do with what had happened the night before.

Then he began to think how frail and crippled A. had looked. It reminded him of the way his father had looked during his last illness. With tears in his eyes, the patient berated himself for his lack of sympathy toward his father during the last years of the latter's life. As the patient, an adolescent, grew taller, stronger, and more manly, his father had become progressively more feeble and childish. At the time, the patient had been secretly scornful of his father's seeming lack of courage and of his babyish demands for care and attention. When, on one occasion, the patient's mother had expressed similar critical thoughts, the patient had joined in and had expressed contempt for his father's weakness in sarcastic, derisive terms. That was, however, the only time the patient had given expression to his thoughts about his father. The latter died, unexpectedly, a few weeks later.

All these memories were recalled with sorrow and remorse. They made the patient feel just as he had felt about forgetting A.'s name. It was only after several more months of analysis that the patient could experience triumphant satisfaction over his father's death, which had left the patient in sole possession of his mother, a satisfaction which gave rise, at the same time, to fears that his father would take revenge by killing and castrating the patient.

Here again the parapraxis is seen to be a compromise formation among parricidal, castrative drive derivatives, fears of retributive castration, defenses that include repression, displacement, and reaction formation, and superego manifestations, particularly shame, remorse, and self-castigation. All contributed to the parapraxis. All were blended together in it.

Although it would be easy to cite further examples, it is unnecessary, since in every instance for which analytic data are available the parapraxis is discovered to be a compromise formation. The examples cited can serve an additional purpose, however. They can help formulate a suitable definition of the term parapraxis, one which fits the psychoanalytic data available about these phenomena.

What, for instance, was the parapraxis in the second of the two examples just given? The answer seems obvious. It was a lapse of memory. The patient forgot A.'s name. But is it so obvious? What actually happened was this: The patient saw A. and wished to go over to him and greet him. As he started to do so, he realized he could not remember A.'s name. Instead of greeting A., therefore, and chatting with him in a friendly way, he turned away from him, feeling very embarassed. In effect, he snubbed him in a way that hurt A.'s feelings. If one focuses merely on the lapse of memory, it is clear that one is in danger of taking something out of context. The psychic event, whose determinants were discovered from the analytic data, included the lapse of memory, to be sure, but it included also the act of insulting A. by snubbing him, and it included feelings of shame and remorse.

Thus, the phenomenon that deserves to be called a parapraxis was not simply a lapse of memory. What interfered with the patient's conscious intent to be friendly with A. was that he forgot A.'s name, turned his back on him, and made himself suffer by castigating himself for cruelty. All of these together, not the memory lapse alone, deserve to be called a parapraxis and turn out, on analysis, to be a compromise formation resulting from a conflict of childhood origin. A principal drive derivative in the conflict was the patient's jealous, competitive wish to castrate and be rid of his father, a wish that had been expressed in adolescence by despising and ridiculing him when he was feeble and close to death. The memory of having done so, stimulated by A.'s appearance and, to a lesser extent, by his name, was repressed and the wish was displaced to A. He insulted A., but silently, not in words. He did not call him bad names; he forgot his name. He felt no satisfaction at having insulted A. He felt instead, despite the defense of displacement and despite his self-imposed silence, a measure of the guilt and remorse he had experienced after his father's death, an event, it will be recalled, that had occurred soon after the patient had aired his contempt for his father. He castigated himself, he confessed his misdeed in his analysis on the following day, and he wept as he talked of the dead father whom he loved and hated, despised and envied.

If one turns to the first example, similar considerations govern the attempt to define that parapraxis. At first glance it seems obvious that the parapraxis was a faulty visual perception, a faulty reaction to a visual perception, or perhaps a mixture of the two. The groom-to-be brought his car to a halt at a green light as though it were a red one.

When one goes into the matter more thoroughly, however, it is evident that this categorization does not do full justice to the facts. The patient was on his way to his wedding, which he eagerly anticipated. He stopped himself at the green light and, a few seconds later, had an impulse to proceed against a red light, an impulse he promptly checked, feeling momentarily apprehensive. A moment later he felt foolish. To be more precise, he felt childish and inexperienced, as though he were not the competent, experienced driver which, in fact, he was.

In this example, the compromise formation was not simply a faulty perception or a faulty reaction to the perception. These were only part of the compromise formation. Additional elements were anxiety, or apprehension, as he started forward against the light and a feeling that he was childish and inexperienced. The sum total of the patient's reaction at the intersection—the entire psychic event—was the compromise formation that resulted from his incestuous and parricidal wishes. The faulty perceptions and reactions were but a part of the whole event, just as, in the other example, the lapse of memory was but a part of the entire compromise formation.

For a definition of the term parapraxis to be satisfactory, it must take into account the sort of data I have just described. With this in mind, I suggest the following: *A parapraxis is a compromise formation, one or more of the features of which is a faulty perception, a lapse of memory, an unintended action, verbal or otherwise, or an unexpected inhibition of action, judgment, or comprehension.*

Whenever the consequence of psychic conflict of childhood origin significantly affects a familiar, conscious aspect of ego functioning, such as perception, memory, action, the use of language, or comprehension, it is appropriate to speak of a parapraxis. This definition makes evident something that will come as no surprise, but is worth mentioning nonetheless, because it has important implications.

Parapraxes occupy a position that is, figuratively speaking, intermediate between neurotic symptoms and normal psychic phenomena. If a compromise formation affects perception, memory, action, the use of language, or comprehension in a gross and lasting way, it is classed as a neurotic symptom, not as a parapraxis. To use Freud's terminology, it would be an instance of serious psychopathology, not an instance of trivial psychopathology—of the psychopathology of everyday life. Familiar examples are cases of hysterical amnesia, hysterical anesthesia, hysterical paralysis, or fugue states. No sharp line can be drawn between parapraxes and various types of neurotic symptoms. As Freud emphasized by his terminology, the difference is one of degree only.

At the other end of the psychological spectrum, parapraxes become indistinguishable from normal psychic phenomena (Brenner, 1973b, p. 152). A slip of the tongue is easy to distinguish from a metaphor that has been consciously and deliberately sought, but there are metaphors that appear in the course of conversation without having been consciously sought. They bob up spontaneously, without conscious volition, sometimes to the speaker's delight, sometimes to his dismay, and sometimes without any particular reaction except that of routine acceptance by the speaker as part of what he or she wished to say. Arlow (1979) has dealt with the unconscious determinants of metaphor at length.

It appears, therefore, that, although the deliberately chosen metaphor and the slip of the tongue are easy to distinguish, there are intermediate cases. How to distinguish between an unwelcome metaphor, which a speaker then retracts with, "Oh, no! That's not what I meant," from a slip of the tongue?

To continue the same line of argument, it would certainly be a parapraxis if one took a wrong turn during a familiar walk and found oneself heading away from one's consciously intended destination. However, one sometimes varies a familiar walk, without consciously planning to do so, by taking a route other than the customary one to reach one's destination. Should that be called a parapraxis? Or, as still another possibility, a favorite route may be changed for no consciously known reason, so that what was once the customary route becomes the unusual way to go. Under what heading should such behavior be subsumed? Is it parapractic or not?

Clearly one can no more make a sharp distinction on dynamic and genetic grounds between a normal psychic event and a parapraxis than between a parapraxis and a neurotic symptom. Whether normal, parapractic, or pathological, such psychic events are compromise formations arising from conflicts originating in childhood. The study of parapraxes, so often possible in a clinical, psychoanalytic setting, offers evidence in support of the view that much of normal, conscious mental life is a compromise formation, a view that will be developed in this chapter and in the two that follow.

The study of dreams can serve the same purpose. As noted earlier, when Freud first studied the psychology of dreams (1900), the component of conflict that impressed him most was drive derivatives. His formulation at that time was that every manifest dream is the (hallucinated) fulfillment of a childhood wish, however disguised, distorted, and, consequently, unrecognizable its wish-fulfilling character. This formulation continued to be accepted unchanged throughout Freud's lifetime and for many years thereafter, despite the fact that there were substantial difficulties in applying it to commonly encountered features of dreams. In 1955 I noted that for dream psychology to be understood in terms of the structural theory, i.e., in terms of id, ego, and superego, every manifest dream should be viewed as the result of an interaction among those agencies (Brenner, 1973b). This idea was developed further some years later (Arlow and Brenner, 1964). At that time the analytic data that support the idea were given in some detail and Arlow and I discussed the advantages that result from understanding dream psychology in terms of id, ego, and superego functioning, rather than within the outmoded framework of the topographic theory, with its systems Ucs., Pcs., and Cs. I shall not go into detail about this, inasmuch as my present subject is not dream psychology as such, but compromise formation. As will appear from the following example, even a partial analysis of dream material suffices to show that a manifest dream is a compromise among conflicting psychic tendencies.

A male patient in his mid-twenties reported the following dream fragment during the second week of his analysis. He was flying through the air in a dirigible made of concrete. In his dream he was impressed by the airship's solidity.

The patient's associations had first to do with what had impressed him during his dream, namely, the craft's solidity. "No fear of something like that getting damaged," he said, and then remembered the old newsreel he had viewed the evening before on television of the dirigible *Hindenburg*, which had exploded and burned years before, thereby demonstrating the impracticability of lighter-than-air ships inflated with hydrogen. As the patient said, the great thing about inflated aircraft is that they do not fall down. They stay up, even if their engines fail.

At this point the patient was silent for a short time. He then told me about a symptom he had not revealed previously. The reason he had given himself and me for starting analysis was his desire to leave his new wife, with whom he had quarreled constantly from the time they got married, in sharp contrast to the amicable way in which they had lived together for a year before marriage. He now told me that for some time before he began analysis he had been impotent on occasion, losing his erection before or during intercourse. His penis, alas, was not lighter than air. Its "engine" sometimes didn't work, it fell toward earth instead of staying up and, indeed, had done so the evening before his dream.

In this, as in every manifest dream, then, even a few associations suffice to demonstrate that it is a compromise formation. The patient's need to reassure himself in order to avoid castration anxiety and castration depressive affect is clearly evident. This was done with the help of a fantasy of being superpotent, of having an erection that was solid as concrete. In the manifest dream, moreover, he exhibited to the world the airship that symbolized his erection. Thus he could feel superior to any rival, especially to me, as it later turned out, instead of feeling insignificant and unloved, as he had felt throughout his childhood in comparison with his father and his older brother.

At the very least, the patient's dream was demonstrably a compromise involving phallic, exhibitionistic drive derivatives, ideas of calamity that included castration and loss of love, and a variety of defensive efforts. During the session in which the dream was reported, it was not possible to identify superego elements in the manifest dream. Only later, as analysis progressed, it became evident that the calamity of loss of love, which included banishment, i.e., object loss as well, was, in the patient's unconscious fantasies, a punishment for the murderous anger he felt for his mother, who had physically abandoned both him and his brother when the patient was only six years old. There is no doubt that the patient's dream was a compromise formation that arose from conflict related to childhood drive derivatives, even though the analysis of the dream itself was far from complete.

As a second illustration, I offer a dream taken from the analysis of a patient, in his mid-thirties, who had been in analysis for several years. He began one session by recounting he had dreamed he was in an office in which there were two middle-aged women. It was apparently the office both of a brewery and of a printing establishment, since he first complained something was wrong with the beer, that it must have been brewed wrong, and one of the women responded by asking him if he wanted to take some beer she had in the refrigerator. Then he was shown a book written by someone whose name he could no longer recall. The book was just a terrible job of printing. It had not even been proofread. It was full of mistakes in spelling, in grammar, and in style. It was not even logical in places.

The patient's associations began with recollections of a party the night before. His wife had invited a few of their friends for dinner. Wine was served before and during dinner. After dinner a bottle of champagne was opened to celebrate the successful outcome of a professional venture the patient had recently concluded after months of effort. The patient drank several glasses of wine over the course of a few hours, which was rather more than usual for him. Several times during the evening he thought to himself that he was becoming an alcoholic. Each time he had the thought, he realized how ridiculous an idea it was since he did not at any time feel tipsy or even exhilarated. It was his late father, as he remarked to me, who had been in the habit of drinking much more hard liquor than he should. He was the alcoholic, not the patient, who never touched hard liquor and who never drank much wine or beer, either.

Further associations connected the terrible printing job in the dream with the patient's recent professional success, which the patient derogated in his characteristic fashion. In fact, one of his principal symptoms was severe inhibition of his ability to compete, to succeed, or to enjoy whatever success he did achieve, despite his conscious desire to be "number one," like his father. Not unexpectedly, the patient's high opinion of his father's accomplishments and his rivalry with him had been transferred to me. The patient knew some of my written work and he both ardently desired to write like me and despaired of his ability ever to do so.

As for the middle-aged women and the office, the patient had no spontaneous associations. When asked, he recalled that, on waking after the dream, he had thought to himself, with surprise, that, though middle-aged, the women were no older than he was. For the patient to think of himself as a mature adult was a matter of some surprise to him. Until shortly before the dream he had habitually thought of himself as an adolescent, despite his actual age. To think of himself otherwise had the same meaning to him as being competitively successful did. It meant to defeat, to destroy, and to replace his father or me.

On the basis of the data just given, it is obviously not possible to arrive at anything like a full understanding of the unconscious determinants of this patient's dream. Much of its latent content, to use Freud's term, must remain unknown. Just as in the case of the previous example, however, this fact enhances its value in the present context. Even partial knowledge of its determinants suffices to demonstrate that it is a compromise formation. More complete knowledge would only serve to make that fact even more apparent. What we know already justifies the following formulation.

The conflictual components that can be convincingly identified include the following drive derivatives: a wish to surpass his father or me, to destroy us, and to replace us. As for the calamities associated with those drive derivatives and, very likely, with other, unidentified drive derivatives, which were also components of the conflict that gave rise to the dream, both anxiety and depressive affect related to castration and to loss of love were indicated by his derogatory account of his professional achievement, an account that emphasized how unsuccessful, how worthless, and how contemptible he really was. At the same time, his feelings of inadequacy served both as an important defense and as a source of libidinal gratification. They were, on the one hand, a way of reassuring himself he had nothing to fear from his rivals, since he was no match for either of us and was not really competing with us. On the other hand, they were a plea for his rivals' pity, sympathy, and love. It is apparent that there were other aspects of the patient's psychic functioning that also served defensive purposes: repression and displacement, to name but two. As for superego components, the manifest dream as a whole, especially the latter portion of it, fits rather well with what Freud, in the later editions of *The Interpretation of Dreams*, called punishment dreams. To dramatize for effect, the patient's conscience said, "What? You've taken your father's place? You're he? Very well, then, be like him! Be an alcoholic!" And, later, "What? You've killed your analyst and taken his place? Very well, then, all you write will be just terrible stuff, instead of as wonderful as you wish it to be!"

In both examples, drive derivatives, calamities and their related affects of anxiety and depressive affect, defense, and superego—all contributed to the compromise formations the patients reported as their dreams. To generalize from the accumulated analytic experience of many years, drive derivatives, calamities, defense, and superego are the components of the conflicts of which every manifest dream, like every parapraxis, is the compromise formation.

It should be noted once again that I have not attempted anything like a full discussion or even a balanced discussion of dream psychology. All I have done, as far as dreams are concerned, is to illustrate that they are compromise formations which are a feature of normal psychic functioning. What normally appears in consciousness during sleep as a dream arises from conflict as a compromise among its various components.

SUMMARY

Examples have been given to illustrate the thesis that dreams and parapraxes are compromise formations. In addition, a definition of parapraxis is offered which makes it possible to clarify the relation of a parapraxis to pathological compromise formations on the one side and to normal ones on the other.

CHAPTER 12

TRANSFERENCE AND COUNTERTRANSFERENCE

Transference is a concept which is, in the mind of every analyst, firmly connected with the analytic situation. Analysts are generally agreed that transference can develop fully only in the setting of an analysis, and many insist that analysis is not really analysis unless a patient develops a full-blown transference neurosis, although, admittedly, there is no generally accepted definition of what a full-blown transference neurosis is. Still, all agree that the development of transference, that transference as a phenomenon in psychic life, stands in a special relation to psychoanalysis as therapy and to the psychoanalytic situation.

The fact is otherwise. Wishes for gratification, anxiety, depressive affect, defense, and superego derivatives, all originating in early childhood, play major roles in every object relation of later childhood and adult life. It is true that a patient's relation to the analyst is profoundly influenced by childhood wishes, i.e., by childhood drive derivatives, and the conflicts they gave rise to. It is true that in an analytic situation the wishes and conflicts of early childhood are transferred to the analyst. It is not true, however, that there is anything unique or special about such a transference. *Every* object relation is a new edition of the first, definitive attachments of childhood. A patient's relation to his or her analyst is no exception.

It is not even true that in the relation of patient to analyst the importance of childhood wishes and conflicts is of greater relative importance than it is in other human relations. As Freud (1915a) remarked, there is no fundamental, psychological difference between transference love and "ordinary" love. The dynamics, i.e., the influence of infantile, conflictual factors, is the same in both. Transference is ubiquitous. It develops in every psychoanalytic situation because it develops in every situation where another person is important in one's life.

As I have pointed out elsewhere (Brenner, 1976), what is unique about transference in psychoanalysis is not its presence, but the way it is dealt with. In other situations of transference, i.e., in the object relations of everyday life, one's counterpart responds in any of the myriad ways with which one is familiar from experience—with friendship, affection, love, admiration, indifference, enmity, disgust, hate, etc. Amplification is unnecessary, since the possibilities are so familiar. In an analytic situation, an analyst responds to a patient's transference in a way that is unique. An analyst analyzes a patient's transference instead of responding to it in any other way. It is analysis of the transference that is unique to analysis, not transference itself.

The analysis of transference, however, is a topic that belongs to a consideration of the problems of psychoanalytic technique (see Brenner, 1976). It lies outside the scope of my present discussion. The points I wish to emphasize here are: (1) Transference is characteristic of every object relation. What happens between patient and analyst is one example of what happens whenever two people have close, continuing contact with one another. (2) Like every other object relation, it derives from the drive derivatives of early childhood, i.e., from the libidinal and aggressive wishes of that time of life, wishes that have to do with mother, father, siblings, and similar figures. Since these wishes give rise to conflicts and to compromise formation, the compromise formations to which they gave rise in childhood determine the object relations of later life.

Freud first called attention to transference as a feature of the psychoanalytic situation in the epilogue to "A Fragment of the Analysis of a Case of Hysteria" (Freud, 1905a, pp. 116-120). He defined it in this way. When a repressed sexual wish or impulse of childhood is aroused during analysis, the patient, instead of remembering what he or she had felt at that time and to whom the feeling was directed, applies it to the analyst as a current wish. Freud recognized that transferences of wishes occur in every analysis and, for that matter, in the nonanalytic treatment of every patient suffering from hysteria. "Psychoanalytic treatment," he wrote, "does not *create* transferences, it merely brings them to light . . . 'transferences' . . . are regularly directed by patients [with hysteria] on to their physicians" (Freud, 1905a, p. 117).

It appears from this and from his later papers on the subject, however, that Freud distinguished between transference and normal object relations (Freud, 1912, 1915a). The normal outlet for sexual wishes, Freud believed, is in sexually gratifying object relations or in sublimations. Only the sexual wishes of childhood which repression has rendered incapable of gratification appear in therapy as transferences. In other words, Freud saw transference as one of the pathological phenomena properly subsumed under the heading, return of the repressed. He did not believe it to be an example of a normal object relation, as I maintain it is.

Another of Freud's views on transference, worth noting because of the great influence it had on later generations of analysts, was that there are mentally ill patients whom the very nature of their psychopathology has rendered incapable of developing a true, analytic transference (Freud, 1914, 1915d). Thus the capacity to develop a transference was made a criterion of analyzability and the basis of a nosology of sorts. Analyzable psychoneuroses, which were thought to be the hysterias and the obsessional neuroses, were grouped together as the transference neuroses, while the others, which included severe depressions and other types of psychosis, were called the narcissistic neuroses. In the latter, as Freud saw it, pathologically repressed libido was self-directed rather than transferred or capable of being transferred onto the person of an analyst. One might say that, according to Freud, transference characterizes only the pathology of the psychoneuroses. For sicker patients it is impossible; for the normal it is unnecessary.

In consequence of Freud's understanding and treatment

of the matter, transference, as I have already noted, is nearly always discussed as though it were only a technical problem, with the result that it was not possible until recently (Brenner, 1976) to reach a correct understanding of it as a phenomenon of all psychic life. However, gradual progress was made before that time toward understanding transference as a complex compromise formation.

Freud first conceived transference to be a manifestation of the id. That is to say, he saw transference as an expression of repressed childhood sexual wishes or drive derivatives. Much later, after Freud had introduced the structural theory of the mind and had revised his theory of anxiety (Freud, 1923, 1926), A. Freud (1936), and Fenichel (1941) called attention to what they called defense transferences, i.e., to the role of defense in transference. They observed that certain manifestations of transference in analysis serve the function of warding off or defending against drive derivatives of childhood origin, rather than expressing libidinal or aggressive wishes. Such transference manifestations, they noted, originate in childhood conflict, like the drive derivatives they oppose. As for the role of the superego in transference, once the concept of superego was introduced by Freud (1923), it rapidly became a commonplace observation, even an obvious one, that patients often attribute to their analysts the guilt or moral condemnation they themselves feel for their own thoughts and actions.

Thus the role of drive derivative, of defense, and of superego functioning in one or another example of transference has gradually become apparent. What was not appreciated until recently, however, is that every one of these components of conflict plays a role in every example of transference (Brenner, 1976). Transference always contains elements of all three. It is invariably a compromise formation that includes among its determinants the components of conflict I have listed and discussed, as the following example will illustrate.

The patient was a woman in her mid-twenties. A striking feature of her behavior during the second year of her analysis was the frequency with which she argued with me. Even when, after her attention had been called to her need to argue, she resolved she would cooperate at least to the extent of listening to whatever I might say without arguing with the first word out of my mouth, her good resolution would evaporate as soon as she came into my office and lay down on the couch. Arguing seemed as natural and as inevitable as breathing. She argued even if I repeated what she herself had said just a moment before.

The patient soon realized that arguing with me in analysis was like arguing with her father during her adolescence. Since it happened daily for many months and under many different circumstances, its various determinants gradually came to be well understood. For one thing, it gratified both aggressive and libidinal drive derivatives. It was intended both to defeat and humiliate me in a special way and to gratify her wish for sexual intercourse with me.

The special way of defeating and humiliating me was this. If she could remain relatively calm and goad me into losing my temper and becoming excited and unreasonable, victory would be hers. This idea was one she remembered from her adolescent arguments with father. If she became uncontrolled and unreasonable, she would feel defeated. If her father lost his temper, if he shouted at her, swore, and was otherwise unreasonable, she would feel triumphant.

That quarreling with me also gratified the sexual wishes she had unconsciously cherished for her father in her adolescence was made clear somewhat later, when she became aware, after yelling at me angrily, rushing out of my office in tears, and locking herself in the lavatory, that she felt like masturbating. Her analogous behavior in adolescence had been to shout angrily at her father, rush out of the room, run into her own room, slam the door shut, and fling herself on her bed in tears. Though she could not recall masturbating while lying on her bed on such occasions, her experience in the lavatory convinced her she must have done so.

Another meaning of the patient's arguing with me had to do with anxiety and depressive affect, both of which, like the drive derivatives expressed in and gratified by arguing, had their origins in her oedipal phase of development. In her childhood she believed that, had she been born a boy, she would have been her father's favorite, as she longed to be. In her relationship with me she consciously wanted to be my most interesting patient, i.e., my favorite. Her anger at me, as at her father, for not showing her the preference she longed for, and her consequent desire to take revenge by besting me in an argument was a defensive reaction that minimized the castration depressive affect caused by her not having a penis. Whenever she felt conscious affection and yearning for me, she simultaneously felt worthless, humiliated, and immeasurably inferior to me. She felt no better than the despicable bevy of adoring female patients who she imagined hung on my every word and were delighted to defer to my every wish, just as her "stupid" mother had behaved with her father. Thus, to argue, to be independent, to be angry and rebellious, meant to be the equal of any man, rather than to feel castrated, worthless, inferior. It will be noted that, in this connection, castration and loss of love were inseparable in the patient's mind. At the same time, her wish to outargue me—unconsciously to castrate me—involved the danger of retributive vengeance on my part. When she felt she had gone too far, she became frightened by her urgent need to argue. At such times she accused me of trying to do to her what she was, in fact, trying to do to me, i.e., arguing involved for her, unconsciously, anxiety over castration and loss of love as well as depressive affect related to both calamities.

I have already noted the defensive function of the patient's anger at me. Being angry minimized or eliminated depressive affect, the content of which was both castration and loss of love. It did so by opposing her wishes to possess my penis, to have a baby from me, and to be my beloved wife. When she argued with me, she could belittle such wishes, ignore them, or put them comfortably in the past. In addition, her troublesome wishes, her fears, and her misery were all displaced and disguised in their transference manifestation of arguing with me, as they had been in adolescence when she argued with her father. She argued with me, as far as she knew at first, not to avoid feeling castrated and humiliated, but because it seemed to her I was trying to ram down her throat something that was untrue. Or she was angry and argued, she believed, because *I* provoked *her* by my insolent, condescending manner, or tone of voice, or both. The defensive function of all these aspects of her arguing with me is obvious.

Finally, arguing had superego aspects as well. All through childhood the patient was guilty about wanting what did not belong to her or what she felt was more than her share. This attitude had pervaded her relationship with father during her oedipal phase as well as thereafter. She was guilty at wanting me all to herself and was remorseful when she felt she had me. To feel that I was provocative, ungiving, contemptuous of her, or otherwise disagreeable represented the punishment and penance she unconsciously felt she deserved and must have if she was to be forgiven by mother and by her other rivals. Thus her bitterest and most cherished reproaches concerned my refusal to advise her how to help the members of her family—mother and siblings—who were the surviving rivals of her childhood.

The illustration just offered has to do with but one feature of my patient's transference reaction during a particular phase of her analysis. I have made no attempt to present all the manifestations of transference in her analysis or even all the transference manifestations that could be identified during a limited period of time. It would be neither novel nor to the point to document the fact that some transference elements could be seen as sexual wishes, others, as defensive, and still others, as related, unconsciously, to guilt, to anxiety, or to depressive affect. The point I wished to illustrate is that *every* transference manifestation is a compromise among *all* the components of psychic conflict.

It is useless and potentially misleading to ask about any transference manifestation whether it is gratifying, defensive, or self-punitive, i.e., whether it derives from id, ego, or superego. One must understand in advance that a transference manifestation is a compromise among all three. The question is never, "Is this a drive derivative, transferred to the analyst?" or, "Is this transference of defense?" The correct question is always, "What defensive functions does this transference manifestation serve, what drive derivatives does it gratify, and in what ways is it a manifestation of superego functioning?" At a particular time one or another component may be more readily identified than others, but all are invariably present.

For example, a young man who had been in analysis for three years, as he left my office on the last day of the old calendar year, for the first time on such an occasion wished me a happy new year and offered to shake my hand—surely a commonplace, minor, transference manifestation, but how to understand it? Was it drive derivative, anxiety, depressive affect, defense, or superego manifestation? How can one tell?

The answer, as I have already indicated, is that even such a minor, conventional bit of behavior is a transference manifestation that is a compromise among all the components just mentioned, as the action itself and his few associations to it demonstrated.

When asked at the next session what his thoughts were about his leave-taking, he said he had none, that he had merely behaved conventionally, as one is supposed to do at that season. He then went on to tell of his annoyance at his wife's nagging him recently.

One can conclude, first of all, that the patient was annoyed with me for having called his attention to the episode. Something unpleasurable, one can reasonably assume, was connected with it, something he wished not to know more about.

Wishing me happiness and shaking my hand were obvious expressions of affection. They were drive derivatives. They might, in addition, have served a defensive function, warding off the possibility of his becoming aware of derivatives of aggression. This possibility is also suggested by the fact that, when I asked him to associate to the episode, his reaction was one of annoyance with me, which he did not express directly, remembering instead a recent example of annoyance with his wife for nagging him. As for the superego component, the one direct association he offered had to do with good manners—with what one is conventionally expected to do at the end of the old year and the beginning of the new. Thus unpleasure, drive derivative, superego functioning, and possibly defense can all be identified even in this minor transference manifestation. The question is not which it is. That is never the question. In one's analytic work with a patient the question can only be which component(s), if any, to interpret to the patient.

In the example just cited, what determined the answer to

this last question was not anything directly connected with the episode just described. It was what had been going on in his analysis for some time before the incident in question that decided the matter. The patient was engaged in an effort to defend against anger at me, anger which derived from oedipal rivalry with his father and which roused intense castration anxiety in the patient. His leave-taking was only one of many occasions for me to interpret to the patient how he defended against anger at me. It was not, however, a defense. It was a compromise formation in which defense played a part, as it does in every compromise formation.

In calling attention to the fact that whatever manifestation of transference a patient may show is always a compromise formation, I am not offering a prescription for analytic technique. Whether one intervenes, what one interprets, and when and how one does so, are determined in part by a particular bit of transference and in part by other factors. Nevertheless, it is indisputable that a full and accurate understanding of a patient's transference is highly desirable in one's analytic work. When one realizes what I have been emphasizing, i.e., the complex nature of every transference manifestation and the multiplicity of its determinants, one has two great advantages. The first is a clearer, more complete, and a better balanced picture of a patient's motivation than one can otherwise achieve. One has avoided the danger of a skewed or one-sided picture. The second is that one is protected against wasting time and energy in deciding a question that should never be asked, i.e., in deciding whether a particular bit of transference is one or another component of conflict when it is, in fact, a compromise among them all.

The improved understanding of transference as a whole afforded by a realization that transference is both a compromise formation and a type of object relation throws new light on some vexing, hitherto unsettled differences of opinion about various aspects of transference that recur or persist perennially whenever the subject is discussed. One of them has to do with transference neurosis, i.e., with the "true transference neurosis" which, it is said, is the hallmark of a good or successful analysis and which, allegedly, must develop if an analysis is to qualify as genuine. Are these assertions correct? Is a transference neurosis present in every successful analysis? Is analysis, in the true sense of the word, possible without a transference neurosis?

The answers to these questions, endlessly debated in the past, is now obvious. The term transference neurosis is a tautology. The concept is an anachronism. Analysts define neurosis as a symptom, or a group of symptoms, which are compromise formations arising out of conflicts over childhood drive derivatives. As I have indicated, transference manifestations are also compromise formations arising from conflicts over childhood drive derivatives. A transference manifestation is dynamically indistinguishable from a neurotic symptom. To call it neurotic, or to call the totality of the transference a neurosis is to add a word without adding meaning. Transference is enough. Nothing is gained by expanding the term to transference neurosis.

What Freud (1916-1917, pp. 444, 454) meant by a neurosis caused by transference may be described, somewhat schematically, as follows. A patient, within a few weeks after beginning analysis, loses the symptoms that brought him or her to seek analysis as the origin and meaning of each symptom in turn is interpreted by the analyst. However, what seems to be a consequence of analytic insight soon proves to be, instead, a consequence of the love the patient bears the analyst, i.e., of the transference (Freud, 1915a). Since the analyst does not satisfy the patient's wishes for sexual satisfaction, the patient, like a disappointed would-be lover, takes revenge by denigrating the analyst, by ceasing to heed the analyst's interpretations, and by reconstituting the neurosis, which had, till then, seemed so skilfully analyzed and so satisfactorily cured. It was the reappearance of a patient's neurosis under these conditions to which Freud referred when he wrote of a neurosis caused or transformed by transference. A. Freud essentially concurred in this definition when she wrote that a true transference neurosis, in her opinion, is one in which the original, primary objects have been replaced by the analyst in the patient's psychic life. The fact that intense transference manifestations have developed does not mean that a true transference neurosis exists, she asserted. The analyst must have wholly taken the place of the primary objects if one is to speak of a true transference neurosis

(A. Freud, 1974). That is to say, according to Freud and A. Freud, a true transference neurosis is defined as one in which the dynamics of conflict have changed from conflict over drive derivatives involving childhood objects—mother, father, siblings, etc.—to conflict over drive derivatives involving the analyst.

The phenomena Freud explained by the concept of transference neurosis are both familiar and important in clinical analytic work. It is the explanation that is anachronistic. Analysts, led by Freud himself, have long since become aware of compliance as a manifestation of transference. No analyst in practice today would mistakenly think that a patient was cured, as Freud did in 1915, when, in fact, the patient's symptomatic improvement was due to compliance with the analyst's wishes as an unconscious sign of love and a wish for love in return. An analyst today would understand such an early symptomatic improvement to be just as much a manifestation of transference as any subsequent exacerbation of symptoms and would interpret it to a patient accordingly. A sequence of the sort Freud himself described is not one of cure followed by the development of a "transference neurosis." It is one manifestation of transference followed by another. Nor is A. Freud's (1974) formulation any more satisfactory in the light of current knowledge. She was concerned with the fact that there are significant differences between the transference manifestations children show in analysis and those characteristic of adults in analysis. She attributed these, quite correctly, I think, to the fact that a child's parents play a role in the child's life which is of far greater immediate importance, psychologically speaking, than is the case for an adult. It is quite another matter, however, to assert that the mental representation of one of the important objects of childhood drive derivatives is ever wholly stripped of psychological importance—ever wholly decathected—and replaced by any later object representation, whether in analysis or not. Such an assertion is wholly at odds with the available evidence.

When and how one interprets any given manifestation of transference to a patient will vary from case to case, depending on one's assessment of the analysis as a whole. There can, however, be no question as to one's understanding of the determinants and the dynamics of the phenomena under consideration. To call them a transference neurosis can serve no useful function and is, at least potentially, misleading.

For the sake of completeness I should add my impression that, when analysts today speak of a true transference neurosis, they are giving a different meaning to the term than the one Freud had in mind and one different from that of A. Freud as well. I believe they mean by it no more than that the patient has intense transference manifestations which can be satisfactorily analyzed. "True transference neurosis," it has often seemed to me, is customarily used as a synonym for "analyzable transference."

Only confusion can result from giving it this meaning, though the reason for doing so is easily understood. If one accepts as proved the dictum that, for analysis to be successful, a true transference neurosis must develop, it is but a step to the converse that, when analysis is successful, a true transference neurosis has, necessarily, developed. Thus the usage I refer to begs, in covert fashion, the question, "How essential to a successful outcome in analysis is the development of a true transference neurosis?" In this case, however, more is involved than merely begging a question. True transference neurosis is a term, whatever meaning one gives it, that no longer should have a place in the vocabulary of psychoanalysis.

Another term that deserves to be discarded is erotic transference. An erotic transference, one hears, is invariably a resistance and is often a formidable or even an insuperable one. The fact is, however, that every transference manifestation expresses, in however distorted or disguised a way, childhood sexual wishes, i.e., childhood drive derivatives. Every transference is erotic. It is true that, when he first used the term, Freud (1912, 1915a) did say that when an analytic patient expresses sexual desires for her analyst, whether these be spoken or unspoken, the analyst must understand two things. The first is that such erotic wishes are not a tribute to his charm. They are a transference. The second is that such wishes are invariably in the service of resistance. A patient who is in love with her analyst, said Freud, has fallen in love in order to avoid analyzing. For Freud to have had so penetrating an understanding at that early date of such a subtle phenomenon is a mark of his genius. To speak of an erotic transference today, however, is to use a confusing misnomer. Transference always includes among its components both libidinal and aggressive drive derivatives. It always includes childhood sexual wishes.

If one observes as a transference manifestation during an analysis that a patient behaves or talks in such a way as to make it clear that he or she is in love with the analyst, one should say so. Being in love with or being consciously sexually stimulated by thoughts of the analyst is a transference manifestation that may or may not be analyzable, but it is no different from every other transference manifestation insofar as it contains "erotic" components. One should not think or speak of an "erotic transference" as though there were some other kind.

Neither should one speak of positive transference or of negative transference. One can speak appropriately of manifestations of negative or positive transference feelings or of negative or positive transference wishes, or both, in an analysis. Transference as a whole, however, is never simply positive or simply negative. It is always ambivalent, as decades of analytic experience attest.

That love is invariably mixed with hate and vice versa is a matter of empirical observation, not a matter of logic or of definition. It is a practical matter with practical consequences for analytic work. Whenever one speaks of positive and negative transference as though they were separate and distinct from one another, one runs the risk of neglecting, perhaps even of overlooking, the transference manifestations of the opposite side of a patient's ambivalence. It is of great practical importance to recognize and to take into consideration the role played by positive wishes and feelings in a patient whose transference manifestations are so predominantly negative as to seem to be exclusively so, just as it is of great importance to recognize the role of negative wishes and feelings when positive ones dominate the scene.

Benign positive transference, a term also introduced by Freud (1912), is another concept which is best discarded. What value it had originally has vanished long since. In the light of the understanding of transference as a compromise formation, benign positive transference is at best a poor name for whatever aspects of transference help, at the moment, to further the work of analysis. As Stein (1981) pointed out, it often happens that the very manifestations of transference which are helpful at one time during an analysis are formidable resistances at another. It may be added that not all helpful transference manifestations are positive. Competitive, negative strivings, perhaps disguised and undetected at the moment, may be as helpful to the work of analysis as positive ones at a particular stage of therapy.

Another obscurity or misconception concerning transference which is corrected when one takes into account that transference is always a compromise formation has to do with the idea that transference entails regression. The phenomena on which this idea is based and which it is supposed to explain are familiar. In every analysis that proceeds satisfactorily the patient's transference, that is, the patient's wishes and attitudes concerning the analyst become more recognizably or identifiably infantile. The explanation usually offered for this is that transference to an analyst, by its very nature, entails or enforces regression. The descriptive terms transference regression, regressive transference, regression in the transference, and the like, all derive from and allude to this explanatory idea.

The fact is, however, that transference manifestations are not increasingly infantile because transference, in and of itself, entails regression. When a patient's analysis proceeds satisfactorily, the patient becomes more and more able to tolerate childhood drive derivatives and, indeed, to enjoy the gratification of many of them. Thus, as analysis progresses, childhood drive derivatives appear with less disguise than formerly in the patient's thought and behavior and, at the same time, the patient's associations to them become more meaningful, i.e., they indicate more clearly what role those drive derivatives played in the psychic life of the patient's childhood, psychic development, and subsequent functioning. It is primarily for this reason that the infantile determinants of a patient's transference manifestations are increasingly identifiable or detectable as analysis progresses. Whatever part regression plays in this aspect of improvement in analysis, it is clearly far from being the whole explanation of it.

It is important to remember, moreover, that the very first transference manifestations in analysis, no less than later ones, are a blend of infantile drive derivatives, the calamities of childhood, both feared and experienced as having already occurred, defenses whose origins date back to early childhood, and early, as well as later, aspects of superego functioning. To say that infantile determinants of transference manifestations are more apparent later in analysis than they are early on is not to say that they become either more frequent or more important as analysis progresses. It says only that they are more readily detected for the reasons already noted. Whether a transference manifestation occurs early or late in analysis, it is always a compromise formation. In every instance it results from a conflict which, with its components, can be traced back to childhood drive derivatives.

As a final example of a misconception about transference, I may mention the idea that there are patients who never develop a transference. To speak thus of any patient is to assert the impossible. As noted earlier, transference is ubiquitous. It develops in every psychoanalytic situation, not because of the unique features of that situation, but because it develops in every situation where another person is important in one's life. Every object relation expresses the drive derivatives of childhood and the conflicts to which they have given rise. A patient may deny, ignore, or otherwise defend against such thoughts and wishes. He or she may react so negatively, so suspiciously, or with such a need to withdraw from the analyst that analysis becomes impossible. But that does not mean that there is no transference. On the contrary, the indifference, the lack of conscious emotion, the absence of conscious personal interest, the suspiciousness, the antagonism, the withdrawal *are* the manifestations of transference. Such a transference may be an insuperable resistance, but it results from the psychic conflicts of infantile origin of the particular patient in whom it appears just as much as does an analyzable transference reaction in another patient. Whatever a patient's reaction to the analyst may be, whether it is readily analyzed or impenetrable to one's best efforts, it is a compromise formation arising from conflicts of childhood origin.

What I have said about transference has important implications for countertransference. Transference develops in analytic patients because every object relation in every individual is a new edition of the first, definitive attachments of childhood. What is true for patients in analysis is equally true for analysts practicing analysis. An analyst's relation with each patient is also determined, genetically and dynamically, by childhood drive derivatives and the conflicts to which they gave rise. Analysts, like patients, are human beings.

It follows that countertransference, like transference, is ubiquitous and that its manifestations are compromise formations among wishes for gratification, anxiety, depressive affect, defense, and superego derivatives, all originating in early childhood, however modified they have become in the course of development. Neither transference nor countertransference manifestations appear because of unique properties of the psychoanalytic situation, as is often erroneously assumed to be the case. What is called transference in psychoanalysis are manifestations of the ubiquitous phenomena of object relations as they appear in a patient's reactions to the analyst. What is called countertransference in psychoanalysis are manifestations of the same ubiquitous phenomena in the analyst's reactions to the patient. Transference and countertransference are indistinguishable dynamically and genetically.

That there are differences between the two is obvious. For example, manifestations of transference in analysis are analyzed rather than dealt with or responded to in other ways. In this respect psychoanalysis is unique both as a form of psychotherapy and as a social situation. Manifestations of countertransference, on the other hand, are not analyzed with the patient's participation or, at any rate, they should not be (Brenner, 1976). For them to be analyzed in that way complicates analysis unnecessarily and, usually, to a patient's disadvantage. The analogue to analysis of transference is not analysis of countertransference. It is an analyst's knowledge of his or her childhood wishes and conflicts, gained from personal analysis, whether therapeutic, didactic, or self-conducted. One may add that an analyst's self-knowledge, though not unique, is certainly a special and necessary characteristic of a psychoanalytic situation (Brenner, 1968).

One might suppose that other important differences between transference and countertransference must follow from the fact that patients usually seek analysts for therapy, while analysts see patients as a matter of vocational choice. It is clear that the conscious motivation of a patient is, as a rule, very different from that of an analyst when the two establish a relation with one another. What analytic data demonstrate, however, is that the similarities are much closer than one would expect from the differences in conscious motivation. When one chooses a vocation, whether analysis or any other, one's choice is necessarily a compromise formation of childhood origin (see Chapter 13). In this important respect childhood drive derivatives and the conflicts arising from them play as determinative and important a role in the choice and pursuit of one's vocation as they do in object choice and in object relations in general. The dynamic and genetic similarities between transference and countertransference far outweigh the apparent psychological differences between them. As I have said above and have noted elsewhere (Brenner, 1976), the practical importance of transference is its analyzability, i.e., its accessibility to analysis. The practical importance of countertransference is whether it interferes with psychoanalysis or whether it assists the process.

It was because of their practical importance in these respects that transference and countertransference were first identified and subjected to analytic scrutiny (Freud, 1905a, 1912). However, their special importance to the topic of technique, i.e., their special practical importance in the conduct of every psychoanalysis, should not mislead one as to their nature and their genesis. From the point of view of psychoanalytic theory, i.e., of psychoanalytic psychology, both transference and countertransference are but subheadings under the rubric of object relations. Both are major topics when one is chiefly interested in psychoanalytic technique. There is less to be said about either when one's principal interest, as is the case here, is not in technique, but in conflict and in compromise formation.

What is of greatest importance here is that transference

and countertransference are compromise formations. In this respect they are no different from any other object relation, a fact that should be kept in mind whenever either transference or countertransference is being considered. A clear appreciation of the fact that transference is an object relation and that, as such, it shares with all other object relations the characteristics of a compromise formation leads to simplification of the psychoanalytic theory of transference on the one hand, and to a substantial improvement of one's ability to understand or analyze its manifestations in the psychoanalytic situation on the other. With suitable modifications, the same can be said for the advantages that accrue from the recognition that countertransference, too, is a compromise formation and, in this respect, an object relation like every other.

SUMMARY

1. Transference in psychoanalysis is but one example of an object relation. Like every object relation, it is a compromise formation.

2. What is unique about transference in psychoanalysis is not its presence. It is the fact that it is analyzed.

3. Examples are offered to illustrate that every transference manifestation is a compromise formation.

4. Transference neurosis is a concept that is both anachronistic and tautologous.

5. Erotic transference is likewise a tautologous concept. Every transference manifestation is, among other things, erotic.

6. Transference is never positive or negative. It is always both. It is always ambivalent.

7. Benign positive transference is a concept that is anachronistic and valueless.

8. The role of regression in the development of transference in psychoanalysis should be reevaluated.

9. To assert that a patient does not or cannot develop a transference is to assert the impossible.

10. Like transference, countertransference in psychoanalysis is a compromise formation. The practical value of transference lies in its being analyzed. The practical value of

CHAPTER 13

FURTHER REMARKS ON NORMAL COMPROMISE FORMATIONS

Some normal compromise formations have been discussed in earlier chapters. The superego is one example. Dreams and parapraxes are two others. Each of these subjects was treated separately for a special reason: in the case of superego formation and functioning, because of the intrinsic importance of the topic; in the case of dreams and parapraxes, because each has a place of exceptional importance in the history of psychoanalysis. Freud studied each of them in great detail. What he discovered about their dynamics and genesis played an important role in the development of his theories of psychic functioning and of psychic development.

In this chapter I shall discuss the relation to psychic conflict of a wide range of normal psychic functioning. My intention in doing so is to demonstrate the scope and the importance in psychic life of compromise formation arising out of conflict. As I have already emphasized, not only psychopathology is characterized by compromise formation. The compromise formations that result from conflict are the chief stuff of all of psychic life, the normal no less than the pathological.

It is because of this fact, which is based on data acquired by the application of the psychoanalytic method, that psychoanalysis truly deserves to be called a depth psychology. Psychoanalytic data have made evident that all of psychic life has a dimension, a depth, one may say figuratively, which was unsuspected prior to the discovery and application of the psychoanalytic method. Childhood drive derivatives are timeless, as analytic data demonstrate. They never lose their force, their driving quality in psychic life. The conflicts to which they give rise and the compromise formations that result from those conflicts persist throughout every person's life with protean changes in myriad forms.

When Freud first gave to psychoanalysis the name, depth psychology, he meant by it simply that psychoanalysis was concerned with exploring only one aspect of psychic life, namely, the part of psychic life that is unconscious in the sense that it is inaccessible to consciousness—the system Ucs., as Freud called it. Precisely because it is inaccessible to consciousness, it is potentially pathogenic, Freud then believed, and it was the psychic depths of the system Ucs. which he claimed as the province of psychoanalysis when he called it a depth psychology. Today, however, the term is applicable in a much broader sense, a sense that is, in fact, the overall message of this book.

My principal goals in writing it have been, first, to substantiate the proposition that a dynamic interaction among the components of psychic conflict underlies much or all of the subjectively conscious and objectively observable phenomena of adult psychic life and behavior and, second, to explicate as fully as I could what that proposition really means, i.e., what its observational referents are and what data substantiate it.

It is easy to illustrate the role of conflict and of compromise formation when one uses examples drawn from clinical practice, i.e., from the psychoanalytic situation. In such cases psychoanalytic data are available to substantiate the determinative role of conflictual components and their interaction in the resulting compromise formation. Even to conclude from illustrative examples, drawn from analytic practice, that *all* dreams and *all* parapraxes, for instance, are compromise formations is to generalize in a plausible, acceptable way. On the basis of all the available data, any other conclusion is distinctly less likely. Enough dreams and enough parapraxes from enough individuals have been studied analytically to justify the generalization that all dreams and all parapraxes are compromise formations.

It is much more difficult to marshal evidence to support the proposition that all instances of a given class of psychic phenomena are compromise formations when they cannot be studied clinically. In such cases, psychoanalytic data are not available, and one must usually apply to the phenomena under scrutiny conclusions that have been drawn from psychoanalytic data about conflict and compromise formation which one has reason to believe are related to the problem in hand.

The various ways in which this can be done, the criteria one uses in deciding that such a relation exists, the uncertainties involved, and the limitations of the method will become apparent in the course of discussion. Sometimes one can show by illustration that each of the components of conflict plays at least some role in the compromise formation. In less favorable cases the most one can do is to illustrate that childhood conflict is involved in a determinative way in the production of a class of psychic phenomena, without being able to identify the specific role of each component.

Additional complication is introduced by the very nature of some of the phenomena to be discussed. When one calls a dream a compromise formation, the meaning is clear. What one is saying is that whenever someone has a dream, the dream is a blending of that person's drive derivatives, depressive affect and anxiety, defense, and superego functioning. To interpret a dream, to discover its meaning—better, its meanings—is to describe the interaction of the conflictual components that gave rise to it. It is a very different matter to interpret a work of fiction, for example, or the meaning of a myth, a legend, a religious belief, or of any other communal or societal phenomenon. Such phenomena have no meaning in and of themselves any more than a dream has a meaning which is independent of the dreamer. When they are discussed, as they will be in what follows, due allowance must be made for this fact.

To repeat, when one can use the psychoanalytic method, one can see most clearly beneath the surface of psychic life. For that reason, I shall begin with examples drawn from psychoanalytic practice. As appeared in the chapter on dreams and parapraxes, one often has an opportunity to study normal psychic phenomena in analyzing a neurotic patient. My first two examples are of normal character traits. They will illustrate what was said earlier about character traits, namely, that those which are normal, no less than those which are pathological, are compromise formations resulting from conflicts of childhood origin which are related to drive derivatives.

NORMAL CHARACTER TRAITS

A woman in her mid-twenties came to analysis because of rather severe neurotic difficulties. Conspicuous in her lifestyle was her generous devotion to charitable causes. Analytic data demonstrated that this character trait was as closely connected with psychic conflict as were the symptoms of which she complained, yet it was clearly not to be classed as pathological. Her charitable generosity gave her conscious pleasure, it was not self-injurious, and it did not bring her into conflict of any serious degree either with her family and close friends or with society in general.

The patient had been separated from her mother repeatedly and for long periods of time, beginning very early in her childhood. As far back as she could remember, moreover, her relation with her mother was frustrating and unhappy for her when they were together, and the circumstances of the many separations suggest strongly that, from the very earliest months of the patient's life, the moody, self-centered, undependable woman who had borne her was a most unsatisfying parent.

The patient's intensely ambivalent ties to her mother and the conflicts they engendered were of principal importance in every aspect of the patient's neurotic symptomatology. In addition, they were the principal determinants of her devotion to charitable causes. From a very early age she was the protector of her younger siblings, babes as forlorn as the patient herself and as exposed to their mother's unpredictable moods and rejecting behavior. Though she was only slightly older than the others, since they were all born within a few years, she championed them, argued their causes, tried to shield them from punishment, and solaced them in distress, as though she were herself their mother, rather than their sister. She acted to them throughout her childhood and adolescence as a good mother should behave to her children. Later, in her adult life, she experienced and lived out the same urge to help the poor, mistreated ones of the world of which she had now become part. She had an urgent need to help those whom she called the little people of society and took great satisfaction in doing so, giving generously of her time, her effort, and her money. Coupled with her generosity to the oppressed was an equally strong contempt and hatred for the oppressors who, by and large, made up what is called the establishment. Those she succored were unconsciously equated with herself and her siblings as children. Those she hated were unconsciously equated with her mother.

What were the components of the conflict of which the character trait in question was the resultant compromise formation?

Among the drive derivatives were longing for mother's love and attention, murderous rage at mother, and murderous jealousy of her siblings. The first of these was gratified by proxy. Her charity, she felt, made happy the poor, downtrodden, neglected, little people who were the objects of her charity. She imagined they must feel that someone was looking after them at last, that someone was taking care of them, and she was happy in their happiness. Her rage at her mother found expression in her anger at the individuals and the social institutions that mistreated little people. As for jealousy and a desire to get rid of her siblings, that, too, achieved expression in her ideas about little people being hated, persecuted, and destroyed.

Both her longing for her mother's love and her rage at her mother, which meant, in part, wanting to be rid of her forever, gave rise to intense anxiety and depressive affect. It was nearly impossible for the patient to be alone for any length of time. To be away from her home and family was the occasion for intense unpleasure. When, for example, she had a baby, she tried to persuade her obstetrician to deliver her in her own apartment. When she failed, she did the next best thing. She curtailed her hospital stay drastically, leaving the hospital thirty-six hours after delivery. In connection with her charitable generosity, it made her both sad and anxious to think of anyone in want or in danger.

As for defense, she obviously identified with mother in the sense that she acted as, in her mind, her mother should have acted. To do so, to be charitable, made her happy instead of anxious and depressed. As an adult, moreover, she was consciously angry, not at her mother, but at the uncaring members of the establishment. In addition, as a generous person, she gave to the little ones, in the sense that she nourished, protected, and befriended them, instead of being aware that she wanted to be rid of them. Finally, in her charitable work she was actively in charge rather than helpless, frightened, and miserable.

A sense of moral rectitude was an important part of the character trait under discussion. She was good, not bad. She shared instead of being greedy and selfish. She would not rest if she knew of some wrong to be righted.

The data just presented demonstrate without question that this young woman's charitable generosity, a normal character trait, was a compromise formation among drive derivatives, anxiety and depressive affect, defense, and superego. It was one among the many results, some normal and some pathological, of her conflict over childhood drive derivatives. I should add, in further support of this statement, that she had little interest in any charitable work other than the kind I have described. Other charities had little appeal for her. When she gave to them, she did so in a perfunctory way which contrasted dramatically with her fervent devotion to the favorite objects of her loving generosity.

To avoid misunderstanding, I must also emphasize that the above is by no means a complete survey of the determinants of my patient's charitable generosity. I have made no attempt at an exhaustive analysis of the conflictual determinants of this normal compromise formation. All I have done is to include enough of the data to substantiate and to illustrate my point, which is that the trait in question is, in fact, a compromise formation that includes the usual components of psychic conflict of childhood origin.

My second example is a thirty-year-old male patient. In addition to the psychological difficulties that brought him to analysis, he was characteristically a cheerful, pleasant, sensible, diligent, and cooperative person. His good spirits and good manners involved no conscious effort. They came naturally to him, as naturally as breathing, it seemed. He was, in fact, the product of a well-bred, highly moral, upper middle-class family and of the best schools, and he behaved as such a person is supposed to.

That the aspect of his personality which I have just described was a normal character trait is beyond question. It was socially acceptable, it often served him well in life, and it caused him neither pain nor distress. He had his moments of discouragement from time to time, as everyone does when failure or danger threaten, but with him these emotions never lasted very long. He would quickly adopt the sensible attitude that what cannot be cured must be endured, that one is better off if one is cheerful than if one complains, and that if one gets on with it and keeps doing what one is supposed to be doing, things are likely to work out satisfactorily in the end.

There were, indeed, times when I wondered whether he was imbued with the homely philosophy of Poor Richard or of Aesop, but, as it turned out, it was not any talent for philosophy that accounted for his attitude and behavior. It became clear during the course of his analysis that the grim realities of his childhood had so reinforced the conventional virtues of his cultural milieu that they had become for him a vitally important and highly necessary part of his personality.

At the age of nine years the patient had been suddenly threatened with the prospect of losing the person who was to him the most important adult member of his family. For three days he was acutely and profoundly depressed. Then, fortunately, the danger of loss passed. But never permanently, as far as he was concerned. The possibility of abandonment remained ever-present in his mind. He reacted to it in two different, logically inconsistent, but easily understandable ways. The first was to assure, by his behavior, that it would never happen. The second was to prepare himself for the time when it would inevitably happen, so that he would not be helpless and overwhelmed when it finally did.

The first set of reactions had basically to do with warding off drive derivatives. Before the threatened loss the patient had been a hot-tempered boy with occasional temper tantrums.

Never again. From that time until the time he entered analysis he could recall but one occasion when he felt really angry. His sexual activities were also curtailed, though by no means as drastically. He became a very good boy, in other words, one who no longer showed the faults of sexual and aggressive behavior which he had been sure had occasioned the threat of desertion he experienced at age nine.

The second set of reactions consisted essentially in identifying with the adult whose loss he feared. He became, like that adult, cheerful, sensible, practical, and optimistic in an unquestioning sort of way. He also became able to take care of himself by means of this identification and, later, he did so in the literal sense when he left home for boarding school in early adolescence.

The character trait I have just described is one in which the most obvious or, perhaps, the most striking role is played by defense. Closer inspection makes clear, however, that it involves more than just defense. It is as much a compromise formation, as much a blend of all the components of conflict, as was any of the other examples in this and previous chapters. That aggressive and libidinal drive derivatives were warded off needs no special demonstration, but they also achieved partial satisfaction. His wishes for love, for approval, and for closeness were abundantly gratified by his being so good, so obedient, so well mannered, so diligent. His angry, vengeful wishes achieved some expression also in his feeling that he could take care of himself. An attitude, "I'll never need *that* person again," is often a blend of defense and revenge; and so it was in the case of my patient. In addition, by identifying with the adult whose loss he feared, the patient became not just sensible and optimistic; he became moralistic as well. His readiness to condemn wrongdoers and his lack of sympathy for them gave partial satisfaction to the angry wishes of his childhood, wishes for revenge on the adult who, he felt, condemned and punished him for his wrongdoing.

As for anxiety and depressive affect, they were conspicuous by their absence. Their pleasurable opposites, optimism and cheerfulness, prevailed in the patient's consciousness. He was for the most part unaware of the fears and misery which were among the legacies of his childhood, a testimony to the success of his defensive efforts. These efforts involved a great variety of defensive reactions, as is usually the case. I have already mentioned identification and, by implication, repression, as well as his habitual emphasis on the opposite of anxiety and depressive affect—a tendency or need to look on the bright side of things, to speak colloquially. When the patient thought of danger, of failure, or of misery, he did so with the consoling feelings that it was not as bad as it seemed, that it could be changed, that it would come out all right in the end.

Finally, the superego element in the patient's compromise formation is also obvious. The character trait I have described was an expression of his morality: "I know you almost left me because I was bad, but now I am good and just like you, as you want me to be, so I am sure you will love me and stay with me."

I should add that, in this example, as in the preceding one, I have made no attempt to present a full or thorough exposition of all the determinants of the patient's character trait. I have tried only to demonstrate that this patient's cheerful, pleasant, sensible, diligent, and cooperative nature was a compromise formation of the usual sort. My next example has to do, not with a character trait, but with choice of vocation.

VOCATION AND AVOCATION

A forty-year-old obstetrician was the oldest of six siblings. Like himself, all his brothers and sisters were born in the farmhouse where the patient spent his childhood. Each delivery was a major event about which he was intensely curious, but which he was never permitted to witness, though witnessing animal births was a commonplace experience from his earliest years.

Thus the patient's choice of vocation gratified his wish, originating in childhood, to watch his mother give birth. It also gratified his childhood wish to be superior to his father, who was always deferential to the physician who attended the patient's mother during her frequent confinements and eager to help him during the delivery. It was also related to the anxiety and depressive affect associated with his childhood wishes. As an obstetrician, he felt competent and, for the most part, self-confident whenever a new baby was born, instead of insignificant and helpless, as he had felt when he was a boy.

His vocational choice involved defense against childhood wishes as well. As an obstetrician he watched and assisted hundreds of women giving birth and took precedence over their husbands during the time of delivery, but none of the women was his mother and none of the men, his father. His curiosity and his attitude of superiority were displaced. In addition, his kindness and helpfulness as an obstetrician defended against his murderous childhood impulses toward both mother and siblings. He felt correspondingly virtuous, rather than guilty, as his childhood wishes made him feel. In brief, his vocational choice was a compromise formation of the usual kind.

The same is true of the vocational choice of another physician, a man in his mid-thirties. He had been separated from his mother for several weeks when he was in his fourth year because she was hospitalized for a major surgical procedure. Among the principal consequences of this experience was the patient's decision to become a physician—in fact, a surgeon, a doctor "who cuts 'em up," as he thereafter told anyone who asked him what he was going to be when he grew up.

Without going into detail, it is clear that here again is an example of a vocational choice that is a compromise formation. Drive derivatives, anxiety and depressive affect, defense, and superego are all involved as determinants. My reason for citing it, however, is not simply to multiply examples. In this case the patient not only became a surgeon in later life, he had a fantasy of becoming one while still a young child.

Although no direct evidence is available, since the patient was not in analysis as a child, one can assume with confidence that his ambition to be a surgeon—"a doctor who cuts 'em up"—was a compromise formation whose components were oedipal wishes, fears, depressive affect, and defense, as was the case with his becoming a surgeon years later as a grown man. The continuity between childhood ambition and adult choice is not only plausible in this case, it was conscious. The patient was three when his mother was operated on and he remembered wanting to be a doctor as early as the age of five.

Clearly there are many differences between a child's wish and an adult's career. Even a child's persistent wish to be a surgeon, or a fireman, an engineer, or an astronaut does not always lead to fruition in adult life. Many factors intervene whose influence is often decisive and wholly out of the control of the person involved. To say that vocational choice is a compromise formation is not to say that psychic conflict is the only determinant of vocation. It is, however, the determinant of what one wishes and tries to do in life. Vocation may be imposed, limited, or favored by external circumstances. However, the choice one makes, insofar as one has a choice, is always determined by the components of conflict resulting from childhood drive derivatives, as can be demonstrated in every instance in which analytic data are available.

The same is true for avocational choice, as illustrated in the following example.

A woman of thirty-one had a considerable avocational interest in music. She enjoyed listening to music, was well educated musically for an amateur, and had studied and enjoyed playing a musical instrument for several years, without ever achieving great proficiency. At the time the patient entered analysis, her interest in music was a pleasurable part of her life, and it was often mentioned incidentally early in analysis. The patient had no knowledge of its conflictual, childhood determinants. Her interest in music was not one of the problems that had brought her to analysis and she paid it correspondingly little attention. She had grown up in a family in which music was important and it seemed to her natural that she should be interested in it. The evidence that her interest in music was a compromise formation emerged unexpectedly in connection with a dream.

She dreamed she was playing in an orchestra. Her associations led to memories of a musician with whom she had been in love a number of years before and who, she had recently heard, had become the conductor of a well-known orchestra. He was, she said, not at all like her father either in age or in physical appearance, yet he reminded her of her father, perhaps because both used the same toilet water as an after-shave lotion. She then recalled that her interest in music had begun in her childhood as conscious imitation of her older sister, a woman who was an accomplished professional musician at the time of the patient's dream. Their father prized his older daughter's musical ability and achievements very highly. When my patient was a child it seemed to her that her sister was their father's favorite because of her musical talent. The patient herself studied music in imitation of her sister, with the hope of rivaling her in his affections.

Thus, throughout her life, my patient's interest in music and in musicians was simultaneously an expression of her libidinal wishes toward her father and of her admiring and envious, competitive wishes toward her sister. It also served the defensive function of avoiding anxiety and depressive affect in a way that was in accord with her moral demands and prohibitions.

Whenever analytic material is available that relates to avocational choice, it bears out the findings of the illustration I have just given. Every avocation, whether it be hobby, game, sport, or whatever else, is a normal compromise formation among the components of psychic conflict of childhood origin.

At this point I wish to enlarge upon something I said earlier. What I have to say is best expressed as the answer to the question, "If avocations, and vocations, are compromise formations that result from conflicts associated with childhood drive derivatives, what of the obvious role played in each by environmental and societal influences?"

Society and environment determine the range and the nature of the vocational and avocational choices available to every individual. In this respect their role is similar to the part played in psychic life and development by constitutional endowment or by physical capacities and incapacities of whatever sort. A blind person is not likely to become a draughtsman nor a deaf one a musician, just as a career in calligraphy is impossible for a member of an illiterate society. Societal and environmental circumstances are factors that set the stage for the drama of each person's life. Every individual exploits the available opportunities for gratification in his or her personal social and cultural milieu and finds in it appropriate ways of expressing childhood anxiety and depressive affect, useful means of defense, and both personal and institutionalized ways of expressing superego functioning. The environment sets the psychological stage by furnishing material that is seized upon and utilized by each of the components of conflict that give rise to compromise formations in psychic life.

I wish to emphasize that this formulation is applicable to all compromise formations. It applies equally to normal compromise formations other than the choice of vocation and avocation. More than that, it applies with equal force to pathological compromise formations. The role in neurosogenesis of the environmental influences of later childhood and of adult life is to be understood in just such terms as is their role in vocational and avocational choice. Environmental factors are important in neurosogenesis through their influence on the components of psychic conflict. However important the influence of environment may be on neurosogenesis in a given case—and it is, at times, of the greatest importance—that influence is always of the sort just described. The environment influences compromise formations because of the opportunities it offers for the satisfaction of drive derivatives and the impediments it places in the way of their satisfaction; because of the fear or misery it brings, or even hints at, and the reassurances it offers against fear and the ways in which it assuages misery; because of the ways in which it reinforces defense as well as the ways in which it undermines it; and because of the opportunities it affords for supporting or for subverting morality in all its many aspects.

In the same way, an individual's overt, sexual behavior is never determined exclusively by the sexual customs or mores of the society in which he or she lives. The same path of gratification may lead to normal compromise formation in one person and to increased anxiety, depressive affect, defense, and self-punishment—pathological compromise formation—in another. In this area of psychic life, as in every other, the thoughts, fantasies, and behavior of adult life are compromise formations that, though influenced by the adult's environment, are determined by antecedent childhood conflicts to a degree which can be appreciated only when psychoanalytic data are available. The sexual troubles and difficulties of adolescents and of adults cannot be eliminated or avoided simply by changing the sexual mores of adult society, as social reformers have so often dreamed of doing.

The choice of sexual partner is an important aspect of adult sexual life in our society. In the chapter on transference I pointed out that every object choice in later childhood and adult life is a compromise formation. No analyst has as yet discovered and described an exception to the rule that every later object is psychologically a substitute for the original objects of early childhood. Every such person, real or imaginary, becomes the focus and target of the manifold, ambivalent wishes of one's childhood and of the conflicts associated with them. What I wish to add here is that what is true in general for object choice in later life is true as well for the special case of choice of a sexual partner or love object.

Every experienced analyst will agree that, in the case of every patient about whose sexual life analytic data are available, the patient's choice of a sexual partner was a compromise formation. For every one, a sexually gratifying relationship in adult life not only provided for satisfaction of libidinal and aggressive drive derivatives of childhood origin, it was also determined by anxiety and depressive affect, by defense, and by superego functioning. There is no difficulty, therefore, in presenting clinical material to illustrate this thesis. The difficulty lies in a different quarter.

As Freud discovered early in his work as an analyst, it is an empirical fact that overt psychosexual pathology is so frequently found among patients whose symptoms lead them to seek analysis that it can reasonably be considered a hallmark of the kind of psychopathology for which analysis is the treatment of choice. Put in other words, virtually every analytic patient has some degree of sexual pathology. It would, therefore, be difficult to present illustrative material with adequate analytic data, i.e., to present material from an analytic case, as an example of a *normal* choice of a sexual or love object.

In addition to this source of difficulty, there is another, which is probably related to the first. Long before Freud devised the psychoanalytic method, long before analytic data were even thought of, it had become common knowledge that sexual object choice, particularly when intense feelings of love are involved, is indistinguishable from psychopathology. To put the matter colloquially, that love is kin to madness. In all, one must be tentative about presenting analytic material to illustrate the normal psychology of choice of a sexual object. Of the example that follows, I can say only that I classify it as normal and that it was, at least, not grossly pathological.

The patient was a woman who entered analysis at the age of thirty-eight. She had felt no need for analysis prior to her husband's death a year before and, as far as one could judge, her marriage of fourteen years' duration had been stable.

When the patient and her older sister were little girls, their closest male playmate had been a boy her sister's age, who lived next door. He and the patient's sister were so fond of one another that it was common talk that when they grew up they would marry. The patient felt excluded by her two playmates and was jealous of them, just as she was of her parents, who also had a close relation which, naturally, excluded the patient in the sense under discussion.

In later childhood the sisters saw little of their former neighbor, since the two families moved apart. Many years later, when the patient was in late adolescence, circumstances reunited the three young people. This time the patient made a conscious effort to get the young man to prefer her to her sister while the latter was away at college. She was successful in accomplishing her aim, but she rebuffed his sexual advances, preferring to be instead what she called good friends. She then fell in love with and married a close friend of the young man whom she had just won away from her sister, a friend who was himself engaged to be married to another young woman at the time the patient met him. Thus the patient, in her adult life, successfully accomplished in her sexual life what she had keenly desired as a young girl: to be the successful, rather than the unsuccessful woman in a family triangle. In the process she took revenge on the man who had, in childhood, preferred her older sister to herself. She threw him over for another man. She lived out, in her sexual life, a compromise formation resulting from her childhood oedipal wishes. Drive derivatives, anxiety and depressive affect, defense, and superego functioning were all components of the conflict that determined the patient's object choice.

DAYDREAMS

Daydreams constitute the final class of normal psychic phenomena I shall discuss on the basis of clinical, psychoanalytic data.

No knowledge of psychoanalysis is necessary to realize that daydreams have to do with unfulfilled wishes. Everyone knows from experience as well as by information from others that one often imagines in a daydream or reverie that what one wishes for is actually in one's grasp. Lovers parted from one another imagine they are blissfully together. Children daydream of being grown up. In fantasy they are handsome, accomplished, and successful at whatever they do. A hungry person daydreams of eating a delicious meal, a thirsty one, of drinking, a tired one, of rest. True, there are exceptions. There are unpleasant, even frightening daydreams. In the great majority of daydreams, however, conscious wishes are consciously gratified.

All I have said so far is common knowledge. What psychoanalytic data have to add is this. Daydreams, at least in adult life, are never simply fantasies that gratify conscious wishes or needs. They are compromise formations that derive from conflicts arising from childhood drive derivatives even when, at the same time, they are determinatively influenced by conscious wishes. The following will serve to illustrate the role of each factor.

A twenty-eight-year-old, male patient was annoyed with me for having to change his daily schedule to suit my convenience. He felt like telling me to go to hell. At the same time, he was ashamed of himself for being angry, since he was appreciative of the help he felt he was getting and was generally well disposed toward me. Under these circumstances he had the following daydream, which he reported at the start of an analytic session.

As he was walking toward my office on his way to the session, he imagined turning the corner and seeing police cars and an ambulance in front of the office entrance. There had been a terrible accident, he imagined. A patient had become violent and had shot me. I was lying on the floor in a pool of blood. When he got to that point, the patient revised his fantasy. I was not shot. An insane patient was threatening me with a gun, but the patient was there. He grappled with my assailant and disarmed him before he could shoot me.

The patient's associations began with a motion picture he had seen the evening before, which was filled with scenes of violence and murder. It had also contained frankly erotic scenes, which had been sexually stimulating to the patient. In one of the scenes a man seduced the widow of someone he himself had murdered. This had horrified the patient and yet, at the same time, he had been fascinated by the idea of someone doing such a thing. Later he mentioned that one of the characters, an older man, had reminded him of his father—not that he really looked like him, it was just that the glasses he wore were like the ones his father used to wear. The patient then went on to speak of how reliable his father had always been, how he could always count on him, and from there to his annoyance with me because of the change in schedule.

In this daydream the patient's conscious feelings for me were expressed in a form clearly influenced by the film which he had seen the night before. He gratified his anger by imagining that someone had killed me or, in the revised version, had threatened to do so. He gratified his friendly feelings by rescuing me. The guilt he consciously felt for wishing to tell me to go to hell as well as the need to ward off his anger found expression in the fantasy that it was not he but another patient who was my murderer, and in the fact that, in fantasy, he exposed himself to danger by grappling with my assailant.

These motives were all conscious. The patient was readily aware of them. However, they were by no means the only determinants of the patient's daydream nor even, in this instance, the ones that were of principal importance. The patient's father had been shot to death in his office by an employee who was mentally ill, at a time when the patient was in early adolescence. He had missed his father very much after the latter's death and had often imagined scenes in which he had been in his father's office, had disarmed his assailant, and had saved his father's life. The patient expressed in his daydream not only his conscious, ambivalent wishes and feelings for me, but also murderous and loving wishes and feelings for his father, which had been transferred to me as his analyst. Moreover, the transferred wishes and feelings had not by any means originated during his adolescence, though they had been powerfully influenced by his father's murder at that time. As his associations suggested, his transferred wishes and feelings were of oedipal origin. An important stimulus for the daydream had been provided by the sexually exciting scenes of the film he had seen the night before, in which a man was portrayed as murdering another man and seducing his widow, something the patient had found to be both horrifying and fascinating and to which he associated thoughts of his own father.

Thus, without presuming to say that the daydream under consideration has been fully or exhaustively analyzed, one can say on the basis of the evidence available that it is a compromise formation in which the components of a conflict of childhood origin are blended. In it are combined oedipal drive derivatives, castration anxiety, symbolized by my being shot and by the patient disarming my assailant, defense, and superego functioning.

For my present purpose a more thorough, more nearly complete analysis of the daydream is unnecessary, since it would do no more than reinforce the statement that this patient's daydream was a compromise formation that resulted from psychic conflict originating in childhood.

The conscious wishes of everyday life vary, superficially, with everyday circumstances, with daily needs, impressions, and interests. The drive derivatives of childhood persist essentially unchanged throughout one's life, even though largely unconsciously. The result is that while one's daydreams constantly vary in accordance with one's conscious wishes, they also, in a very important sense, remain the same, since they reflect the various components of conflicts associated with and originated by childhood drive derivatives. Thus, for example, the patient just referred to had repeated daydreams of saving his father's life during his adolescence. His boyhood reveries were regularly concerned with parricide in the same way as was the transference daydream just discussed.

Another patient, during childhood, had recurrent fantasies of being in the army and operating a machine gun. In his daydreams he killed thousands of his imaginary enemies. He also had a buddy, a beloved comrade, in each daydream. The buddy would always be wounded, nearly fatally, only to be saved by the patient in a heroic, self-sacrificing way.

In this case, the military setting was determined by external circumstances, namely, the second world war. The patient, a boy during the war, consciously wished to be grown up and a manly soldier. The unconscious determinants of his repeated daydream were both more complex and more important.

The patient's playmate in real life, his real buddy, was a sister, four years younger than himself, who was his mother's darling. The patient's jealous rage encompassed the entire family, but it could never be expressed openly. Instead, it found a partial or substitute outlet in fantasies of patriotic slaughter. His jealous wish to take his sister's place as the beloved girl baby of his family was associated with intense castration anxiety, which also found expression in his daydreams, as did defense and superego functioning. Thus, in his daydreams, it was not he who was a girl, but his sister who had become a man. Moreover, he had a large machine gun in his hands as symbolic reassurance that his penis was intact. In addition, he did not kill his sister in fantasy. It was the bad enemy who tried to kill her, while he rescued her and tended her wounds with loving care, always at the risk of his own life.

Thus daydreams are still another class of normal, psychic phenomena which are compromise formations resulting from psychic conflicts of childhood origin. This is important in itself, but it has broader implications for many other aspects of psychic functioning in addition.

Most daydreams are of purely personal significance to the daydreamer. They are disclosed to another person only under special circumstances, one of which is being a patient in psychoanalysis. There are daydreams, however, that are communicated to others and come to play an important role in the psychic lives of those to whom they have been told. Daydreams are the basis of folk tales, of fictional literature, of myths, and of religious beliefs. They can become communal by being adopted by persons other than the person who originated them (Sachs, 1942).

FOLK TALES

I shall begin with folk tales, since they are in many ways the simplest examples of communal daydreams. Perhaps their simplicity is due to the fact that what one most often thinks of as folk tales today are those anonymous narratives whose chief appeal is to children and to childish adults.

The original version of every folk tale, whatever it may have been, was the daydream of the crone or gaffer who first told it. Every new version was the daydream of the teller who introduced changes into the story as first told. For those who listen to a folk tale and make it their own, it is a readymade daydream that serves the same functions in their psychic lives as do daydreams of their own. A folk tale is a compromise formation for the unknown author, for each new teller, and for every member of the large or small audience who makes it his or her own.

Clearly, this generalization cannot be tested directly. Those who formed any folk tale are both unknown and long since dead. One cannot analyze them nor can one hope for much if anything in the way of psychoanalytic data from the children and simple folk in whose psychic lives folk tales play an important role. Substantiation must come from a different source.

Most genuine (and synthetic) folk tales that have had wide appeal and have enjoyed perennial popularity greatly resemble one another in their content. They have similar plot lines and similar casts of characters. In each there is a young hero or heroine, or both, who triumphs over a wicked old villain, either male or female, kills the villain, and marries a beautiful youth or damsel who was formerly in the villain's family, the villain's care, or the villain's power. What constitutes the principal evidence for the generalization offered above is the similarity between this stereotyped plot and the typical wish of children in the oedipal phase of development to marry the parent of the opposite sex and to displace and kill the rival who stands in the way of their doing so. Most folk tales, in a disguised way which is nevertheless easy to understand, portray the satisfaction of oedipal drive derivatives. They are, for children, readymade, wish-fulfilling daydreams that gratify each child's oedipal drive derivatives. It is difficult to account for their persistent popularity on any other basis.

Moreover, as one would expect, folk tales are not merely portrayals of drive gratification. Readymade daydreams, like individual ones, contain elements that can be identified as representing each of the other components of conflict. Anxiety, depressive affect, defense, and superego functioning are so evident as to be unmistakable. Danger and misery are part of every folk tale; father, mother, and siblings are disguised as strangers; and it is understood that the action took place long before the listeners or readers were born—or even that there is no truth to the tale at all, that it is just make-believe. As for superego elements, transparent devices suffice there as well. The motives of the hero and heroine are always good. They are never bad people, never jealous, cruel, or vengeful. Hero and heroine kill only to punish evildoers. The latter are the bad people. It is they who are punished as they deserve.

Take the Cinderella story, for example. It appeals especially to younger sisters, for obvious reasons. In the story, a younger sister outshines her mother and her older sisters and marries a prince who loves only her, despite the efforts of mother and sisters to prevent it. The story explicitly sets out to satisfy the libidinal and aggressive drive derivatives of little girls who are jealous of mother and sisters and who wish father to love them best. At the same time, however, both misery and anxiety figure largely in the plot. Cinderella, as her name indicates, is languishing in misery, clad in rags, and treated like a servant by her rivals until the very end of the story. In addition, there is great anxiety about being punished for her disobedience, thoughtless and unintentional though it is made out to be, as midnight approaches and she continues enjoying the favors and attention of the prince. There is also a good mother, the fairy godmother, whom Cinderella loves and who loves Cinderella in return. So much so, that it is she who helps Cinderella win the prince's love. In short, the contributions of drive derivatives, anxiety and depressive affect, defense, and superego are as evident as such things can be without actual, analytic data.

The same is true for the most popular of the British folk tales about Jack, the one called *Jack and the Beanstalk* or, alternatively, *Jack the Giant Killer.* It tells of a boy who robbed a giant of his possessions and then killed the giant by chopping down a magic beanstalk. The most obvious drive derivatives have to do with envy, castration, and parricide. Fear of retributive destruction by the giant, who is repeatedly about to kill Jack by eating him, is a prominent part of the story, though misery is by no means absent: At the start of the story, Jack and his mother are poor and faced with starvation. As for defense, in addition to the make-believe element alluded to above, the giant in the story is a stranger, not Jack's father. Indeed, in some versions of the story, he had murdered Jack's father and stolen his possessions, so that Jack appears as an avenger of his father's murder, rather than as having committed parricide himself. These defenses are in the service of morality as well. Jack was good, not bad; the giant deserved what was done to him; the giant's possessions rightfully belonged to Jack, so he was not a robber after all.

And so it goes from one folk tale to the next. They are readymade fantasies—compromise formations that offer to children the pleasure of the imaginary gratification of their libidinal and aggressive drive derivatives blended with anxiety, depressive affect, defense, and superego manifestations. For an adult with any knowledge of psychoanalysis, it is not difficult to guess at the nature of at least some of the drive derivatives and other components of the conflicts associated with them in any folk tale. Thus, monotonous and uninteresting as they are to adults simply on their merits as fiction, folk tales, particularly the ones with wide appeal to many generations of children, are useful and interesting for the insight they afford adults into the mind of the child. They offer an unparalleled panorama of the components of childhood conflicts arising from drive derivatives, a panorama of children's wishes, fears, miseries, defense, and morality, of fateful childhood conflicts that persist throughout life.

MYTHS AND LEGENDS

Like folk tales, myths and legends are communal daydreams. The evidence that they are compromise formations is of the same sort as the evidence just advanced for the proposition that folk tales are compromise formations. The myths people share are sufficiently similar to one another and sufficiently similar to personal daydreams which have been subjected to psychoanalytic study to justify the conclusion that they, too, are compromise formations related to conflicts of childhood origin which have been adopted readymade.[1]

It must be kept in mind that there are differences as well as similarities between folk tales and myths or legends. The former are for amusement. The latter have a more serious purpose. They profess to explain the origin of a people or tribe, they attempt to explain the nature and origin of men's occupations and of their environment, or they are attempts at cosmology. In short, they deal with serious, realistic problems that are of grave concern to the members of the community who share them. In a very real sense, as has been observed more than once, myths are precursors of scientific theories. Nevertheless, their relation to psychic conflict is direct and intimate.

To westerners the Homeric version of the Greek myths is among the best known. Current shortly after 1000 B.C., it portrays gods and goddesses as a large family, living in a palace on a mountaintop with a father, Zeus, a mother, Hera, and many children. Incest, jealousy, fighting, and intrigue are as common on Homer's Olympus as they are in the mind of any oedipal child. Murder, however, is impossible. The Homeric gods are immortal and, sinze Zeus is the strongest, he is always the victor or the final arbiter. The Homeric myth precludes parricide. It never ends in tragedy for the father.

In other myths, however, including many Greek ones, the theme of parricide appears directly. The father god meets the same fate as the giant in the folk tale of *Jack and the Beanstalk.* He is killed, castrated, and, often, eaten by his children, frequently with their mother's help. The children usurp his power

[1]For a more complete discussion of the psychology of myths, see Arlow, 1961.

and sexual prerogatives only to be destroyed in turn by their own offspring.

In the legend of Oedipus, which was dramatized in the fifth century B.C. by Sophocles, the hero slew his father, became king in his place, married his mother, and was, eventually, punished by being blinded—a not infrequent symbol of castration—and by being cast out of his city to wander the earth as a beggar.

It was because the Oedipus legend tells directly of parricide and incest that Freud used the name as a label for the oedipal period of development. The Oedipus legend, however, is as much a compromise formation as any other. As it has come down to us, and as Sophocles presented it, Oedipus was ignorant both of the fact that the man he slew was his father and that the widow he married was his mother. The gods knew, according to the legend. They predicted as much at Oedipus's birth, in fact, but Oedipus himself is portrayed as being as horrified as any of his fellow men to learn he had committed the double crime of parricide and incest. According to the story, he had no wish at all to do either. He was innocent of any such intent. It was all a terrible accident for which he was not to blame. In a sense, it was the fault of his father, Laius, according to the legend, since it was Laius who refused to rear Oedipus as his son, who cast him out, and who ordered him to be left to die. Moreover, when Oedipus finally discovered what he had done, even though he had done it in all innocence, he punished himself by blinding himself. All the components of conflict are clearly present in the legend. It is a compromise formation. On its very face, it is a blend of drive derivatives, anxiety, depressive affect, defense, and superego manifestations.

The Greek stories of Olympus and of Oedipus were religious myths. We call them myth and legend because we give no credence to the religion of which they were a part, to the religion of classical antiquity. The religious belief, the articles of faith of one religionist, are the myths and superstitions of those who disbelieve them and who subscribe instead to another set of beliefs and myths. Whether revered and accepted as true now, or whether accepted only in the past and discredited in the present, such myths are nonetheless compromise formations.

The religious tradition that superseded the Greek and consigned it to history is the Judaeo-Christian-Moslem one. Of its many myths and legends, two may be given particular attention, those of Moses and of Jesus. They are useful for my purpose because each has to do unmistakably with the relation between father and son. The Jesus legend portrays Jesus as the son of God in so many words. The Moses legend is less forthright in this respect. In it Moses appears as God's favorite and his deputy in dealings with other mortals—God's junior partner, so to say. In addition, according to pious tradition among the Jews, God customarily addressed Moses as his son.

It is neither possible nor necessary for my purpose to attempt to survey either legend completely here. My discussion will be based on a few of the principal elements of each.

Moses, supposedly born a Jew, was reared as a prince in the Egyptian court. In time he rebelled against the king, defeated him, caused him to die, and became himself a king with a people and country of his own. By contrast, in his attitude toward his other father, God, Moses was loving and obedient. He is depicted as serving God faithfully and as punishing those who would rebel against him by worshipping other Gods, i.e., as punishing those who would kill Moses' God and replace him by another. In short, the legendary Moses was thoroughly identified with God and was submissive to him.

By thus giving Moses two fathers, whoever (collectively) created the legend disguised the theme of parricide. In the legend, Moses is not to be blamed for getting rid of the Egyptian king. It was the king who was bad, it was he who disobeyed God, it was God who decided to get rid of the king and, besides, the king was not Moses' real father. Moses was really a Jew, not an Egyptian prince. In the legend, then, Moses is no parricide. He is a good son to God, a son who is faithful, loving, and obedient. True, Moses is supposed to have disobeyed God in a minor way, for which disobedience God punished Moses by refusing to let him enter his promised homeland, but the main message of the legend is how faithful and obedient Moses was to God.

Like folk tales, like the Oedipus myth, and like other, similar myths, the legend of Moses, thus condensed, is so similar to parricidal, oedipal fantasies with which analysts are familiar from their experience with many patients in analysis that it is plausible to assume the legend springs from conflicts over parricidal, oedipal wishes. One can say with a reasonable degree of confidence that whoever the person was who invented the legend did so as a compromise among his parricidal, competitive drive derivatives, the anxiety and depressive affect they aroused in his mind, and their consequences in defense and superego functioning. The legend was a compromise formation for its author or authors, if what psychoanalysis has learned about psychic functioning is to be trusted. It serves the function of a readymade compromise formation for the pious who believe it, again, if one can confidently trust the findings of psychoanalysis about the way children and adults think. In place of direct psychoanalytic data one must, in this instance, rely on the assumption that those who are not patients in analysis nevertheless resemble, in their psychic functioning, those who are. Assuming that this is so, the only reasonable conclusion one can draw on the basis of the available evidence is that the Moses legend is a compromise formation in the same sense that folk tales are.

The same is true of the legend of Jesus. As in the Moses story, the principal and explicit emphasis is on the love of son for father. Jesus and his father, God, are represented as so closely identified that they are actually one and the same. The hero never rebels. On the contrary, he is so obedient to his father's will that he permits his father to have him killed, after which Jesus and God, son and father, are lovingly united forever. The theme of parricide appears only incidentally in the story, but it is there, nevertheless. It is not the hero who is a parricide either in wish or deed. It is bad men, Jews and Romans, who crucify the young Jesus, who is also, in the legend, the father-God. It is they who commit parricide, not the hero. He is their victim instead of their leader.

The theme of incest is even less prominent in the legend. It appears incidentally, as a mere hint. According to the legend, Jesus came to earth and let himself be killed in order to redeem man from original sin, which God would otherwise punish implacably. One must think for oneself that man's original sin was the sin of Adam and Eve in the garden of Eden, namely, the sin of sexual intercourse against God's express command. That is why Jesus died, although the legend does not say so in so many words.

One way to defend against parricidal wishes is by displacing them and, in fantasy, killing someone else who is only a stepfather and who deserves to die anyway, as in the Moses legend. Another way is to submit to mutilation, which symbolizes castration, by one's father in order to win his love and forgiveness, as in the Jesus legend, which ends, be it remembered, with Jesus on God's throne, ruling heaven and earth. It is reasonable to conclude that, despite their many differences, the two legends have in common that they were conceived as compromise formations and are readymade compromise formations in the mental lives of those who believe them, provided one accepts the assumptions outlined earlier.

RELIGION

A consideration of myths and legends leads directly to the psychology of religion, as the examples above indicate. No aspect of societal life is more interesting psychologically than this one. Since the dawn of history it has occupied a central position in the great drama called civilization during the past fifteen thousand years. It is only in the last two centuries that there has been even a threat to its preeminently important role.

A cosmogony, a moral and ethical code, and a catalogue or system of rewards for obeying the code and of punishments for transgressing it—these are the constituents to be found in every known religion (Freud, 1933). Every religion tells its believers how they and the earth on which they live came to be, as well as how to behave so as to prosper and be happy. Not every religion has an anthropomorphic god, as do the Judaeo-Christian-Moslem ones. Some have many gods in human form, some have animal or other gods, some have no gods whatever. Some promise life after death, while some do not. Some are warlike, while others preach peace and brotherhood. Whatever their differences from one another may be in these and in other respects, all religions teach, prescribe, and protect or threaten in the ways Freud described. Religions treat adults as parents treat children (Freud, 1933).

If Freud's assessment is correct, as I believe it is, religion is the outgrowth into adult life of a child's relation to his parents. Since, from a child's side, this relation is so largely composed of drive derivatives and of the conflicts to which those drive derivatives give rise, it can come as no surprise that religious beliefs and practices are compromise formations. In Chapter 8 I discussed in some detail the psychological significance of communion in Christian religions and of circumcision among the Jews. What can be added here is that every code of morality, together with its system of rewards and punishments, derives from and serves the functions of each believer's superego. Institutionalized morality derives from individual morality. Since superego formation and functioning represent a compromise formation in every instance, this part of religion must of necessity be a compromise formation also. That religious myths and legends, including those dealing with cosmogony, are also compromise formations, seems likely also.

Though it is impossible to make a really reliable estimate, it is probably correct to say that religious beliefs play an important role in the conscious mental lives of most people on the earth today. At the same time, it is clear that a growing percentage of the world's population do not subscribe to any religious belief and that religion as a social institution is on the decline.

The most important factor in this decline is almost surely the psychological impact of the scientific and technological developments of the past three centuries. Galileo is chiefly responsible for having initiated the events that are leading to just the consequences the Roman Curia hoped to prevent by forcing him to recant and then holding him prisoner for the rest of his life. It took many decades, however, and the discoveries of many scientists who followed Galileo before the progress of science, great as it was, affected the religious beliefs of mankind to a noticeable degree. As recently as the time of the first world war, every government espoused some religious belief. Not a single one was officially atheistic. By now the situation is substantially different. The governments of two countries, China and the Soviet Union, whose combined populations include one third of the population of the globe, condemn all religions. So do the governments of many smaller countries. What has happened to the religious belief of these one and a half billion people?

No doubt millions still cling to conscious belief in one religion or another, but hundreds of millions of them are consciously in agreement with their political and intellectual leaders, with their rulers and their teachers, that all religions are factually incorrect. They are convinced that the gods their parents or grandparents worshipped are nonexistent, that assurances of a life after death are illusory, whether those assurances are promises of heaven or threats of hell, and that religious cosmologies are nothing but the charming myths of primitive, ignorant, unscientific people, however poetically gifted they may have been.

Since religion comes from sources in psychic life which are as deep as psychoanalysis has shown them to be, since religious beliefs have been such useful compromise formations for countless generations of mankind, it seems impossible that religion could simply disappear without substitute. There is, by now, more than enough evidence to show that Marxist socialism neither alters childhood drive derivatives nor eliminates the conflicts associated with them. The psychic forces that have motivated people to participate in organized religion for countless centuries are as strong among inhabitants of socialist countries as they are in those of the rest of the world. What, then, are their manifestations in an atheistic, irreligious society?

To answer this question reliably, one would have to have psychoanalytic data on which to base one's answer. One would have to assess the accumulated relevant findings of the analyses of many consciously atheistic persons, preferably of the second or third generation, who live in officially atheistic countries. Unfortunately, there are no such findings. The officially atheistic countries of the world today, like many others that officially subscribe to one or another religious belief, are police states in which all mental health workers are dependent on the state for a livelihood. Under such conditions it is virtually impossible either to learn to do psychoanalysis or to practice it if one has been trained elsewhere.

One might hope to substitute data obtained from the analyses of atheistic patients living in societies that are not officially atheistic, but in which large segments of the populace are, in fact, atheists. The answer suggested by such data from this source as are available is that religious beliefs tend to persist, though disavowed. Often enough the same thing, or something similar, is true for religious practices as well as for religious beliefs. For example, atheistic patients in modern society react to religious holidays as do those who professedly believe in their significance. They dream of babies at Christmastime and of infanticide or parricide at the time of Passover and Easter. They call on God to bless themselves and to curse others. They enjoy sacred music—a Bach cantata or a mass by Mozart, for instance—while professing disinterest in the words for which the music was written. Not infrequently they attend religious services which, at the same time, they sincerely maintain have no meaning for them whatsoever. In short, they seem to have adopted at least some of the religious beliefs and practices of the society in which they were born and raised, while consciously disavowing both belief and practice. In attempting to assess the significance of such data it must be kept in mind that they come in large part, if not entirely, from the analyses of persons who were exposed to some kind of religious influence during childhood or even to formal religious instruction.

The rather unsatisfactory data available to bear on the question point in the direction that religious beliefs and practices persist in the minds of atheists, though disavowed, repressed, or defended against in other ways. For how many generations they would continue to persist in an avowedly atheistic society, there is no way of knowing. Perhaps the following, admittedly speculative answer to the question posed originally has some merit.

It may be that politics and political beliefs occupy the same psychological position and serve the same psychological functions in the officially atheistic countries of the world today as religion and religious beliefs do elsewhere. In atheistic countries there are political processions and festivals for people to participate in instead of religious ones. Instead of religious icons, there are political banners and pictures. Instead of divine or semi-divine personages of the past, there are Marx, Engels, and Lenin. Instead of priests, there are political leaders who command obedience, love, and reverential awe. In addition, there is a strong moral trend in socialist or communist teachings as they exist today. Belief and conformity are not merely rewarded in a material sense; they are valued as good. Believers in socialism who support the regime are considered to be good in the moral sense. Unbelievers and those who are antagonistic to the regime are valued as bad by the community at large. In addition, socialism promises reward for good behavior and punishment for bad, just as religions do. It promises that the advent of true socialism will bring with it a kind of heaven on earth, the equivalent of the stereotyped folk tale ending, ". . . and they lived happily ever after."

What has just been said about the psychology of politics in countries with atheistic regimes in the world today is not intended to discredit in any way either the economic and political theories of socialism or its ideal goal of economic plenty for all. Indeed, if it is true that imitation is the sincerest form of flattery, all of the major capitalist countries of the world have only the highest praise for the socialist ideal of social justice. Without exception they offer to their citizens the same promise of material prosperity and security for all. My speculation goes only to the point that, in nonreligious societies, the psychic trends otherwise expressed in religious practices and beliefs have made a kind of religion of politics and politicians. One should add that this development was neither intended nor foreseen. The reformers who were the architects and leaders of the revolutions that created the nonreligious societies of today had no conscious desire to have those societies become themselves a kind of religion. Quite the contrary. Such an idea would have been abhorrent to them. Nevertheless, this may be what has happened.

If so, it is not really a novelty in societal organization. In many societies men and women have deified their rulers from the most ancient times. In Egypt and in the valley of the Tigris and the Euphrates rivers, where the first empires we know of arose, king, high priest, and god were one and the same. Even after the birth of rationalism in the golden age of Greece, Aristotle's pupil, Alexander, was deified, as were countless other Greek and Roman rulers who succeeded him. It seems strange to us to think of a living person who claims to be a god and even stranger when such a person is considered to be one by others, yet until very recently most of the world was ruled, at least in name, by men and women who claimed to have been selected for the position of king or queen by God himself. In their own opinion and in the opinion and belief of their subjects they ruled by divine right—*Dei gratia*. Even today the conservative faithful consider the Pope (in Italian, *il Papa* = father), whose official title is bishop of Rome, to be the direct representative of God on earth. This position, psychologically speaking, surely is close to that of a living deity—not the equal of one of the great gods, to be sure, but like them, though on a smaller scale.

The fact is that analytic data strongly support the conclusion that anyone who is looked up to as older and as being in a position of superior wisdom can and often does unconsciously represent a parent. This generalization does not apply only to authoritarian regimes, whether they be religious or atheistic ones Any ruling establishment is not just imposed from above. It is supported from below as well, and the attitude of the humble toward their rulers in any society is inevitably a reflection of childhood drive derivatives and of the conflicts attendant on them. The president of a republic is unconsciously viewed as a father no less than is God, or a dictator, or a divinely anointed king, or an imperial demigod. The accepted sobriquet of the first president of the U.S.A., George Washington, is *The Father of His Country*. It is given him as the first president. It was never given to Franklin, to Jefferson, to Madison, or to Hamilton, all of whom arguably played indispensable roles in the unification of the thirteen colonies, something Washington also did. It is Washington, the successful warrior and first president of the new nation, who is by consensus revered as the country's father.

What differences there are in the attitude of the general public to a god, a demigod, a divinely appointed king, a dictator, and a president who was elected by the people themselves seem to be differences of degree. The differences seem to lie in the forcefulness with which a particular society or social organization insists that *in reality* one person, or a relatively few people, do indeed possess the attributes with which young children endow their parents: that they are so wise as to be omniscient, so strong as to be omnipotent, and so good as to be without sin or flaw. That to love and obey them is to be good, i.e., to be deserving of love and reward in return, while to fail to love and obey is to be bad and to deserve whatever punishment they impose.

The more closely any religious organization or political system approaches such criteria, the more obviously it is an adult reproduction of the psychic life of childhood and the more obviously does it serve the function of a compromise formation for each of its members. With respect to both politics and religion, the urge to duplicate the world of childhood is unmistakable. It is observable in societies today no less than in those of fifty centuries ago.

It must be apparent that this discussion of religion and, to a lesser extent, of sociopolitical organization has merely touched on one aspect of two immensely complex subjects. I have done no more than to adduce evidence in favor of the view that the psychology of each is that of compromise formation arising from childhood drive derivatives. Even in this task I have limited myself. I have said little of the role of sensual or libidinal drive derivatives as compared with the role of aggressive ones, for example, although the importance of each is, if not equal, at least fully comparable. For example, female members of many Christian religious orders marry God (Jesus) on entering the order.

I say this to ensure that it will not be wrongly assumed that I believe that what I have said represents anything approaching a thorough exposition of even the psychology of the aspects of human psychic life which I have been discussing, to say nothing of a thorough exposition of the whole of them. Whatever generalizations one may suggest at present about the psychology of religion or of sociopolitical organizations on the basis of a knowledge of psychoanalytic psychology cannot be more than provisional. However, when one considers how little is known in either field and how much remains to be learned, one may be persuaded, as I am, that even formulations that cannot yet be adequately substantiated or satisfactorily tested nonetheless deserve serious consideration, provided their provisional nature is kept in mind.

As a final generalization of this sort, the following is of interest.

The two hundred years since the French and American revolutions have often been called the age of revolution. Never before has revolution been so widespread. Never before have so many revolutions been so successful in their immediate aim of overthrowing existing governments and establishing new ones, each based on the, by now, universally accepted principles of liberty, equality, fraternity, popular sovereignty, and the rights of man.

In the course of recording these many political upheavals, it has not escaped the attention of at least some historians that a foe of tyranny, once successful in deposing the ruling tyrant, often becomes equally tyrannical. The explanation most often cited to account for this sequence of events is the epigram attributed to the British historian, Acton, to the effect that power corrupts, while absolute power corrupts absolutely.

Psychoanalytic data suggest that being a revolutionary, like being a tyrant, a priest, a demigod, or anything else, for that matter, has important determinants that derive from conflicts arising from childhood drive derivatives. They suggest that to be a revolutionary is to choose that particular compromise formation as a vocation. If this is indeed the case, as I believe it is, it is easy to surmise some of the psychological determinants likely to be responsible for the evolution of liberators into tyrants.

As noted earlier, the relation between adult subject and ruler, tyrant or not, reflects and, in important respects, repeats the relation between child and parent. It is a compromise formation that arises from conflicts over childhood drive derivatives among which are included wishes to supplant the parent and to assume his or her place in the family constellation. The data available from the psychoanalysis of patients suggest that admiration, envy, and a desire to imitate are among the determinants of the vocational choice and behavior of political revolutionaries. Whether they are aware of it or not, they wish to supplant and to imitate whomever they revolt against. It is to be expected that such a ruler would follow in the same mold. If the deposed ruler was a tyrant, one would expect the deposer to become one as well. When one has the power, one can do as one wishes. If what one wishes is to become a tyrant, the power one has achieved enables one to become a tyrant.

Psychoanalytic data suggest that power does not "corrupt." There have been, after all, beneficent despots as well as evil-doing ones. Psychoanalytic data suggest that power, i.e., the power to coerce other persons to one's will, permits, even encourages the gratification of childhood wishes to do so, wishes that, in adult life, would otherwise find other means of gratification. As already noted, environmental circumstances simply set the stage for the drama of each person's life. Every individual, whether ruler or subject, master or slave, exploits whatever opportunities are at hand for gratification.

SUPERSTITIONS

Another aspect of normal psychic functioning comprises what are called superstitious beliefs and practices. As noted earlier, they overlap religious beliefs and practices in the sense that what believers see as revealed truth, a nonbeliever sees as mere superstition. The sacred character of any religious belief or practice that involves magical, supernatural ideas is inseparable from faith in the religion of which it is a part.

A common superstition among urban children is that it is bad luck to step on a crack in the sidewalk. Youngsters aged five to ten will at times take great pains to avoid doing so, once they have been told this, usually by another child. I know of no psychoanalytic data derived from analyses of children who subscribe to this superstition that illuminate the question of the psychic determinants of the superstition. The determinants may well be different in different children or even, from time to time, different in the same child, since the superstition is one that usually waxes and wanes before it is finally given up altogether. The evidence that points to a common meaning is analogous to psychoanalytic evidence, as children's play often is—not to the children themselves, to be sure, but to adults who observe them in the light of psychoanalytic knowledge. There is a ditty that accompanies the superstitious behavior. Children sing it either to themselves or aloud as they walk along a sidewalk, taking care to avoid stepping on a crack:

> Step on a crack and break your mother's
> [or father's] back.
> Step on a line and break your father's
> [or mother's] spine.

Moreover, the same children sometimes run along a sidewalk in great glee, repeating the same ditty and stepping, or jumping forcefully, on every crack or line they come to.

It seems reasonable to conclude that, for many children, the superstition in question is a compromise formation that derives from conflict arising from parenticidal wishes, i.e., from well-known, universally troublesome drive derivatives of childhood origin. It may be that libidinal and castrative wishes are also involved for many children, but these drive derivatives are not alluded to unmistakably by either speech or behavior. Moreover, one cannot tell from the available evidence what calamities each child associates with the murderous and, possibly, incestuous and castrative wishes. As for defense, the practice of avoiding stepping on the cracks has the explicit meaning that the child is avoiding breaking the parent's back or spine. In addition, it is all make-believe. The children all know they cannot really break either parent's back by stepping on a sidewalk crack. They can only pretend they are doing so, as when they step or jump on every crack. Finally, for manifestations of superego functioning, "bad luck" means that one will be punished in one way or another.

As far as the available evidence goes, it is reasonable to conclude that all the usual components of psychic conflict contribute, at least in many cases, to the superstition about stepping on cracks in a sidewalk. The superstition is a compromise formation, one which I would classify as normal. To those who argue that it is not normal, that it is, on its face, pathological, I can say only, "It is certainly no more so than a slip or an error. It is everyday psychopathology at most."

It should be kept in mind that what has been said so far is by no means the whole story with respect to the superstition in question. A superstition of this sort is intended by the one who practices it to have a magical effect. It is intended to ensure good luck or, at least, to avoid bad luck. It is as though the practitioner is saying to omnipotent fate, "I do not wish to be bad. I wish to be good. Therefore be good to me."

This is an attitude, as we have seen earlier, which is part of religious belief in general. It is an attitude or belief about the world that is also a compromise formation: fate or God will be good to me if I do what they want me to. The probable derivation of this belief from psychic conflicts originating in childhood should be apparent from what has been said on the matter already.

Another superstition, which also proposes to avoid bad luck, concerns the number thirteen. The belief that thirteen is an unlucky number is so widespread that many buildings have no floor marked "13," lest people refuse to go there, theatre seats are numbered so as to avoid "13," etc. As in the case of the previous example, there are no psychoanalytic data adequate to the task of reaching an understanding of the dynamics and genesis of the superstition that the number thirteen brings bad luck. The only available evidence is as follows.

This is a Christian superstition. In its original form, it was a belief that it is bad luck for thirteen people to sit at table. The reason given is that there were thirteen at the last supper: Jesus and his twelve disciples. Another, closely related Christian superstition has it that Friday is a day of ill omen, an unlucky day, since it was on a Friday that Jesus was crucified. A combination of the two superstitions has it that Friday the 13th is particularly unlucky.

To return to the number thirteen itself. According to superstitious belief, if thirteen people sit at table, as Jesus and his disciples did, it will bring bad luck. One of the thirteen will die before the next meal, as happened to Jesus in the legend, or something else bad will happen.

At first glance the reason for the connection between the last supper and death is puzzling. Why should such importance be attached to a meal, rather than to some other incident that preceded the crucifixion? The connection becomes more understandable if one recalls that the last supper was not merely a meal shared by thirteen persons. It was the first communion. The legend states that on that occasion twelve persons, the disciples, ate their god in the form of their master, Jesus. Here is the description (Matthew, 26): "Jesus took bread and blessed it and brake it and gave it to the disciples and said, 'Take, eat; this is my body.' And he took the cup and gave thanks, and he gave it to them, saying, 'Drink ye of it, for this is my blood. . . .' "

It would appear, therefore, that for a Christian to seat thirteen at table expresses the gratification of a childhood drive derivative, namely to kill and eat one's parent. It is understandable, in light of this, that many Christians believe they will be punished if they seat thirteen at table—in one version of the superstition, by dying themselves. On the basis of the evidence available, one may reasonably assume that the idea that bad luck will come if thirteen, no more and no less, sit at table is, for those who believe the superstition, a compromise formation from conflict associated with a murderous, cannibalistic wish of childhood origin. Anxiety, defense, and fear of punishment all play easily identifiable roles in this superstitious belief, just as they do in the minds of children who believe that it is bad luck to step on cracks in a sidewalk.

As I observed earlier with respect to folk tales and legends, for those who hear or believe them superstitions can best be described as readymade daydreams. Since the origins of all of these phenomena are never identifiable, one cannot be sure whether their originators conceived them while awake or asleep—whether they began, so to speak, as nocturnal dreams or as daydreams. As communal phenomena, however, they function as daydreams do.

FICTION

Works of fiction constitute another group of psychic phenomena that function as readymade daydreams for those who read them, who listen to them, or who view them (Sachs, 1942). In their function, which is primarily to entertain, they most clearly resemble folk tales. They differ in that their authors are known. They are not, like folk tales, of anonymous origin.

Works of fiction, which include stories, novels, poems, plays, and films, have been discussed by analysts from several points of view. My own purpose is a limited one. I wish to present evidence to support the view that in the minds both of those who create them and of those who enjoy them, works of fiction are compromise formations.

It must be granted in advance that the evidence in favor of this view is largely indirect. There are relatively few psychoanalytic data available. However, what evidence there is weighs heavily in favor of the view advanced.

Libidinal and aggressive drive derivatives, i.e., lust and violence, abound in popular works of fiction. One cannot say that their presence assures the popularity of any such work, but it seems that none can hope to be popular without them. Interwoven with them are the calamities of mutilation, death, loss of love, desertion, and loneliness. Anxiety and depressive affect, in other words, are as important and regular elements of works of fiction as are lust and violence. At the same time, the explicitly fictional nature of these works guarantees against too great a degree of unpleasure, as do many other defenses, which vary from one work of fiction to another. Finally, superego manifestations are never lacking: reward, punishment, remorse, and often a moral message, which is sometimes explicit and sometimes implicit.

It is true that none of these are data acquired by the psychoanalytic method, yet taken all together, they render it highly probable that works of fiction are also compromise formations which are consequences of conflicts over childhood drive derivatives (see Brenner, 1973b, pp. 255-257).

Neurotic symptoms and character traits, dreams, daydreams, the slips and errors of daily life, object relations in and out of analysis, normal character traits, vocational and avocational activities, religion, superstition, folk tales, myths, legends, works of fiction—taken together these occupy a large portion of one's psychic life. But what about the very prosaic, apparently trivial parts, like what clothes one decides to wear on a particular day, or what one has for breakfast tomorrow, or whether to go for a walk or to stay home and do something about the house or apartment? Are all these compromise formations? The answer, I think, is that they are. Whenever such a trivial matter can be analyzed, one is surprised to discover how many conflictual components determine it. I do not think that compromise formation is a mark of either neurosis or of immaturity. A pathological compromise formation has characteristics that distinguish it from a healthy or normal one. The differences are of great practical importance. The same is true for immaturity. Children and adolescents are not adults. Some adults are less mature than others. Again, the differences are of great practical importance. What is the same for all, however, is the role played by compromise formation in psychic life.

CONCLUSION

To repeat what I wrote earlier, psychoanalytic data have paved the way for an understanding of psychic life that is both unique and of far-reaching importance. It has shown that childhood drive derivatives never disappear, that they never lose their impelling quality, that the conflicts they give rise to likewise persist, and that the compromise formations which are the consequences of those conflicts make up the ever-changing manifestations of psychic activity of which we are conscious in ourselves and which we observe in those about us. The fabric of psychic life as we know it is woven of drive derivatives, of anxiety and depressive affect, of defense, and of superego manifestations.

This includes not only the entire gamut of neurotic symptoms and characterological disorders, but also an extremely wide range of normal mental phenomena. Psychic conflict is importantly involved in dreams, in the psychopathology of everyday life, in jokes, in fantasies, plans, thoughts, object choice, vocation, avocations, scientific and artistic creativity, even in the ordinary activities of life that rarely attract more than slight and fleeting attention. Compromise formations arising from psychic conflict comprise virtually all of psychic life which is of emotional significance to us.

It has been truly said that a knowledge of psychoanalysis gives one another window through which to view the works of man. The perspective it affords is not only unique, it is essential to an understanding of what would otherwise seem to be fragmentary, disconnected phenomena. Just as a telescope trained on the starry sky resolves the blurred and condensed images visible to the naked eye into components whose existence and connection with one another were previously unsuspected, so psychoanalysis resolves behavior and conscious mental life into its unsuspected, apparently unconnected components. It demonstrates the interacting forces or tendencies that are the component elements of psychic conflict, and it shows their relation to the myriad compromise formations that are its consequences.

REFERENCES

Arlow, J. A. (1951), The consecration of the prophet. *Psychoanal. Quart.*, 20:374-397.

——— (1959), The structure of the *déjà vu* experience. *J. Amer. Psychoanal. Assn.*, 7:611-631.

——— (1961), Ego psychology and the study of mythology. *J. Amer. Psychoanal. Assn.*, 9:371-393.

——— (1979), Metaphor and the psychoanalytic situation. *Psychoanal. Quart.*, 48:363-385.

——— & Brenner, C. (1964), *Psychoanalytic Concepts and the Structural Theory*. New York: International Universities Press.

——— ——— (1966), The psychoanalytic situation. In: *Psychoanalysis in the Americas*, ed. R. E. Litman. New York: International Universities Press, pp. 23-43.

Brenman, M. (1952), On being teased and the problem of "moral masochism." *The Psychoanalytic Study of the Child*, 7:264-285. New York: International Universities Press.

Brenner, C. (1953), An addendum to Freud's theory of anxiety. *Internat. J. Psycho-Anal.*, 34:18-24.

——— (1957a), The nature and development of the concept of repression in Freud's writings. *The Psychoanalytic Study of the Child*, 12:19-46. New York: International Universities Press.

——— (1957b), The reformulation of the theory of anxiety. In: *A General Selection from the Works of Sigmund Freud*, ed. J. Rickman. New York: Doubleday, pp. 236-246.

——— (1959), The masochistic character: genesis and treatment. *J. Amer. Psychoanal. Assn.*, 7:197-226.

——— (1966), The mechanism of repression. In: *Psychoanalysis—A General Psychology*, ed. R. M. Loewenstein et al. New York: International Universities Press, pp. 390-399.

——— (1968), Psychoanalysis and science. *J. Amer. Psychoanal. Assn.*, 16:675-696.

——— (1973a), Psychoanalysis: philosophy or science. In: *Psychoanalysis and Philosophy*, ed. C. Hanly & M. Lazerowitz. New York: International Universities Press, pp. 35-45.

——— (1973b), *An Elementary Textbook of Psychoanalysis* (2nd ed.). New York: International Universities Press.

——— (1974a), Depression, anxiety, and affect theory. *Internat. J. Psycho-Anal.*, 55:25-32.

——— (1974b), Some observations on depression, on nosology, on affects, and on mourning. *J. Geriat. Psychiat.*, 7:6-20.

——— (1974c), On the nature and development of affects: a unified theory. *Psychoanal. Quart.*, 43:532-556.

——— (1975a), Affects and psychic conflict. *Psychoanal. Quart.*, 44:5-28.

——— (1975b), Alterations in defenses during psychoanalysis. *Monogr. Kris Study Group N.Y. Psychoanal. Inst.*, 6:1-22. New York: International Universities Press.

——— (1976), *Psychoanalytic Technique and Psychic Conflict.* New York: International Universities Press.

——— (1979a), Depressive affect, anxiety, and psychic conflict in the phallic-oedipal phase. *Psychoanal. Quart.*, 48:177-197.

——— (1979b), The components of psychic conflict and its consequences in mental life. *Psychoanal. Quart.*, 48:547-567.

——— (1980), Metapsychology and psychoanalytic theory. *Psychoanal. Quart.*, 49:189-214.

Cannon, W. B. (1929), *Bodily Changes in Pain, Hunger, Fear, and Rage.* New York: Appleton.

Dahl, H. (1979), A new psychoanalytic model of motivation. *Psychoanal. & Contemp. Thought*, 1:373-408.

Darwin, C. (1872), *The Expression of the Emotions in Man and Animals.* New York: Philosophical Library, 1955.

Fenichel, O. (1935), A critique of the death instinct. In: *The Collected Papers of Otto Fenichel*, 1:363-372. New York: Norton, 1953.

——— (1939), The counter-phobic attitude. In: *The Collected Papers of Otto Fenichel*, 2:163-173. New York: Norton, 1954.

——— (1941), *Problems of Psychoanalytic Technique.* Albany, N.Y.: The Psychoanalytic Quarterly.

——— (1945a), Neurotic acting out. In: *The Collected Papers of Otto Fenichel*, 2:296-304. New York: Norton, 1954.

——— (1945b), *The Psychoanalytic Theory of Neurosis.* New York: Norton.

Ferenczi, S. (1923), *Thalassa. A Theory of Genitality.* Albany, N. Y.: The Psychoanalytic Quarterly.

——— (1925), Psychoanalysis of sexual habits. *Internat. J. Psycho-Anal.*, 6:372-404.

Freud, A. (1936), *The Ego and the Mechanisms of Defense. The Writings of Anna Freud*, 2. New York: International Universities Press, 1966.

——— (1952), Mutual influences of ego and id. *The Writings of Anna*

Freud, 4:230-244. New York: International Universities Press, 1968.

——— (1969), Difficulties in the path of psychoanalysis: a confrontation of past with present viewpoints. *The Writings of Anna Freud*, 7:124-156. New York: International Universities Press, 1971.

——— (1974), Introduction. *The Writings of Anna Freud*, 1:xii-xiii. New York: International Universities Press.

——— (1975), Introduction. In: *Female Sexuality and the Oedipus Complex*, by H. Nagera. New York: Aronson.

——— (1976), Changes in psychoanalytic practice and experience. *Internat. J. Psycho-Anal.*, 57:257-260.

——— (1977), Fears, anxiety and phobic phenomena. *The Psychoanalytic Study of the Child*, 32:85-90. New Haven: Yale University Press.

Freud, S. (1894),* The neuro-psychoses of defence. *S.E.*, 3:41-61.

——— (1895a), On the grounds for detaching a particular syndrome from neurasthenia under the description 'anxiety neurosis'. *S.E.*, 3:85-117.

——— (1895b), Studies on hysteria (with J. Breuer). *S.E.*, 2.

——— (1896), The neuro-psychoses of defence. *S.E.*, 3:159-185.

——— (1898), Sexuality in the aetiology of the neuroses. *S.E.*, 3:261-285.

——— (1900), The interpretation of dreams. *S.E.*, 4 & 5.

——— (1901), *The Psychopathology of Everyday Life*. *S.E.*, 6.

——— (1905a), Fragment of an analysis of a case of hysteria. *S.E.*, 7:1-122.

——— (1905b), Three essays on the theory of sexuality. *S.E.*, 7:125-245.

——— (1905c), *Jokes and Their Relation to the Unconscious, S.E.*, 8.

——— (1911a), Psycho-analytic notes on an autobiographical account of a case of paranoia (dementia paranoides). *S.E.*, 12:1-82.

——— (1911b), Formulations on the two principles of mental functioning. *S.E.*, 12:213-226.

——— (1912), The dynamics of transference. *S.E.*, 12:97-108.

——— (1912-1913), *Totem and Taboo*. *S.E.*, 13:1-162.

——— (1914), On narcissism: an introduction. *S.E.*, 14:67-102.

——— (1915a), Observations on transference-love. *S.E.*, 12:157-171.

——— (1915b), Instincts and their vicissitudes. *S.E.*, 14:109-140.

——— (1915c), Repression. *S.E.*, 14:141-158.

——— (1915d), The unconscious. *S.E.*, 14:159-215.

——— (1916), Some character-types met with in psycho-analytic work. *S.E.*, 14:309-333.

*All references to S. Freud are to the *Standard Edition of the Complete Psychological Works of Sigmund Freud*. London: Hogarth Press.

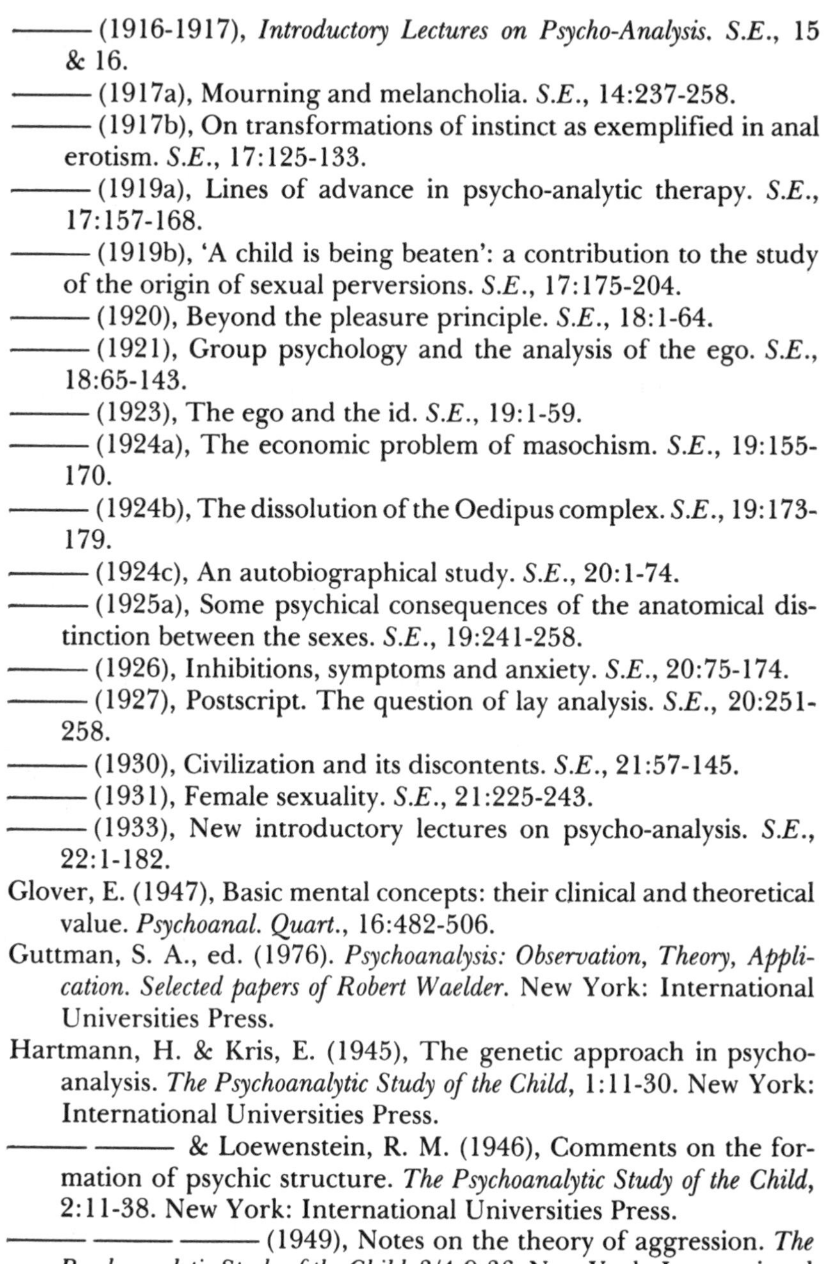

——— (1916-1917), *Introductory Lectures on Psycho-Analysis. S.E.*, 15 & 16.

——— (1917a), Mourning and melancholia. *S.E.*, 14:237-258.

——— (1917b), On transformations of instinct as exemplified in anal erotism. *S.E.*, 17:125-133.

——— (1919a), Lines of advance in psycho-analytic therapy. *S.E.*, 17:157-168.

——— (1919b), 'A child is being beaten': a contribution to the study of the origin of sexual perversions. *S.E.*, 17:175-204.

——— (1920), Beyond the pleasure principle. *S.E.*, 18:1-64.

——— (1921), Group psychology and the analysis of the ego. *S.E.*, 18:65-143.

——— (1923), The ego and the id. *S.E.*, 19:1-59.

——— (1924a), The economic problem of masochism. *S.E.*, 19:155-170.

——— (1924b), The dissolution of the Oedipus complex. *S.E.*, 19:173-179.

——— (1924c), An autobiographical study. *S.E.*, 20:1-74.

——— (1925a), Some psychical consequences of the anatomical distinction between the sexes. *S.E.*, 19:241-258.

——— (1926), Inhibitions, symptoms and anxiety. *S.E.*, 20:75-174.

——— (1927), Postscript. The question of lay analysis. *S.E.*, 20:251-258.

——— (1930), Civilization and its discontents. *S.E.*, 21:57-145.

——— (1931), Female sexuality. *S.E.*, 21:225-243.

——— (1933), New introductory lectures on psycho-analysis. *S.E.*, 22:1-182.

Glover, E. (1947), Basic mental concepts: their clinical and theoretical value. *Psychoanal. Quart.*, 16:482-506.

Guttman, S. A., ed. (1976). *Psychoanalysis: Observation, Theory, Application. Selected papers of Robert Waelder.* New York: International Universities Press.

Hartmann, H. & Kris, E. (1945), The genetic approach in psychoanalysis. *The Psychoanalytic Study of the Child*, 1:11-30. New York: International Universities Press.

——— ——— & Loewenstein, R. M. (1946), Comments on the formation of psychic structure. *The Psychoanalytic Study of the Child*, 2:11-38. New York: International Universities Press.

——— ——— ——— (1949), Notes on the theory of aggression. *The Psychoanalytic Study of the Child*, 3/4:9-36. New York: International Universities Press.

Jacobson, E. (1953), The affects and their pleasure-unpleasure qualities in relation to the psychic discharge processes. In: *Drives, Affects, Behavior*, ed. R. M. Loewenstein. New York: International Universities Press, pp. 38-66.

——— (1964), *The Self and the Object World.* New York: International Universities Press.

——— (1971), *Depression. Comparative Studies of Normal, Neurotic, and Psychotic Conditions.* New York: International Universities Press.

Jones, E. (1911), On 'dying together,' with special reference to Heinrich von Kleist's suicide. In: *Essays in Applied Psycho-Analysis,* 1:9-15. New York: International Universities Press, 1964.

——— (1912), An unusual case of dying together. In: *Essays in Applied Psychoanalysis,* 1:16-21. New York: International Universities Press, 1964.

——— (1931), *On the Nightmare.* New York: Liveright.

Katan, A. (1972), The infant's first reaction to strangers: distress or anxiety? *Internat. J. Psycho-Anal.,* 53:501-503.

Klein, M. (1948), A contribution to the theory of anxiety and guilt. *Internat. J. Psycho-Anal.,* 29:114-123.

——— et al. (1952), *Developments in Psycho-Analysis.* London: Hogarth Press.

Kramer, P. (1958), Note on one of the preoedipal roots of the superego. *J. Amer. Psychoanal. Assn.,* 6:38-46.

Kris, E. (1935), The psychology of caricature. In: *Psychoanalytic Explorations in Art.* New York: International Universities Press, 1952, pp. 173-188.

——— (1939), On inspiration. In: *Psychoanalytic Explorations in Art.* New York: International Universities Press, 1952, pp. 291-302.

Kubie, L. S. (1939), A critical analysis of the concept of a repetition compulsion. *Internat. J. Psycho-Anal.,* 20:390-402.

Lewin, B. D. (1950), *The Psychoanalysis of Elation.* Albany, N. Y.: The Psychoanalytic Quarterly.

——— (1961), Reflections on depression. *The Psychoanalytic Study of the Child,* 16:147-157. New York: International Universities Press.

——— (1965), Reflections on affect. In: *Drives, Affects, Behavior,* ed. M. Schur. New York: International Universities Press, pp. 23-37.

Loewald, H. (1972), Freud's conception of the negative therapeutic reaction, with comments on instinct theory. *J. Amer. Psychoanal. Assn.,* 20:235-245.

Loewenstein, R. M. (1957), A contribution to the psychoanalytic study of masochism. *J. Amer. Psychoanal. Assn.,* 5:197-234.

Malev, M. (1966), The Jewish orthodox circumcision ceremony. *J. Amer. Psychoanal. Assn.,* 14:510-517.

Novey, S. (1959), A clinical view of affect theory in psycho-analysis. *Internat. J. Psycho-Anal.,* 40:94-104.

Panel (1956), Re-evaluation of the libido theory, reported by C. Brenner. *J. Amer. Psychoanal. Assn.,* 4:162-169.

Pollock, G. H. (1978), Process and affect: mourning and grief. *Internat. J. Psycho-Anal.,* 59:255-276.

Rado, S. (1933), Fear of castration in women. *Psychoanal. Quart.*, 2:425-475.

Rangell, L. (1955), On the psychoanalytic theory of anxiety: a statement of a unitary theory. *J. Amer. Psychoanal. Assn.*, 3:389-414.

——— (1978), On understanding and treating anxiety and its derivatives. *Internat. J. Psycho-Anal.*, 59:229-236.

Rivera, J. de (1977), *A Structural Theory of the Emotions. Psychol. Issues*, Monogr. #40. New York: International Universities Press.

Rochlin, G. (1953), The disorder of depression and elation. *J. Amer. Psychoanal. Assn.*, 1:438-457.

Róheim, G. (1950), *Psychoanalysis and Anthropology*. New York: International Universities Press.

Sachs, H. (1942), The community of daydreams. In: *The Creative Unconscious*. Boston: Sci-Art Publishing.

Schafer, R. (1960), The loving and beloved superego in Freud's structural theory. *The Psychoanalytic Study of the Child*, 15:163-188. New York: International Universities Press.

——— (1968), The mechanisms of defence. *Internat. J. Psycho-Anal.*, 49:49-62.

Schur, M. (1966), *The Id and the Regulatory Principles of Mental Functioning*. New York: International Universities Press.

——— (1969), Affects and cognition. *Internat. J. Psycho-Anal.*, 50:647-653.

Stein, M. (1981), The unobjectionable part of the transference. *J. Amer. Psychoanal. Assn.*, 29:869-892.

Stone, L. (1954), The widening scope of indications for psychoanalysis. *J. Amer. Psychoanal Assn.*, 2:567-594.

——— (1971), Reflections on the psychoanalytic theory of aggression. *Psychoanal. Quart.*, 40:195-244.

——— (1979), Remarks on certain unique conditions of human aggression (the hand, speech, and the use of fire). *J. Amer. Psychoanal Assn.*, 27:27-64.

Strachey, J. (1961), Editor's note. In: *Standard Edition of the Complete Psychological Works of Sigmund Freud*, 19:243-247.

Waelder, R. (1930), The principle of multiple function. Observations on overdetermination. In: *Psychoanalysis: Observation, Theory, Application*, ed. S. A. Guttman. New York: International Universities Press, 1976, pp. 68-83.

——— (1937), The problem of the genesis of psychic conflict in earliest infancy. *Internat. J. Psycho-Anal.*, 18:406-473.

Yorke, C. & Wiseberg, S. (1976), A developmental view of anxiety: some clinical and theoretical considerations. *The Psychoanalytic Study of the Child*, 31:107-135. New Haven: Yale University Press.

NAME INDEX.

SUBJECT INDEX